No Whine with Dinner

150 healthy, kid-tested recipes from
THE MEAL MAKEOVER MOMS

Liz Weiss, MS, RD
Janice Newell Bissex, MS, RD

M3 Press

Library of Congress Control Number: 2010911464

ISBN-13 978-0-615-38122-0
ISBN-10 0-6153812-2-7

Edited by Wendy Smolen
Cover and Interior Design by Carol Shufro
Food Photos by The Meal Makeover Moms
Author Photo by Lynne McGraw
Ginger Drizzle Cookies Photo by Colin Campbell
Nutritional Analysis by Janice Newell Bissex, MS, RD

Other books by The Meal Makeover Moms:
The Moms' Guide to Meal Makeovers (Broadway Books 2004)

Published by M3 Press
Melrose, MA
www.MealMakeoverMoms.com

Manufacturing and Distribution:
Favorite Recipes Press
An imprint of FRP Books, Inc.
P.O. Box 305142 Nashville, TN 37230
800-358-0560
www.frpbooks.com

The recipes and recommendations in this book are not intended to replace the advice
of a qualified health professional. The authors and publisher expressly disclaim responsibility
for any adverse effects incurred as a consequence, directly or indirectly,
of the use and application of any of the contents of this book.

Printed in the United States of America

This book is dedicated to our moms,
Sylvia Weiss and Carol Newell,
whose delicious homemade meals instilled
in us the importance of
gathering our own families around the table,
to our husbands, Tim and Don,
and our children, Josh and Simon
and Carolyn and Leah,
and to the hundreds of moms and kids
who tested and tasted our recipes
and shared their best mealtime "secrets."

~ Liz and Janice

Contents

Introduction

We all want the best for our children, and eating a well-balanced diet is certainly up there in terms of "what's best." But when kids hit the reject button every time you serve a new food (especially if it's green), it sets the stage for dishes like mac & cheese, chicken nuggets, and hot dogs to become staples at the dinner table. Taking this path of least resistance — the wrong fork in the road, if you will — can certainly keep mealtime complaints at bay, but it establishes a pattern of poor eating habits, and feeds right into the demands of your pickiest eater.

As registered dietitians, we understand the importance of serving healthy, well-balanced meals, but as moms ourselves, we realize that no matter how super nutritious a meal may be, unless it appeals to kids in a big way, *they just won't eat it.* Since our first book, *The Moms' Guide to Meal Makeovers*, was released in 2004, we have been networking with moms around the country (and the world). Via our website, *MealMakeoverMoms.com*, through our blog, *Meal Makeover Moms' Kitchen*, our weekly radio podcast, *Cooking with the Moms*, Facebook, Twitter, and our e-newsletter, we have built strong online relationships based on the sharing and exchange of ideas.

Our followers are constantly on the lookout for nutritious recipes to add to their nightly repertoire, new ways to get vegetables on the table, and meals that appeal to both parents and kids. From a survey we conducted in 2009 of nearly 600 moms nationwide, we learned that the number one obstacle to getting children to eat healthy, well-balanced meals is "picky eaters who whine and complain." Their mealtime challenges inspired us to write *No Whine with Dinner*, a book designed to give busy parents nutritious recipes the whole family will enjoy.

We know this book comes at a critical time. Today's youth are heavier than ever with 34% overweight or obese. We have a nation of children overfed on fat, sugar and salt, and underfed on fruits, vegetables and whole grains. Recently, high profile advocates from doctors and dietitians to chefs and even First Lady Michelle Obama have stepped forward to tackle the growing crisis of childhood obesity. We believe that by turning childhood nutrition into a national priority, the quality of foods available in school cafeterias, supermarkets, restaurants, and, of course, at the family dinner table will improve dramatically. And to that end, so will our children's health. To support the effort, we have filled these pages with practical, real-life advice and easy-to-follow, taste-tested recipes that moms and dads everywhere can use to deliver fresh, flavorful, and nutrient-rich foods to their families.

Yes, there are skeptics who believe feeding kids a healthy diet is a lost cause. Others believe that adding pureed vegetables to everything from brownies to the breading on chicken nuggets is the best way to get more nutrition into kids' diets. Our approach is more optimistic and revolves around the simple premise that kids will eat an array of nutritious foods — colorful fruits and vegetables, hearty whole grains, seafood, and even beans, if — *and here's the catch* — they are presented in a way that appeals to their senses. The way a food crunches, how it smells, and the way it looks can make or break a child's willingness to try it. Presentation is key. Just imagine the surprise when your child, once labeled as "picky," gobbles up his broccoli because now it's steamed until crisp-tender — versus cooked to death — and topped with a golden cheese sauce. Don't drop your jaw when he favors a smoothie brimming with bananas and frozen berries over a sugar-sweetened juice "drink," or slurps every last spoonful of homemade soup because our recipe calls for crushed tomatoes instead of the usual "lumpy" diced ones. We didn't just dream up this mealtime utopia. We've actually seen it happen. Again and again.

We don't believe in "kid foods." All of our recipes — *Perfect Parsnip Fries*, *Banana Brownie Waffles*, *Chicken Pot Pie Bundles*, *Ginger Drizzle Cookies* — have widespread appeal, are made with color and flavor in mind, and incorporate nutritious ingredients into their essence. We don't go overboard on the "nutrition" thing either, so you'll never see recipes like sugar-free, fat-free, oat bran muffins or dishes packed with so many vegetables even the most open-minded eater would balk. It takes time for kids' taste buds to come around to liking new foods, which is why we ease them in with familiar flavors and preparations. A cup of whole wheat flour in *Peanut Butter Power Cookies*, a grated carrot in *Garden Turkey Meatballs*, or some ground flaxseed in *Nutty Fruit Crumble* are subtle additions, but all up the ante on good nutrition without causing pushback at the table.

Making over the eating habits of today's youth (and their families) for the better is a lofty goal. By no means do we claim to have all the answers. That's why we gathered ideas and feedback from hundreds of fellow moms — those embedded deep in the mealtime trenches — to bring you kid-friendly recipes and practical advice. These moms generously tested, tasted — *and had their kids taste* — every single recipe in this book, and their feedback is included on each one. Their insightful comments helped us fine-tune the recipes, clarify instructions, and even toss out a few dishes that, well, made their kids whine. Their remarks were encouraging too. Here's what Jackie, a mother of two from Roseville,

MN had to say about our *Chicken Broccoli Crunch* casserole: "My 3-year old daughter, Danika, made this dish with me, and she willingly ate broccoli for the first time!" When we say our recipes are kid-tested, we mean it!

The creative and savvy strategies presented in our *50 Moms' Secrets for Getting Picky Eaters to Try New Foods* chapter offer more ways to turn the tables on finicky eaters. The tips are positive, not punitive. And they are as unique as the moms themselves. Kim, a mother of three from Dexter, MI turns trying new foods into a game: "We always pick out a 'try it' item when we go to the grocery store. One rule: No junk food! We have tried star fruit, kefir, and plantains. Each week we pick one new thing and look up what to do with it. My kids are always excited to try it, and as a result, we have added quite a few new foods to our diet."

What we aim to present in *No Whine with Dinner* is a whole new family food dynamic — one that fosters excitement and appreciation for fresh, nutritious food and gives children a choice and a voice in what's for dinner. In the words of our own kids, we want to turn mealtime whines into "wows!"

Let us know what works for your family.

Liz & Janice

Liz, with her husband Tim, and her sons, Simon and Josh.

Janice, with her husband Don, and her daughters, Leah and Carolyn.

CHAPTER 1

The Meal Makeover Moms' Healthy Basics

Our goal in writing *No Whine with Dinner* is to show parents how easy it can be to make healthy meals and snacks that kids will really want to eat. Aside from upping the ante on nutrition, we kept two other priorities in mind: kids' taste buds and busy parents' lifestyles. After using (and re-using) our own families as the initial guinea pigs, we enlisted the help of fellow moms to prepare and serve our recipes to their families. Their feedback, along with the reactions from their kids, enabled us to fine tune the ingredients, tweak the directions, and ultimately decide which ones were good enough to make the cut. The moms (and one dad) who took part in our testing process not only gave us valuable insight, they also sent us photos as their families cooked each dish. You can see them — along with pictures we took in our kitchens — online on the photo-sharing website, Flickr. We provide the link on the introductory page of each recipe chapter.

All of the recipes in this cookbook were nutritionally analyzed using a software program from ESHA Research called Food Processor SQL. The nutrients we include are calories, fat, saturated fat, sodium, carbohydrate, fiber, and protein, plus vitamin A, vitamin C, calcium, and iron if the recipe provides at least 10 percent of the Recommended Dietary Allowance (RDA). These percentages are based on a diet of 2,000 calories, the standard used on the Nutrition Facts label on food packages. We list omega-3 fats if a recipe contains at least 0.2 grams. When alternative ingredients are listed, we analyze using the first one suggested, and optional ingredients are not included in our nutrient analysis.

Using the latest software program ensures our nutrient analysis is as accurate as possible. It's not an exact science, however, because nutrient levels may vary between brands, or differ based on where a food is grown and how it's stored before it arrives at your local market. Also, the software does not account for nutrients lost or gained by cooking, and occasionally food companies reformulate recipes for their products, which may change the nutrient breakdown.

We have worked hard to make our recipes low in saturated fat, added sugars, and sodium; moderate in total fat and calories; and high in fiber, good quality protein, omega-3 fats, vitamins A and C, calcium, and iron. To meet our nutrition goals, we rely on everyday, easy-to-find ingredients — things such as whole grains, fruits, vegetables, lean meats and poultry, eggs, low-fat dairy products, nuts, canned beans, and healthy oils — and we keep our recipes simple and streamlined.

Flavor

Even though we're dietitians and nutrition is clearly of the utmost importance to us, taste is still a top priority. Healthy foods that kids refuse to eat won't make them healthier, so we try to make every recipe too delicious to resist. We tend to keep the flavors on the mild side since young palates need time to grow accustomed to spicier, more intense tastes. Feel free to follow a recipe as written or add an extra kick here and there in the form of a spicier salsa, a few extra pinches of chili powder, or a sprinkling of fresh herbs.

Calories

Two thousand calories a day is the standard reference used on food labels, although it's just an average, and not the amount everyone needs. Calorie requirements vary depending on age, gender, and activity level. For example, a toddler might only need about 1,000 calories a day, while an active teen might need 2,500. When you see calorie amounts listed on our recipes, rest assured we do everything in our culinary power to make each one counts toward good nutrition.

Portion Size

With two thirds of all Americans, and over one third of our children overweight or obese, we pay close attention to portion size. Our portions are designed to leave you comfortably full; they're not supersized to the point where you feel stuffed. Calculating how many people a recipe will serve can be a challenge since appetites can vary between family members. We take that into account, so if a recipe says it serves four, we understand that a toddler might eat less than a teen, and that a family with two small children may have leftovers.

Fat

There's a belief that dietitians are anti fat, but that is certainly not the case with us. We incorporate fats into our families' diets and our recipes, but we're careful to choose the "right" kinds of fats. Research shows that switching from saturated fat (found in things such as the skin on chicken, the marbling in red meat, or full-fat dairy products) to monounsaturated fats and omega-3 polyunsaturated fats can lower blood cholesterol levels, so we like to use mono and poly fats in moderation. As a general rule, it's best if you consume no more than 30 percent of your daily calories from fat, and keep saturated fat to seven to 10 percent of total calories. So, if you consume a 2,000 calorie diet, your saturated fat intake should be no more than 15 to 20 grams per day.

As you read our recipes, you'll notice that we often use canola oil in our baked goods and for high heat sautéing. Of all the popular oils, canola contains the most health-enhancing omega-3 fats, and it's the lowest in saturated fat. Extra virgin olive oil is a good source of the heart-healthy monounsaturated fat and adds great flavor when drizzled over vegetables, mixed in salad dressings and used for moderate heat sautéing, so we use that too. And we use toasted sesame oil and peanut oil in some recipes for their pronounced flavor. We strive to keep recipes under five grams of saturated fat per serving, and we keep artificial trans fats out entirely because we avoid foods made with partially hydrogenated oils.

Omega-3 Fats

Omega-3s have many health benefits. They've been shown to lower heart disease risk, decrease inflammation in the body, and promote healthy brain and eye development in growing babies both in utero and in the first year of life. Seafood is the best source of omega-3 fats. It contains docosahexaenoic acid (DHA) and eicosapentaenoic acid (EPA) omega-3s, and experts suggest eating seafood twice a week. Some plant-based foods such as walnuts, flaxseed, and canola oil also contain omega-3, but in a less potent form called alpha-linolenic acid (ALA). Omega-3 eggs, which we use every time eggs are called for in a recipe, may contain either type of this health-promoting fat. The following daily intake of ALA omega-3 is recommended: Adult men; 1.6 grams, women; 1.1 grams, children; 0.7 to 1.2 grams. Ideally, at least ten percent of your omega-3s should come from the more potent DHA and EPA.

Protein

Some kids subsist on diets of pizza, hot dogs, and chicken nuggets. While these dishes provide protein, many are high in sodium and saturated fat, and are made with artificial fillers. We prefer high-quality protein foods such as lean cuts of meat and lean ground beef (look for 90% lean or higher), seafood, poultry, pork, and non-meat alternatives including tofu, eggs, nuts, beans and other legumes. As a guideline, about 20 percent of daily calories should come from protein. That means a toddler consuming 1,000 calories a day should strive for about 50 grams of protein, while a teen who consumes 2,000 would need about 100 grams. Many protein-rich foods, especially lean meats, beans, seafood, and tofu, are also rich in iron, an important mineral that many teen girls lack.

Carbohydrates

Carbs tend to get a bad rap, mainly because most people eat too many refined versus whole grain carbohydrates. When grains are refined, the nutritious germ and bran are stripped away. Even though refined carbohydrate foods such as white bread, white pasta, white rice, and refined breakfast cereal provide the body with energy, they're not nearly as nutrient-rich or fiber-filled as their whole grain counterparts: whole wheat bread, whole wheat or whole wheat blend pasta, brown rice, and whole grain cereals. Experts suggest shifting the focus to quality carbs. According to the US Dietary Guidelines, half of all the grains we eat should be whole grains. About 50 percent of your daily consumption of calories should come from carbs.

Fiber

When children choose white bread over whole wheat, shun fruits and veggies, and turn their noses up to beans, getting the recommended amount of fiber can be a tall order. On average, Americans consume just 14 grams of fiber a day. The daily requirement for children ranges from 19 grams for 1-to 3-year olds to

38 grams for 14-to 18-year old boys. Eating fiber-rich foods is good for heart health and digestion (parents of constipated kids take note of this). Because fiber is also filling, some studies show it may play a positive role in weight control. Truth be told, we're actually a bit fixated on fiber, which is why we use so many fiber-rich foods in our recipes. You'll find whole wheat flour, oats, wheat germ, ground flaxseed, and cornmeal in our pancakes, waffles and baked snacks and desserts; we use canned beans in soups and main dishes; fruits and veggies in everything we can cram them into; and whole wheat blend pastas in everything from our *Spaghetti Zucchini Pie* to our *One-Pot Pasta and Beef Dinner*.

Sugar

Most children consume way too much added sugar. In fact, on average, kids gobble up over 20 teaspoons of added sugar every day, usually from soft drinks, sweetened fruit drinks, candy, cookies, and cake. As a reality check, most experts suggest consuming no more than 10 teaspoons of sugar a day — half of the average. We're not opposed to a little bit of sugar, but we prefer it come packed with great nutrition. When we add maple syrup to our recipe for *Sweeeeet Brussels Sprouts*, it makes them taste sooooo good that kids are more likely to eat them. And, even though our recipe for *Blueberry Cornmeal Pancakes* calls for two tablespoons of brown sugar in the batter, the overall nutrition per serving makes up for the bit of sugar found in each pancake. We tend to avoid foods made with artificial sweeteners.

Salt and Sodium

On average, Americans consume as much as 4,000 milligrams of sodium a day, well above the recommended 2,300 milligram limit (some experts support an even stricter limit of 1,500 milligrams). Research shows that too much sodium may contribute to high blood pressure, so it's important to keep it in check. Sodium is prevalent in our food supply, found in everything from breads and baked goods to the more predictable processed meats and fast food fries.

To keep our recipes as low in sodium as possible, we use kosher salt; Diamond Crystal kosher salt, for example, contains half the sodium of regular table salt and has a nice, clean flavor. We also turn to reduced-sodium products such as reduced-sodium teriyaki and soy sauces, lower-sodium deli meats and cheeses, and we drain and rinse our canned beans to wash off about 40 percent of the sodium. While we don't hesitate to add a little bit of salt to our recipes, we use the smallest amount necessary to enhance the flavor. If you or someone in your family is on a sodium-restricted diet, feel free to leave it out. We consider 800 milligrams of sodium as an upper limit for our recipes, though most fall well below that number. Many food manufacturers are already reformulating their products in an effort to lower the amount of sodium, and we applaud their efforts.

Calcium

Calcium is critical for strong bones and teeth, but more than half of all children fail to meet the daily recommendation. The calcium-rich foods we like to use include low-fat milk and yogurt, reduced-fat cheeses, calcium-fortified juices, and other lesser known calcium-containing foods including almonds, broccoli, tofu, and oranges. The chart below outlines the milligrams of calcium children should strive for each day:

Age	Calcium (milligrams)
Birth to 3 years	500
4 to 8 years	800
9 to 18 years	1,300

To put those numbers in perspective, a glass of milk has about 300 milligrams, one cup of yogurt, 275 milligrams, a one-ounce slice of cheese, 200 milligrams, an ounce of almonds, 65 milligrams, and one cup of broccoli, 45 milligrams.

Fruits and Vegetables

Often the biggest gap in children's diets is fruits and vegetables, so we incorporate them into our recipes whenever possible, and go to great lengths to make them appealing. The USDA Food Guide Pyramid recommends children eat about two cups of fruit and two and a half cups of vegetables each day (based on a 2,000-calorie diet). If you visit the website, *MyPyramid.gov*, you can calculate recommended servings of fruits and vegetables (as well as grains, milk, and meat/beans) by plugging in your child's age, gender, height, weight, and activity level.

Eggs

Eggs are rich in high-quality protein, and you won't catch us throwing away the yolks. While yolks do, in fact, contain cholesterol, they are low in saturated fat, the real culprit in heart disease. Yolks are also rich in lutein (an antioxidant important for healthy eyes), as well as vitamin A, folate, and choline (a B vitamin needed for normal brain function). While we don't specifically call for heart-healthy omega-3 eggs in our recipes, we use them exclusively. Omega-3 eggs come from chickens fed a special diet containing such things as grains, rice bran, alfalfa meal, and kelp. The eggs we use contain 115 milligrams of omega-3 fat, about 10 percent of the daily recommended intake. While omega-3 eggs cost more than regular eggs, we think they're worth it.

Nuts

We're huge fans of walnuts, pecans, almonds, and peanuts (technically a legume, not a nut). Nuts add flavor, texture and a long list of important nutrients including fiber, protein, vitamin E, manganese, and good-for-you fats. Walnuts have the added benefit of being a good source of ALA omega-3 fat. Nuts are heart healthy — a handful a day just might keep the doctor away — and they're delicious as a stand-alone snack or as an added ingredient in salads, the crispy breading on fish or chicken, and scrumptious desserts. Since lots of kids are averse to big chunks in their food, our recipes often call for finely chopped nuts — the consistency of coarse grains of sand. If someone in your family is allergic to nuts, by all means leave them out.

Local & Organic

While we don't specify locally-grown or organic ingredients in our recipes, we support shopping at farmers' markets, buying organic produce if it fits your budget, joining a CSA (Community Supported Agriculture, where consumers can buy a share in a local farm), and planting a backyard vegetable garden. For CSA information visit *localharvest.org*, and for a shopper's guide to pesticides and a list of the fruits and vegetables with the highest pesticide levels, check out *foodnews.org*.

Convenience Foods

We use convenience foods, but we choose them wisely. We prefer all-natural brands, free of artificial colors, flavors, and monosodium glutamate (MSG). As a rule, we look for products with few ingredients and with names that are easy to pronounce! We often find ourselves comparing labels for things like sodium and saturated fat, opting for the lowest choices out there. We're also mindful of our kids' taste and texture preferences. For instance, when choosing a pasta sauce or a salsa, we're inclined to go with the brands with the smoothest consistency since lumps don't seem to cut it with our kids.

Meal Makeover Moms' Pantry Picks

We spend a lot of time at the supermarket, comparing labels, debating the best brands, and discovering new products on the shelves. As you read through our 150 recipes, you will notice that we rarely list specific brands, although we do have our favorites. Listed below are the brands we turn to again and again. Overall, they work well in our recipes, our kids — Josh and Simon and Carolyn and Leah — like their tastes and textures, and we appreciate their stellar nutrient profiles.

Within each category we often list several brands, because we realize that what may be available in New England, where we live, may be hard to find where you live. Although we don't list store brands, many are now made with wholesome ingredients and are free of artificial colors and flavors, making them just as healthy as their national counterparts. Whether you shop at Kroger, Albertson's, Stop & Shop, Trader Joe's, Whole Foods Market, a warehouse store like Costco, or your regional chain, in-store brands can be less expensive, and we encourage you to seek them out and compare their nutritional merits.

We hope the list below guides you in a healthy direction as you prepare our recipes. For updates on the newest food products to hit the market, you can read our blog and subscribe to our monthly e-newsletter.

Eggs:
Eggland's Best
Land O Lakes Omega-3 All-Natural Eggs
The Country Hen
Organic Valley

Reduced-Fat Cheese:
Cabot 50% Reduced Fat Cheese
Kraft Natural Reduced Fat Cheese
   made with 2% milk
Sargento Reduced Fat Cheese
Galaxy Veggie Shreds

Yogurt:
Dannon All Natural Yogurt
Stonyfield Farm Lowfat Yogurt
Horizon Organic Yogurt

Greek Yogurt:
Stonyfield Farm Oikos Organic Greek Yogurt
Fage Total 0% Yogurt
Chobani 0% Greek Yogurt

Kefir:
Lifeway
Organic Valley

Soy Milk:
Silk Soymilk
Eden Soymilk

Cream Cheese:
Philadelphia ⅓ Less Fat Cream Cheese

Canned Soup:
Health Valley Organic
Amy's Kitchen Organic
Campbell's Healthy Request

Chicken, Beef, Vegetable Broths:
Imagine Natural Creations Organic Broth
Pacific Natural Foods Organic Broth
Swanson Natural Goodness or
   Certified Organic Broth
College Inn Organic Broth
More Than Gourmet Culinary Stock

Frozen Potatoes:
McCain Smiles
Alexia Waffle Fries
Ian's Alphatots
Cascadian Farm Hash Browns
Ore-Ida Country Style Hash Browns
  Shredded Potatoes

Breads and Bagels:
Thomas' 100% Whole Wheat English Muffins
Thomas' Hearty Grains Double Oat
  Golden Honey Bagels
Pepperidge Farm 100% Whole Wheat
  Cinnamon with Raisins Swirl Bread
Pepperidge Farm Whole Grain Mini Bagels
Pepperidge Farm Wheat Sliders
Lender's Bagels 100% Whole Wheat

Whole Wheat Blend Pasta:
Barilla Plus
Ronzoni Healthy Harvest
Heartland Perfect Balance

Lasagna Noodles:
Prince Oven Ready Lasagna
Barilla No Boil Lasagna

Pizza Crust:
Boboli
Mama Mary's

Pasta Sauce:
Light Ragu Tomato & Basil
Newman's Own Marinara
Classico Tomato & Basil

Light Mayonnaise:
Cains Light Reduced Calorie Mayonnaise
Spectrum Organics Light Canola Mayo
Hellmann's Light Mayonnaise

Salad Dressing:
Newman's Own Lighten Up
Ken's Light Options
Annie's Naturals

Soy and Teriyaki Sauces:
Kikkoman Less Sodium Soy Sauce
Kikkoman Less Sodium Teriyaki Sauce

Enchilada Sauce:
Hatch Chili Company

Peanut Butter:
Smucker's Natural
Skippy Natural Creamy
Peanut Butter & Co.
Jif Omega-3
Teddy

Tofu:
Nasoya

Canned Beans:
Bush's Best
Goya
Eden Organic

Canned Tuna and Salmon:
Bumblebee
Chicken of the Sea
Wild Planet
Bear & Wolf

Nitrite-Free, Uncured Hot Dogs:
Coleman Natural
Applegate Farms
Nature's Rancher
Lightlife Smart Dogs (vegetarian)
Yves The Good Dog (vegetarian)

(continued)

Sausage:
Coleman Organic
Al Fresco All Natural
Aidells
Hans All Natural
Niman Ranch

Nitrite-Free, Uncured Bacon:
Applegate Farms
Niman Ranch
Wellshire Farms
Nature's Rancher

Deli Meats:
Boar's Head
Applegate Farms Organic
Dietz & Watson

100% Juice:
Minute Maid Enhanced Pomegranate Blueberry
Welch's Blueberry Pomegranate
   Concord Grape
Ocean Spray Cranberry & Raspberry Blend
Tropicana Pure Premium Orange Juice
Dole Pineapple Juice

Ground flaxseed:
Bob's Red Mill Whole Ground
   Flaxseed Meal
Spectrum Organic Ground Flaxseed

Wheat Germ:
Kretschmer
Mother's

All-Natural Applesauce:
Mott's
Musselman's
Earth's Best

Tortilla Chips:
Tostitos Multigrain Tortilla Chips
Food Should Taste Good
   Multigrain Tortilla Chips
Green Mountain Gringo Tortilla Strips
Garden of Eatin' Tortilla Chips

Spreads:
Smart Balance Light Omega-3
Olivio Light
I Can't Believe It's Not Butter Light

Kosher Salt:
Diamond Crystal Kosher Salt

Visit our website to download our customized
supermarket shopping list.

Ham and Cheesy Breakfast Sandwich

CHAPTER 2

Morning Makeovers

It's true that breakfast is the most important meal of the day. Kids who eat a healthy breakfast end up with a diet higher in vitamins and minerals, have better concentration and performance in the classroom, and more energy for the playground. Even when you're racing against the clock, there are plenty of nutrient-rich options that you can toss together quickly. Our *Blueberry Breakfast Parfait* and *Nest Eggs* take just minutes to prep. And although pancakes, waffles, and French toast require more time, they too can be made quickly if you organize your ingredients ahead. For kids who tend to skip breakfast, our tasty recipes made with whole grains, eggs, nuts, dried fruit, and good-for-you oils may be the ticket to lure them back to the table.

Kiran helps his mom make our *Ham and Cheesy Breakfast Sandwich* recipe, and he shares one with little brother, Aidan.

See more photos of our young cooks and moms cooking their favorite breakfast recipes on Flickr http://www.flickr.com/photos/mealmakeovermoms

Pumpkin Chocolate Chip Pancakes

MAKES 4 TO 5 SERVINGS (ABOUT FOURTEEN 4-INCH PANCAKES)

When Liz's son Josh entered middle school, she was disappointed to learn they no longer allotted time for a mid-morning snack break. Worried that Josh would be starving by the time lunch rolled around (not to mention, so hungry he'd find it hard to concentrate), Liz began beefing up his breakfast. These pumpkin pancakes are one of his favorites. They're jam-packed with nutritious ingredients — whole wheat flour, ground flaxseed, eggs, milk, and pumpkin. Drizzle them with pure maple syrup, and any kid would be happy to start his day with a stack.

1 cup all-purpose flour

½ cup whole wheat flour

2 tablespoons ground flaxseed or wheat germ

2 tablespoons granulated sugar

2 tablespoons mini semi-sweet chocolate chips

1 tablespoon baking powder

2 large eggs, beaten

1⅓ cups 1% low-fat milk

½ cup canned 100% pure pumpkin

1 teaspoon vanilla extract

1 Whisk together the all-purpose flour, whole wheat flour, flaxseed, sugar, chocolate chips, and baking powder in a large bowl.

2 In a separate bowl, whisk together the eggs, milk, pumpkin, and vanilla until well blended. Pour the liquid ingredients over the dry ingredients and stir until just combined.

3 Lightly oil or coat a large nonstick skillet or griddle with nonstick cooking spray and heat over medium-high heat. Pour the batter onto the hot skillet using a ¼ cup measuring cup, forming 4-inch pancakes.

4 Cook until bubbles begin to appear on the surface of the pancakes and the bottoms turn golden, about 3 minutes. Flip and cook until the other sides are golden, an additional 2 to 3 minutes. Repeat with the remaining cooking spray and batter.

PER SERVING (3 pancakes): 280 calories, 6g fat (2g saturated, 0.7g omega-3), 330mg sodium, 46g carbohydrate, 4g fiber, 11g protein, 80% vitamin A, 25% calcium, 15% iron

tip Place half-cup portions of leftover canned pumpkin in zip-top bags and freeze for later use. Thaw before mixing into batters.

mom's feedback Pancakes are always a huge hit with my boys. With this recipe, they weren't even aware that there was pumpkin in them.

Julie, mother of Matthew, age 4 months, Joey, age 6 and Patrick, age 9 ▪ Mercer Island, WA

Blueberry Cornmeal Pancakes

MAKES 4 TO 5 SERVINGS (ABOUT FOURTEEN 4-INCH PANCAKES)

For years, all of our kids have been taste-testing recipes for our website, blog, magazine articles, and cookbooks. Leah, Janice's silly 10-year old, got in the habit of simply saying, "Book" every time she loved a new recipe. When we first created these *Blueberry Cornmeal Pancakes*, we knew we had a winner on our hands when Leah took one bite and declared, "Book!" Blueberries are a super fruit, bursting with health-enhancing antioxidants. Coupled with cornmeal and whole wheat flour — both whole grains — these pancakes are a dietitian's dream … and Leah's too!

1 cup all-purpose flour

½ cup whole wheat flour

¼ cup cornmeal

1 tablespoon baking powder

1½ cups 1% low-fat milk

2 large eggs, beaten

2 tablespoons brown sugar

½ teaspoon vanilla extract

¾ cup frozen wild blueberries

1 Whisk together the all-purpose flour, whole wheat flour, cornmeal, and baking powder in a large bowl.

2 In a separate bowl, whisk the milk, eggs, brown sugar, and vanilla until well blended. Pour the liquid ingredients over the dry ingredients and stir until just combined. Stir in the blueberries.

3 Lightly oil or coat a large nonstick skillet or griddle with nonstick cooking spray and heat over medium-high heat. Pour the batter onto the hot skillet using a ¼-cup measuring cup, forming 4-inch pancakes.

4 Cook until bubbles begin to appear on the surface of the pancakes and the bottoms turn golden, about 3 minutes. Flip and cook until the other sides are golden, an additional 2 to 3 minutes. Repeat with the remaining cooking spray and batter.

PER SERVING (3 pancakes): 270 calories, 3.5g fat (1g saturated), 330mg sodium, 49g carbohydrate, 3g fiber, 11g protein, 30% calcium, 15% iron

tip The reason we call for wild blueberries is that they have even more antioxidants than cultivated blueberries, but either type will work.

mom's feedback

I liked the tip about using wild blueberries because they have more antioxidants. Plus, my kids, who don't usually eat blueberry pancakes, tried them because the blueberries were smaller.

Colleen, mother of Logan, age 2, Connor, age 4 and Paige, age 5 ▪ Sandy Hook, VA

Oatmeal Power Breakfast

MAKES 1 SERVING

Good old-fashioned oatmeal may not sound like the most glamorous food, but this hearty whole grain has recently emerged as a hot food trend. Fancy oatmeal recipes are making their way onto restaurant menus around the country, so we figured we'd jump on the oatmeal bandwagon too. Our recipe — already healthy because the fiber in oatmeal has been shown to lower cholesterol levels — gets an extra kick of nutrition with ground flaxseed (a good source of heart-healthy omega-3 fat), blueberries, and nuts if you choose to use them. We guarantee no one will complain that it's boring when topped with a spoonful of maple syrup. Oatmeal sticks to your ribs, so your kids should feel comfortably full and satisfied as they head off to school.

¼ cup quick-cooking oats

1 tablespoon ground flaxseed

⅔ cup 1% low-fat milk

¼ cup fresh or frozen blueberries

2 tablespoons chopped pecans or walnuts, optional

1 teaspoon pure maple syrup

1 Place the oats, ground flaxseed, and milk in a large microwave-safe cereal bowl and stir to combine. If you use a small bowl the contents may overflow when heated.

2 Place in the microwave, uncovered, and heat on high for 90 seconds (if you like your oatmeal thick, check it after 90 seconds and then cook an additional 20 to 30 seconds). Remove very carefully and stir in the blueberries, nuts as desired, and top with the maple syrup.

PER SERVING 230 calories, 6g fat (1g saturated, 1.4g omega-3), 70mg sodium, 34g carbohydrate, 5g fiber, 10g protein, 20% calcium

mom's feedback

We eat oatmeal a lot. I was thrilled that the kids liked the added blueberries ... more fruit!

Molly, mother of Gavin, age 6 and Gwen, age 9 ▪ Coon Raids, MN

Apple-icious Oatmeal Bake

MAKES 6 TO 8 SERVINGS

This recipe was originally sent to us by Kelly, a mom of two from Marietta, GA. Kelly is a fan of our weekly radio podcast, *Cooking with the Moms*. When she heard us talk about our *Recipe Rescue* blog series — where we take a recipe and give it a healthy makeover — she sent us her favorite breakfast dish for a fix. Made with oats, milk, half a stick of butter, half a cup of sugar, and an egg, she hoped we could slim it down with a few simple swaps. Not only did we use less butter and sugar, we took our rescue a step further by adding two nutritious ingredients: an apple, rich in cholesterol-lowering fiber, and chopped pecans, a great source of good-for-you fats and fiber.

⅓ cup brown sugar

2 tablespoons butter, melted

1 large egg

2 cups 1% low-fat milk

½ teaspoon vanilla extract

1½ cups quick-cooking oats

1 medium apple, unpeeled and cut into ¼-inch dice (about 1 cup)

½ cup coarsely chopped pecans

1½ teaspoons baking powder

½ teaspoon salt

¼ teaspoon ground cinnamon, plus more for sprinkling

1 Preheat the oven to 350°F. Lightly oil or coat an 8 x 8-inch baking pan or dish with nonstick cooking spray and set aside.

2 In a large bowl, whisk together the brown sugar and the butter until well combined. Whisk in the egg until creamy and then whisk in the milk and vanilla.

3 Stir in the oats, apple, pecans, baking powder, salt, and cinnamon. Place the mixture in the prepared pan, sprinkle with cinnamon, and bake about 30 minutes, or until the top turns golden and the oatmeal is set.

PER SERVING 250 calories, 12g fat (3g saturated), 300mg sodium, 30g carbohydrate, 3g fiber, 7g protein, 15% calcium

 If you think your kids will be bothered by the crunch of the nuts, chop them up even finer so they blend right in.

 **mom's feedback** Claudette plays competitive softball, and this is the type of hearty breakfast she needs to sustain her on game days. We loved the addition of the apples and nuts.

Kelly, mother of Julia, age 12 and Claudette, age 15 ▪ Marietta, GA

Cheery-O-Granola

MAKES 12 SERVINGS

There is no shortage of breakfast cereals to choose from at the supermarket. Many are high in sugar and low in fiber, while others contain artificial flavors and colors … things we try to avoid with our kids. Our easy, homemade granola combines the nutrition of oats, nuts, grains, and canola oil with the yumminess of cinnamon and maple syrup. Make a batch on the weekend and serve it on school days with low-fat milk, or layer with yogurt and your family's favorite berries for a parfait (see recipe for *Blueberry Breakfast Parfait* on page 27).

3 cups quick-cooking oats

2 cups Cheerios® or other O-shaped cereal

1 cup slivered or sliced almonds

¼ cup ground flaxseed or wheat germ

1 teaspoon ground cinnamon

¼ cup pure maple syrup

¼ cup apple juice

¼ cup canola oil

2 tablespoons brown sugar

1 teaspoon vanilla extract

⅔ cup dried currants or raisins

1 Preheat the oven to 350°F. Lightly oil or coat a large rimmed baking sheet with nonstick cooking spray and set aside.

2 Stir together the oats, Cheerios®, almonds, flaxseed, and cinnamon in a large bowl. In a separate bowl, whisk the maple syrup, apple juice, canola oil, brown sugar, and vanilla until well blended. Pour over the oat mixture and stir until well coated.

3 Spread the mixture evenly on the prepared baking sheet and bake about 20 minutes, or until golden brown. Stir halfway through to ensure even baking. When done, cool about 10 minutes before adding the currants.

4 Store in an airtight container for up to 2 weeks.

PER SERVING (½ cup): 250 calories, 12g fat (1g saturated, 0.9g omega-3), 35mg sodium, 33g carbohydrate, 4g fiber, 6g protein, 15% iron

mom's feedback This recipe was quick, easy, and it keeps well — although we ate it within a week! It was crunchy and we loved it mixed in with yogurt.

— Wendy, mother of Ryan, age 4 ▪ Jacksonville, FL

Blueberry Breakfast Parfait

MAKES 1 SERVING

We would be remiss if we didn't address the issue of kids skipping breakfast. According to a new study, 20 percent of children and 32 percent of adolescents opt out of breakfast. We're not sure why kids leave the house on an empty stomach, but we suspect it has a lot to do with fatigue (we don't know too many kids who enjoy waking up early), a desire to assert independence, and/or a lack of time. To entice kids of all ages to eat breakfast, we created this simple parfait. By layering fiber-filled cereal with protein-rich yogurt and nutrient-dense berries, this one-bowl parfait looks more like a fancy dessert than the power-house breakfast it is.

½ cup low-fat vanilla or fruited yogurt

⅓ cup whole grain cereal or granola

⅓ cup blueberries

1 Place half the yogurt in the bottom of a parfait glass, bowl, or drinking glass. Top with half the cereal and half the blueberries. Repeat with the remaining yogurt, cereal and berries.

PER SERVING 270 calories, 4g fat (1.5g saturated), 70mg sodium, 45g carbohydrate, 4g fiber, 9g protein, 20% calcium

tip For younger kids with smaller appetites, use ⅓ cup yogurt, ¼ cup cereal, and ¼ cup berries. Plenty of other fruits would work great in this recipe too: sliced strawberries, raspberries, diced cantaloupe, mango, peach, kiwi, or banana.

mom's feedback

I liked the ease of making this and the smaller portion size option for my little guys. I also like how it was very healthy and could be made with purchased or homemade ingredients (we make our own granola and yogurt and have frozen blueberries that we picked last summer).

Aj, mother of Josephine, age 8 months, Abel, age 3 and Judah, age 5 ▪ Dundee, OR

Ham and Cheesy Breakfast Sandwich

MAKES 1 SERVING

While getting kids to eat a variety of vegetables is one of the biggest challenges we hear about from moms, protein can be a tough sell too, especially with kids who don't like meat. If you're worried your child isn't getting enough protein, try this easy-to-assemble breakfast sandwich. Between the egg, the cheese, and the deli ham, your child will start the day with nearly 20 grams of high-quality protein.

½ teaspoon canola oil

1 large egg, beaten

1 slice lower-sodium deli ham (¾ ounce)

1 slice reduced-fat Cheddar or American cheese (½ ounce)

1 whole wheat English muffin, halved and lightly toasted

1 Heat the oil in a small nonstick skillet over medium heat. Add the egg and cook until almost set, 2 to 3 minutes.

2 Fold the egg in half and then in half again so it is about the same size as the muffin. Top with the ham and cheese and cook, covered, until the cheese melts, 1 to 2 minutes. Place between the muffin halves.

PER SERVING 260 calories, 9g fat, (2g saturated, 0.4g omega-3), 550mg sodium, 24g carbohydrate, 3g fiber, 19g protein, 15% calcium

mom's feedback

Kiran had one word to describe this recipe: "Yum." The next time I make it, I may toss in some finely chopped mushrooms or bell pepper for even more flavor.

— Melissa, mother of Aidan, age 2 and Kiran, age 5 ▪ San Jose, CA

Nest Eggs

MAKES 2 SERVINGS

Nutrition advice has a habit of flip-flopping from time to time. Take eggs, for example. Although they're an excellent source of high-quality protein and the yolks boast a laundry list of must-have nutrients like lutein, an antioxidant important for healthy vision, and choline, a type of B vitamin needed for normal brain development, the fact that they're high in cholesterol once put them on the "foods to limit" list for some people. The bottom line today, however, is that eggs can fit quite comfortably into a heart-healthy diet. They actually have more of the good monounsaturated fat than the not-so-good saturated fat. And if you buy omega-3 eggs — something we always do — you'll be doing your family's health an even bigger favor. Each omega-3 egg typically provides over 100 milligrams of the heart-healthy fat — about 10 percent of the recommended daily intake. So go ahead and enjoy these eggs without a twinge of guilt.

2 slices 100% whole wheat bread, lightly toasted

1 teaspoon canola oil

2 large eggs

A few drizzles of honey or pure maple syrup

1 Use a cookie cutter or the top of a small drinking glass to cut a 2½-inch round hole in the middle of each slice of toast. Set the "holes" aside.

2 Heat the oil in a large nonstick skillet over medium heat. Place the bread slices in the skillet. Crack the eggs open and drop into the cutout circles; break the yolks. Cover the skillet and cook until the eggs set, 4 to 5 minutes. Flip the bread and cook an additional 30 seconds to 1 minute.

3 Top with honey or maple syrup and serve with the toasted (and buttered, as desired) "holes" on the side.

PER SERVING 180 calories, 7g fat, (1.5g saturated, 0.4g omega-3), 190mg sodium, 16g carbohydrate, 2g fiber, 10g protein, 10% iron

mom's feedback My daughter is two so this was new for her. She took a few learning bites of the egg, and we plan on making it again.

— Deanna, mother of Mia, age 2 ▪ Havertown, PA

Banana Brownie Waffles

MAKES EIGHT 4 ½ X 4 ½-INCH WAFFLES

When Janice and Don got married, they received a waffle maker as a wedding gift. Instead of stashing it in a cabinet, Janice used their waffle maker constantly, until it went kaput about a year ago. The original waffle maker was quickly replaced with a fancy Belgian one. Coincidentally, around that time we heard from an 11-year-old fan from Seattle named Margaret, who asked us to include a chocolate waffle recipe in our next book. Janice got right to work. This waffle batter is chock-full of goodness. In addition to cocoa powder, we use whole wheat flour, wheat germ, bananas, and eggs, and instead of butter, we use canola oil. Top with sliced bananas or berries and a dollop of light whipped cream or a drizzle of maple syrup and your kids won't be hungry 'til lunch. As for Margaret, read on for her family's feedback.

1 cup all-purpose flour

½ cup whole wheat flour

½ cup cocoa powder, sifted

¼ cup wheat germ

3 tablespoons granulated sugar

1 tablespoon baking powder

¾ teaspoon ground cinnamon

½ teaspoon salt

1½ cups 1% low-fat milk

2 ripe bananas, mashed (1 cup)

2 large eggs, beaten

¼ cup canola oil

2 teaspoons vanilla extract

Pure maple syrup or light whipped cream, optional

1 Preheat the waffle iron according to the manufacturer's instructions.

2 Whisk together the all-purpose flour, whole wheat flour, cocoa powder, wheat germ, sugar, baking powder, cinnamon, and salt in a large bowl.

3 In a separate bowl, whisk the milk, bananas, eggs, oil, and vanilla until well blended. Pour over the dry ingredients and stir until just combined.

4 Lightly oil or coat the hot waffle iron grids with nonstick cooking spray. Pour the batter onto the center of the lower grid (about 2 cups, or the amount specified for your waffle iron) and cook on medium to medium-high setting until done, 2 to 4 minutes. Repeat with the remaining cooking spray and batter.

5 Top with maple syrup or light whipped cream as desired.

PER SERVING (1 waffle): 270 calories, 10g fat (1.5g saturated, 0.7g omega-3), 330mg sodium, 37g carbohydrate, 4g fiber, 8g protein, 15% calcium, 15% iron

tip Freeze leftover waffles in individual zip-top bags. To reheat, simply toast in a toaster oven or place in a 350°F oven for 3 to 5 minutes.

mom's feedback

In addition to being delicious, the chocolate waffles were more filling and satisfying than standard waffles. We like them with a few chocolate chips stirred into the batter.

— Elizabeth, mother of Margaret, age 11 and Frances, age 14 ▪ Seattle, WA

Peter Pumpkin-Eater Waffles

MAKES EIGHT 4 ½ X 4 ½-INCH WAFFLES

Frozen waffles are fine when you're in a pinch or need something fast for breakfast. Be sure to look for whole grain options. But when you have time — and a waffle maker — give our pumpkin waffles a try. For this recipe, we slip some needed nutrients into kids' diets — calcium, fiber, and vitamin A — by using whole wheat flour, walnuts, and canned pumpkin.

1 cup all-purpose flour

½ cup whole wheat flour

½ cup walnuts, finely chopped

1 tablespoon baking powder

1 teaspoon ground cinnamon

¼ teaspoon salt

1 pinch ground nutmeg

1¾ cups 1% low-fat milk

¾ cup canned 100% pure pumpkin

3 large eggs, beaten

¼ cup canola oil

3 tablespoons brown sugar

1 teaspoon vanilla extract

Pure maple syrup, optional

1 Preheat the waffle iron according to the manufacturer's instructions.

2 Whisk together the all-purpose flour, whole wheat flour, walnuts, baking powder, cinnamon, salt, and nutmeg in a large bowl.

3 In a separate bowl, whisk the milk, pumpkin, eggs, oil, brown sugar, and vanilla until well blended. Pour over the dry ingredients and stir until just combined.

4 Lightlyt oil or coat the hot waffle iron grids with nonstick cooking spray. Pour the batter onto the center of the lower grid (about 2 cups, or the amount specified for your waffle iron) and cook on medium to medium-high setting until done, 2 to 4 minutes. Repeat with the remaining cooking spray and batter.

5 Serve with additional chopped walnuts on top and maple syrup as desired.

PER SERVING (1 waffle): 310 calories, 16g fat (2g saturated, 1.6g omega-3), 310mg sodium, 32g carbohydrate, 3g fiber, 9g protein, 80% vitamin A, 20% calcium, 10% iron

mom's feedback

We love how the nuts gave the waffles a little more crunch. Topped with some cinnamon whipped cream or frozen vanilla yogurt, these waffles could be served for dessert!

— Michelle, mother of Riley, age 3, Ben, age 6 and Sidni, age 15 ▪ Aurora, CO

Raspberry Breakfast Cake

MAKES 8 SERVINGS

The impetus for this recipe came from a raspberry buttermilk cake we saw in *Gourmet* magazine. It looked like something kids would happily eat; after all, there aren't too many who would kvetch if given cake for breakfast. The original recipe called for half a stick of butter, ⅔ cup sugar, and all white flour. We add a healthier spin by switching to canola oil, less sugar, and some whole wheat flour and wheat germ (rich in heart-healthy vitamin E). Of course, we keep the raspberries. We decided this was so healthy, it was A-OK to serve for breakfast.

½ cup all-purpose flour

½ cup whole wheat flour

¼ cup wheat germ

½ teaspoon baking soda

½ teaspoon baking powder

¼ teaspoon salt

1 large egg, beaten

½ cup plus 1 tablespoon granulated sugar, divided

¼ cup canola oil

½ cup 1% low-fat milk

1 tablespoon lemon juice

½ teaspoon vanilla extract

1 cup fresh raspberries

1 Preheat the oven to 400°F. Lightly oil or coat a 9-inch round cake pan with nonstick cooking spray and set aside.

2 Whisk together the all-purpose flour, whole wheat flour, wheat germ, baking soda, baking powder, and salt in a large bowl.

3 In a separate bowl, whisk the egg, ½ cup of the sugar, and the oil until well blended. Whisk in the milk, lemon juice, and vanilla.

4 Pour the liquid ingredients over the dry ingredients and stir until just combined. Spread the batter evenly in the prepared pan. Arrange the raspberries over the top, and sprinkle with the remaining 1 tablespoon sugar.

5 Bake 20 to 22 minutes, or until the cake is golden and a toothpick inserted in the center comes out clean. Transfer to a wire rack and cool (or serve while it's still warm).

PER SERVING (1 slice): 210 calories, 8g fat (1g saturated, 0.7g omega-3), 190mg sodium, 30g carbohydrate, 3g fiber, 5g protein

tip If raspberries aren't in season, you can use frozen raspberries or ⅔ cup fresh or frozen blueberries.

mom's feedback When my daughter saw cake for breakfast, she wondered if it was someone's birthday! The berries were a big hit.

Marla, mother of Sarah, age 3 ▪ Evanston, IL

Berry Good French Toast

MAKES 4 SERVINGS

For this recipe, we remake classic French toast using whole wheat bread, which usually goes unnoticed, since the bread is cooked. Then we up the ante with the addition of a healthy topping made with berries. The berry sauce is a nice change from maple syrup; and made with two cups of strawberries, each serving provides nearly half a day's worth of vitamin C. We call for frozen strawberries, but you could certainly use fresh — especially when they're in season. The topping is easy to make, but you'll need to budget in about 20 minutes to give the berries time to cook down to a sweet, fruity syrup. To save time, the topping can be made ahead and kept in the fridge for a few days.

2 cups frozen strawberries

½ cup water

2 tablespoons granulated sugar

1 pinch salt

4 large eggs

½ cup 1% low-fat milk

½ teaspoon ground cinnamon

2 teaspoons canola oil, divided

8 slices 100% whole wheat bread

Powdered sugar

1 For the topping, place the strawberries, water, sugar, and salt in a small or medium saucepan. Place over high heat and bring to a boil. Reduce the heat and continue to cook at a low boil, stirring every few minutes, until the berries break down and the mixture is nice and syrupy, 15 to 20 minutes. To speed things up a bit, use the back of a spoon to smoosh the berries against the side of the saucepan as you stir.

2 While the berries are simmering, whisk together the eggs, milk, and cinnamon in a large bowl. Heat half the oil in a large nonstick skillet over medium–high heat. Dip the bread in the egg mixture, one slice at a time, and coat evenly.

3 Place the bread in the skillet and cook until the bottoms turn golden brown, about 3 minutes per side. Remove to a plate, cover, and set aside. Repeat with the remaining oil and bread slices. Sprinkle with powdered sugar and serve with the strawberry topping.

PER SERVING (2 slices): 290 calories, 9g fat (2g saturated, 0.4g omega-3), 340mg sodium, 38g carbohydrate, 5g fiber, 15g protein, 45% vitamin C, 15% calcium, 15% iron

tip You may be tempted (as we were) to cut back on the sugar in the strawberry topping. Resist the urge because the berries won't thicken without it!

mom's feedback Sara doesn't usually like whole wheat bread, but she said the French toast was awesome, and Zack asked if I could make it every Sunday morning from now on.

Lisa, mother of Zack, age 12 and Sara, age 17 ▪ Melrose, MA

Fruity Chicken Kebabs

CHAPTER 3

Lunch Box Winners

The rise in food allergy awareness and peanut-free policies means kids don't often trade their lunches at school anymore. But if they don't like what you've packed, chances are they'll simply throw it away. Hang out by the trash can in your school cafeteria and you'll see what we mean! To guarantee your children will actually eat their midday meal — and it's healthy — you may need to shake things up a bit by switching from the usual turkey and cheese or PB&J on white bread to our better-for-you and better-tasting options. We're confident that our *Sushi Ham and Cheese Roll Ups*, *A-Plus Pasta Salad*, and *Fruity Chicken Kebabs* will never see the inside of a wastebasket. Most of our recipes make one or two servings, but you can certainly double or triple them, depending on the number of lunches you're packing.

Josh, Faith, and Nathan build their own kebabs with chicken, grapes, and strawberries. Mom, Kelly, admires their handiwork.

See more photos of our young cooks and moms making their favorite lunch recipes on Flickr http://www.flickr.com/photos/mealmakeovermoms

Fruity Chicken Kebabs

MAKES 4 SERVINGS

We often hear from moms that an easy way to coax kids into eating more fresh fruit is to put it on a toothpick or skewer. So that's exactly what we do with these playful kebabs. By skewering kid-friendly strawberries and grapes with lean chunks of chicken, we create a colorful lunch box meal that may become the envy of the cafeteria. If your children are prone to sword fights, make smaller kebabs with toothpicks or thin straws. Round out the lunch by packing it with low-fat milk or an all-natural fruit smoothie and a mini whole wheat bagel with light cream cheese or a slice of reduced-fat cheese.

8 ounces lower-sodium deli chicken or turkey, sliced ¾-inch thick

8 8-inch wooden skewers

16 green grapes

12 strawberries, cut in half lengthwise

1 Cut the chicken into ¾-inch cubes. To make the kebabs, thread 3 pieces of cubed chicken, 2 grapes, and 3 strawberry halves onto each skewer in any order that you and your children choose. Be sure to leave enough space at the bottom so the kids can hold the skewers comfortably.

2 To wrap, lay 2 skewers on a sheet of aluminum foil and fold the foil loosely over the kebabs.

PER SERVING (2 kebabs): 100 calories, 1.5g fat (0g saturated), 360mg sodium, 10g carbohydrate, 2g fiber, 14g protein, 80% vitamin C

tip If you have leftover grilled or roasted chicken on hand, cut into chunks and use instead of the deli chicken.

mom's feedback I like that I can pack the kebabs for lunches or a picnic. I was surprised that my 3-year old was able to assemble hers.

Kelly, mother of Faith, age 3, Nathan, age 4 and Josh, age 7 ▪ Downers Grove, IL

Better-For-You B.L.T.

MAKES 4 SERVINGS

When you think of the typical foods dietitians eat, bacon may not be the first thing that comes to mind. That said, a small amount of bacon, cooked, drained, and patted with paper towels to absorb the excess fat, can certainly fit right in with a healthy diet. For this recipe, we start with uncured, nitrite-free bacon and build from there using whole wheat bread (any whole grain bread works well), romaine lettuce (which is higher in vitamins A and C than iceberg), light mayonnaise, and a few slices of tomato. The end result is a sandwich with lots of flavor but not a lot of bad fat.

4 teaspoons light mayonnaise

8 slices 100% whole wheat bread

8 romaine lettuce leaves, washed, trimmed, and dried

8 thin slices tomato

8 slices nitrite-free bacon, cooked

1 Spread the mayonnaise evenly over four of the bread slices. Layer with one lettuce leaf, 2 slices of tomato, 2 slices of bacon, and the remaining lettuce. Place the remaining bread slices firmly on top.

2 Slice in half and wrap in plastic wrap, or place in zip-top bags.

PER SERVING (1 sandwich): 230 calories, 9g fat (2.5g saturated), 550mg sodium, 25g carbohydrate, 5g fiber, 12g protein, 25% vitamin A, 15% vitamin C, 10% iron

mom's feedback

My son — who can be picky — said he wanted to try this sandwich! We all liked it, and I ended up adding even more tomatoes.

— Kim, mother of Genny, age 4 and Jackson, age 6 ▪ North Augusta, SC

Scoop-It-Up Salmon Salad

MAKES 2 SERVINGS

We never miss an opportunity to incorporate more heart-healthy omega-3 fats into our children's diets. That's why this salmon salad is especially near and dear to us. Each serving has nearly a day's worth of omega-3s and the flavor is surprisingly mild … not fishy. With fun scoopers like tortilla chips, cucumber wheels, and whole grain crackers on the side, it's a nice change of pace from the usual sandwich or wrap.

1 5- or 6-ounce can boneless, skinless salmon, drained and flaked

1 small carrot, shredded (about ¼ cup)

2 tablespoons light mayonnaise

1½ teaspoons honey mustard

Kosher salt and freshly ground black pepper

1 pinch fresh or dried dill, optional

Scooper options: Baked tortilla chips, cucumber wheels, mini whole wheat pitas, whole grain crackers

1 Place the salmon, carrot, mayonnaise, honey mustard, salt and pepper to taste, and dill as desired in a medium bowl and stir to combine.

2 Divide the salmon salad between two plastic containers with tight-fitting lids, and place optional "scoopers" in separate containers.

PER SERVING (⅓ cup): 140 calories, 7g fat (1.5g saturated, 1.1g omega-3), 520mg sodium, 5g carbohydrate, 0g fiber, 13g protein, 45% vitamin A

tip You can also make this salad with one 5- or 6-ounce can of solid white or light tuna, packed in water, and drained and flaked.

mom's feedback I like the recipe because I can put it in my daughter's lunch (I'm running out of lunch ideas!), and because I can't usually get my kids to eat carrots. Of course, salmon is also extremely healthy.

— Laura, mother of Meredith, age 4 and Sophia, age 8 ▪ Newmarket, Ontario, Canada

A Sub to Love

MAKES 1 SERVING

When Liz's son Josh entered his freshman year of high school, his appetite suddenly soared. To satisfy his noonday hunger pangs and to fill him up with high-quality calories, Liz began packing larger, more substantial sandwiches ... and this sandwich certainly hit the mark. Made on a whole wheat sub roll — whole grains are more filling than refined — with deli meats and cheese and zesty Italian dressing, it's a teenager's dream. Josh's favorite sandwich sides include fresh fruit such as grapes, a Clementine, or a mini unsweetened applesauce, and 100% fruit juice or a carton of 1% low-fat milk.

1 6-inch whole wheat sub or hoagie roll, halved

1 romaine lettuce leaf, washed, trimmed, and dried

1½ slices lower-sodium deli turkey (about 1¼ ounces)

1 slice deli roast beef (about ¾ ounce)

1 slice reduced-fat provolone cheese (about ½ ounce)

½ teaspoon Italian salad dressing

Freshly ground black pepper, optional

1 Place half the lettuce over one side of the roll. Top with the turkey, roast beef, cheese, salad dressing, pepper as desired, and the remaining lettuce. Place the remaining roll half firmly on top.

2 Slice in half and wrap in plastic wrap, or place in a zip-top bag.

PER SERVING (1 sub): 300 calories, 9g fat (3.5g saturated), 700mg sodium, 35g carbohydrate, 5g fiber, 22g protein, 10% vitamin A, 20% calcium, 15% iron

mom's feedback

The idea of using Italian dressing was phenomenal. My daughter has problems with tomato-based things and can't seem to get over her squeamishness of mayo. Using the dressing as a topping was ideal.

— Stephanie, mother of Emmy, age 8 ▪ Boise, ID

Peanut Butter Swirl Sandwich

MAKES 1 SANDWICH

There is nothing new or different about a peanut butter & jelly sandwich, so for this recipe, we swap the usual white or whole wheat bread with slightly-sweet, whole grain cinnamon-raisin swirl. It's amazing how the flavor upgrade can spark a child's interest in digging into lunch. You can change it up even more by adding a thin layer of sliced apples or bananas.

2 tablespoons peanut butter

1 tablespoon all-fruit jelly or jam

2 slices 100% whole wheat cinnamon with raisins swirl bread

1 Spread half the peanut butter on one slice of bread and the remaining peanut butter on the other slice (this will prevent the jelly from making the bread soggy). Spread the jelly on one side. Place the bread together and slice in half.

2 Wrap in plastic wrap, or place in a zip-top bag.

PER SERVING (1 sandwich): 410 calories, 18g fat (2g saturated), 330mg sodium, 46g carbohydrate, 6g fiber, 13g protein, 15% iron

mom's feedback

I like how just a few simple changes can add even more nutritional punch to a PB&J sandwich. My 7-year old can even make it himself.

Katie, mother of Audrey, age 4 months, Jonah, age 4 and Elliot, age 7 ▪ Littleton, MA

Turkey and Cheese Bagelwich

MAKES 1 SERVING

We do a lot of cooking classes and lectures for teens and tweens and what we have discovered from our many conversations with them is that white bagels are their hands-down go-to breakfast, lunch, and snack food favorite. Our main issue with bagels is that they're pretty ho-hum when it comes to nutrition, especially when there's nothing more than a layer of cream cheese or butter on top. To give kids the foods they love while bolstering the good nutrition, our lunch box bagelwich starts off on the right foot with a whole grain bagel, reduced-fat cheese, and lower-sodium turkey. We stick with familiar cream cheese but choose a light version and add some pesto for a kick of flavor.

2   teaspoons light cream cheese

1   whole wheat bagel, sliced in half

1   teaspoon prepared basil pesto

1   slice part-skim mozzarella cheese (about ½ ounce)

6   baby spinach leaves

1   slice lower-sodium deli turkey (about ¾ ounce)

1 Spread the cream cheese on one side of the bagel and the pesto on the other side. Top either side with the cheese, spinach leaves, and turkey. Place the remaining bagel half firmly on top.

2 Slice in half and wrap in plastic wrap, or place in a zip-top bag.

PER SERVING (1 sandwich): 350 calories, 8g fat (4g saturated), 730mg sodium, 52g carbohydrate, 8g fiber, 20g protein, 15% vitamin A, 25% calcium, 15% iron

mom's feedback This was a perfect recipe. It was simple to make — both of my kids were able to help — and my husband said he would love to take it for his lunch.

Jenette, mother of Makenzie, age 18 months and Hayden, age 3 ▪ Surprise, AZ

Bacon and Egg Salad Rolls

MAKES 2 SERVINGS

Egg salad may sound very 1950's, but as far as we're concerned it's survived the test of time. For our updated, super-flavorful remix, we combine bits of bacon with naturally sweet shredded carrots. The result is an egg salad mixture that's light years from what grandma used to make! Placing the salad on kid-size slider buns — if you're not familiar with sliders, they look like mini burger buns — ups the appeal. For tips on the best way to hard cook an egg, see page 165.

2 large eggs, hard cooked, shelled, and coarsely chopped

2 slices nitrite-free bacon, cooked and coarsely chopped

2 tablespoons shredded carrot

1½ tablespoons light mayonnaise

Kosher salt and freshly ground black pepper

2 romaine lettuce leaves, washed, trimmed and dried

4 slider rolls (preferably whole grain), or 2 mini whole wheat pita pockets

1 Place the eggs, bacon, carrot, and mayonnaise in a bowl and mix until well combined. Season with salt and pepper to taste.

2 Cut the lettuce leaves into 8 smaller pieces; about the same size as the slider rolls. Layer one side of each roll evenly with a lettuce leaf, the egg salad mixture, and another lettuce leaf. Place the remaining slider half firmly on top.

3 Wrap in plastic wrap, or place in zip-top bags

PER SERVING (2 slider sandwiches): 340 calories, 15g fat (2.5g saturated, 0.5g omega-3), 610mg sodium, 37g carbohydrate, 2g fiber, 18g protein, 30% vitamin A, 10% calcium, 20% iron

tip We created this recipe with two school lunches in mind. You can easily double or triple the recipe if you're cooking for the whole family ... or want leftovers the next day.

mom's feedback My 3-year old actually ate eggs! He loved helping — he tore the lettuce leaves, cut the bacon, and enjoyed mixing.

Jamie, mother of Seamus, age 3 ▪ Marinette, WI

Chicken and Cucumber Caesar Wrap

MAKES 1 SERVING

Caesar salad is one of those salads that defies logic. While "salad" is often perceived as too healthy, or as nothing more than rabbit food, Caesar is the go-to salad for our kids … especially when we're eating out. For Liz's boys, it's definitely the crunchy croutons that entice them to dig in. As for Janice's girls, the crisp romaine and creamy dressing are the draw. Given its popularity with so many kids, we take Caesar salad ingredients, add some chicken and cucumber slices, and roll it all up in a tortilla. We pack it along with fresh fruit and extra veggies — bell pepper strips, sugar snap peas, or baby carrots — for a hard-to-resist noonday meal.

1   1-inch piece cucumber

1   10-inch flour tortilla (preferably whole wheat)

2   slices lower-sodium deli chicken or turkey (about 1½ ounces)

6   baby spinach leaves or 1 romaine lettuce leaf, washed, dried, and coarsely chopped (about ½ cup)

2   teaspoons creamy Caesar salad dressing

2   tablespoons shredded part-skim mozzarella cheese

6   seasoned croutons

1 Peel the cucumber, cut in half, remove the seeds and slice into ¼-inch-thick crescent moon shapes. Set aside.

2 Lay the flour tortilla on a work surface. Arrange the chicken, spinach leaves, cucumber, salad dressing, cheese, and croutons evenly down the center.

3 Roll up tightly burrito style and slice in half. Wrap in plastic wrap, or place in a zip-top bag.

PER SERVING (1 wrap) 280 calories, 10g fat (2.5g saturated), 780mg sodium, 29g carbohydrate, 3g fiber, 18g protein, 10% vitamin A, 15% calcium

mom's feedback

I will definitely make this again. My daughter said she would like to have it in her lunch bag! I also prepared the wrap for my 5-year old niece and 3-year old nephew, and they thought it was delicious too.

— Lisa, mother of Lauren, age 15 and Michael, age 19 ▪ North Reading, MA

Thousand Island Roast Beef Wraps

MAKES 2 SERVINGS

Red meat often gets a bad rap, but there are plenty of lean cuts to choose from at the supermarket (29 to be exact). Beef provides high-quality protein as well as iron, zinc, and choline (a brain booster). When portions are kept to three to four ounces — about the size of a deck of cards — beef can fit into a well-balanced diet quite nicely. Our wraps call for deli roast beef which is surprisingly low in saturated fat and sodium. Two ounces of one of our favorite brands (see *Pantry Picks*, page 18) has just one gram of saturated fat and a scant 80 milligrams of sodium — significantly less than the whopping 590 milligrams in the same amount of regular deli ham.

2 romaine lettuce leaves, washed, dried, and coarsely chopped (1 cup)

1 small carrot, shredded (about ⅓ cup)

2 tablespoons lite Thousand Island salad dressing

Kosher salt and freshly ground black pepper

2 10-inch flour tortillas (preferably whole wheat)

4 slices deli roast beef (about 3 ounces)

2 slices part-skim mozzarella cheese (about 1 ounce)

1 Place the lettuce, carrot, and dressing in a medium bowl and stir to combine. Season with salt and pepper to taste.

2 Lay the flour tortillas on a work surface. Arrange the roast beef, cheese, and the lettuce mixture evenly down the center of each tortilla.

3 Roll up tightly burrito style and slice in half. Wrap in plastic wrap, or place in zip-top bags.

PER SERVING (1 wrap): 300 calories, 10g fat (2.5g saturated), 620mg sodium, 33g carbohydrate, 4g fiber, 20g protein, 100% vitamin A, 10% vitamin C, 15% calcium, 10% iron

tip To kick up the flavor, swap the mozzarella cheese for reduced-fat provolone or pepper Jack. The dressing can also be swapped for low-fat ranch or Italian.

mom's feedback This wrap would also be great for a quick meal before sports practice. Cooper loved the wrap and actually asked for more carrots next time!

Kim, mother of Coleman, age 10 and Cooper, age 12 ▪ Tulsa, OK

Sushi Ham and Cheese Roll Ups

MAKES 2 SERVINGS

There's something about sushi — California rolls in particular — that seems to really intrigue kids. Perhaps it's the challenge of using chopsticks that whets their appetites, or maybe it's the salty soy sauce they get to dip in. This recipe isn't technically sushi, but we do our best to mimic the idea by rolling together ham, cheese, shredded carrots, and pickles. Thanks to Leah, the flavor of these cute little rolls gets an extra kick with honey mustard.

- 1 9 x 11-inch soft Lavash bread
- 2 tablespoons light cream cheese
- 1 teaspoon honey mustard
- 1 small carrot, shredded (about ⅓ cup)
- 2 slices lower-sodium deli ham, each cut in half (about 1½ ounces)
- 1 slice reduced-fat Swiss cheese, cut into 6 smaller pieces (about 1 ounce)
- 1 dill pickle sandwich stuffer, patted dry with paper towels and sliced into four long pieces

1 Place the Lavash on a work surface so the 9-inch end of the bread is facing you. Spread the cream cheese and the honey mustard evenly over the entire Lavash, making sure they reach all the outside edges (the cream cheese will be the "glue" that holds the rolls together).

2 Sprinkle the carrots over the Lavash. Cover, as evenly as possible, with the ham slices. Place two pieces of cheese, side by side, about a quarter of the way up the Lavash. Repeat with two more pieces about halfway up the Lavash, and with the remaining cheese three quarters of the way up.

3 Arrange two slices of the pickle, lengthwise, side by side, in the space between the bottom cheese layers and the remaining pickles in the space between the top cheese layers.

4 Starting at the end closest to you, roll up as tightly as you can until the Lavash looks like a giant cigar. Using a serrated knife, slice into twelve ¾-inch rounds. Arrange the pieces in two plastic containers with tight-fitting lids.

PER SERVING (6 pieces): 210 calories, 4g fat (2g saturated), 600mg sodium, 29g carbohydrate, 2g fiber, 14g protein, 60% vitamin A, 15% calcium, 10% iron

tip This recipe may be a bit tough to visualize, so feel free to visit our Flickr page for cooking prep demonstration photos: http://www.flickr.com/photos/mealmakeovermoms/sets/72157623770584306/

mom's feedback

I loved how surprised my younger son, Josh, was that he liked it. He was bracing himself for the first awful bite, but then a big smile came on his face as he said, "Mmmm." I'm so happy to find something healthy that my boys will actually eat and enjoy.

Lisa, mother of Josh, age 10 and Zach, age 12 ▪ Frisco, TX

A-Plus Pasta Salad

MAKES 5 SERVINGS

Ask Janice's 10-year old, Leah, to name her preferred bagged lunch for school and chances are she'll answer PB&J. Recently, however, she decided to venture outside her culinary comfort zone by declaring our *A-Plus Pasta Salad* her new favorite. The fact that big sister, Carolyn, takes it to school at least once a week was probably all the motivation Leah needed to give it a try. Regardless, Janice couldn't be happier. Our cold pasta salad recipe is brimming with high-energy carbohydrates from the pasta, protein from the chicken, vitamin C-rich peppers, and lots of flavor and crunch. It's versatile too: the bell peppers can easily be replaced with diced cucumber or lightly steamed broccoli florets, and the feta can be switched to small cubes of part-skim mozzarella cheese.

8 ounces dried whole wheat blend bowtie pasta (3 generous cups)

1 small red bell pepper, cut into ¾-inch dice (1 cup)

8 ounces cooked chicken, cut into ¾-inch dice (1½ cups)

½ cup crumbled feta cheese

⅓ cup Italian salad dressing

1 Cook the pasta according to package directions. When done, drain, rinse with cold water, and drain again.

2 Place the pasta in a large bowl. Add the bell pepper, chicken, feta cheese, and salad dressing and stir to combine.

3 Pack in plastic containers with tight-fitting lids.

PER SERVING (1½ cups): 330 calories, 10g fat (3.5g saturated, 0.5g omega-3), 480mg sodium, 34g carbohydrate, 4g fiber, 25g protein, 10% vitamin A, 30% vitamin C, 10% calcium

tip If you make this recipe the night before, the pasta may be a bit dry the next day. To add more moisture, stir in a bit more salad dressing before packing in your child's lunch box. Feel free to use a light salad dressing if you're trying to cut calories.

 **mom's feedback** To give it more of a Greek flavor, I'm going to add kalamata olives the next time I make this. I may even bring it to work!

Sandi, mother of Kevin, age 14 and Michelle and Julie, age 21 ▪ Port Orange, FL

Corny Pups and Beans

MAKES 3 SERVINGS

Do your kids suffer from brown bag boredom? If they do, then shake things up by switching from the usual cold lunch to one that's piping hot. This recipe requires just three ingredients — all-natural vegetarian hot dogs (they tend to be lower in sodium than meat-based dogs), a can of fiber-rich baked beans, and frozen corn — as well as a small thermos and a few extra minutes in the morning. Liz's son, Simon, prefers a hot lunch and tends to eat every last bite when *Corny Pups and Beans* is on the menu.

4 vegetarian hot dogs, cooked and sliced into ½-inch rounds

1 15-ounce can vegetarian baked beans

¾ cup frozen corn, thawed

1 Combine the hot dogs, beans, and corn in a small saucepan and heat over medium heat, stirring frequently, until heated through, about 5 minutes.

2 Place in a thermos or serve in a bowl.

PER SERVING (1 cup): 270 calories, 4.5g fat (1.5g saturated), 630mg sodium, 42g carbohydrate, 10g fiber, 20g protein, 10% calcium, 30% iron

tip Any kind of all-natural hot dog works well in this recipe: beef, turkey, chicken, or tofu. For young children and toddlers, cut them lengthwise into quarters before slicing.

mom's feedback
Olivia actually thought it tasted like mac & cheese ... but with beans and corn. The name, Corny Pups and Beans really grabbed her attention.

— Jessica, mother of Hollyn, age 2 and Olivia, age 5 ▪ Surprise, AZ

ABC Chicken Alphabet Soup

CHAPTER 4

Soups to Savor

At their best, homemade soups are simple and soothing. But, they can also be swimming in sodium when recipes call for canned broths and bouillon cubes. Our solution is to use all-natural broths — they're moderate in sodium, and compared to salt-free broths, taste so much better. To add interesting textures, flavors, and good nutrition to our brews, we also use lots of vegetables (cut into small pieces, of course), beans, grains, canned crushed tomatoes, lean meats, and whole wheat blend pastas. Our goal is to make these savory soups as nourishing for developing bodies as they are for developing taste buds.

Lizzie and her son, Simon, make our robust *ABC Chicken Alphabet Soup*. Sydney helps by delivering the pasta.

See more photos of our young cooks and moms cooking their favorite soup recipes on Flickr http://www.flickr.com/photos/mealmakeovermoms

Potato Carrot Soup with Goldfish Croutons

MAKES 6 SERVINGS

Potato soup is one of those recipes that typically goes over big with kids. In fact, when we asked our Facebook fans to share their favorite family soup recipes, potato soup ranked in the top three. The only problem with most hearty potato soups is the use of heavy cream. So to lighten things up and add a big kick of good nutrition, we use the potatoes themselves to give it thickness and add in two extra kid-friendly veggies — carrots and corn.

1 tablespoon extra virgin olive oil

2 stalks celery, trimmed and cut into ¼-inch dice (½ cup)

½ small onion, cut into ¼-inch dice (½ cup)

1 32-ounce carton all-natural chicken broth

2 pounds white potatoes, peeled and cut into 1-inch dice (5 cups)

1 large carrot, peeled and shredded (1 cup)

2 fresh thyme sprigs

1 cup frozen corn, thawed

½ cup shredded reduced-fat Cheddar cheese

Kosher salt and freshly ground black pepper

½ cup whole grain Goldfish® crackers

1 Heat the oil in a large Dutch oven or saucepan over medium heat. Add the celery and onion and cook, stirring frequently, until the vegetables are softened, about 7 minutes.

2 Stir in the broth, potatoes, carrot, and thyme. Cover, raise the heat, and bring to a boil. Reduce the heat and cook at a low boil, uncovered, until the potatoes are tender, about 15 minutes.

3 Remove the thyme, and let the mixture cool slightly. Transfer to a blender and puree in batches until very smooth and creamy. You can also use an immersion blender to puree the soup.

4 Place the soup back in the Dutch oven over low heat. Add the corn and cheese and stir until the cheese melts. Season with salt and pepper to taste. Top each serving with about 9 Goldfish® crackers.

PER SERVING (1 cup): 210 calories, 5g fat (1.5g saturated), 520mg sodium, 35g carbohydrate, 5g fiber, 8g protein, 60% vitamin A, 20% vitamin C, 10% calcium, 10% iron

mom's feedback

My family loved the flavor and the consistency of this soup. My husband even said, "Are you sure this soup is healthy? It tastes too good!" I am definitely going to invest in an immersion blender.

Lisa, mother of Sarah, age 10 and Elizabeth, age 13 ▪ Lexington, MA

Brilliant Bean and Broccoli Cheese Soup

MAKES 6 SERVINGS

Having a well stocked pantry can turn dinnertime drudgery into a downright delight. This recipe relies on some of our favorite pantry staples — all-natural broth, frozen veggies, and canned beans — and it takes just minutes to prepare. All you'll really need are a blender and an appetite for something creamy and delicious. Happily, the "creaminess" in this soup comes from the fiber-rich beans and the reduced-fat cheese — not from cream.

1 tablespoon extra virgin olive oil

1 large clove garlic, minced

1 small onion, cut into ¼-inch dice (1 cup)

1 32-ounce carton all-natural chicken or vegetable broth

1 16-ounce bag frozen chopped broccoli

1 15-ounce can cannellini beans, drained and rinsed

¼ teaspoon black pepper

1½ cups shredded reduced-fat Cheddar cheese, divided

Kosher salt

Seasoned croutons, optional

1 Heat the oil in a large Dutch oven or saucepan over medium heat. Add the garlic and cook, stirring frequently, until golden, 30 seconds to 1 minute. Add the onion and cook, stirring frequently, until softened, about 7 minutes.

2 Stir in the broth, broccoli, beans, and pepper. Cover, raise the heat, and bring to a boil. Reduce the heat and simmer, covered, until the broccoli is tender, 5 to 7 minutes.

3 Let the mixture cool slightly. Transfer to a blender and puree in batches until very smooth and creamy. You can also use an immersion blender to puree the soup.

4 Place the soup back in the Dutch oven over low heat. Add 1 cup of the cheese and stir until it melts. Season with salt and additional pepper to taste. Top each serving with the remaining cheese and the croutons as desired.

PER SERVING (1 cup): 190 calories, 8g fat (3.5g saturated), 580mg sodium, 18g carbohydrate, 6g fiber, 14g protein, 25% vitamin A, 80% vitamin C, 30% calcium, 10% iron

tip We have found that some preshredded cheeses don't melt well in this recipe. We suspect the cornstarch added to prevent caking may be the culprit. For best results, use a block of reduced-fat Cheddar cheese and shred it on the large holes of a box grater.

mom's feedback The flavor and color were great. This is something I can make on any weeknight.

Margot, mother of Mallory, age 1½ ▪ Glen Burnie, MD

Brainy Fish Chowder

MAKES 6 SERVINGS

If you read our blog, *Meal Makeover Moms' Kitchen*, you'll be familiar with an occasional feature called *Recipe Rescue*, where we take family favorites and give them a healthy makeover. When Kristin, co-host of the wildly popular *Manic Mommies* podcast told us her favorite fish chowder is made with a staggering 3 cups of cream and half a stick of butter we went to town with our Moms' Rescue. To slim things down, we take out the cream entirely and make our own luscious sauce with low-fat milk as the base. For kids who shun seafood, this is a simple way to get them hooked.

1¼ pounds white fish such as haddock or cod, cut into 1-inch pieces

1 pound yellow or Yukon Gold potatoes, peeled and cut into ¾-inch dice (3 cups)

12 ounces carrots, peeled and cut into ½-inch dice (2 cups)

1 small onion, cut into ¼-inch dice (1 cup)

2 tablespoons extra virgin olive oil

2 tablespoons sherry wine or ¼ cup white wine

1 tablespoon Worcestershire sauce

1 bay leaf

½ teaspoon kosher salt

¼ teaspoon black pepper

¼ teaspoon dried dill

¼ teaspoon celery seed

1 ounce pancetta ham or 2 slices nitrite-free bacon, coarsely chopped

3 tablespoons unsalted butter

4 tablespoons all-purpose flour

2 cups 1% low-fat milk

2 cups all-natural chicken broth

¼ cup light sour cream, optional

Oyster crackers, optional

1 Preheat the oven to 375°F. Place the fish, potatoes, carrots, onion, olive oil, wine, Worcestershire sauce, bay leaf, salt, pepper, dill, and celery seed in a large Dutch oven or ovenproof pot or casserole, and gently stir to combine.

2 Cover and bake until the fish is cooked through and the vegetables are tender, about 1 hour. Remove from the oven and set aside.

3 About 15 minutes before the fish is done, prepare your "cream" sauce. Cook the pancetta in a medium saucepan over medium heat, stirring frequently, until crispy, about 5 minutes.

4 Add the butter and heat until it melts. Add the flour and whisk constantly until smooth, about 2 minutes. Whisk the milk and broth slowly into the flour mixture. Raise the heat and bring to a low boil, stirring constantly. Reduce the heat and continue to simmer and stir gently until the mixture thickens, about 3 minutes.

5 Remove from the heat, and whisk in the sour cream as desired. Add the sauce to the fish mixture and stir gently to combine. Remove the bay leaf. Top each serving with oyster crackers as desired.

PER SERVING (1 generous cup): 330 calories, 13g fat (5g saturated, 0.2g omega-3), 500mg sodium, 30g carbohydrate, 4g fiber, 22g protein, 180% vitamin A, 25% vitamin C, 15% calcium

> **tip** Kristin's husband suggests adding diced celery along with the carrots and onion, and mixing in baby peas at the end for even more veggies.

mom's feedback

The original recipe was a family favorite, so we were hesitant about giving it a slimdown. But the results were so good, we consider this "the" fish chowder recipe now. I like to make it on the weekends or snow days — it's full of good things like fish and veggies — and makes enough for leftovers.

Kristin, mother of Sophie, age 4 and Anders, age 7 ■ Ashland, MA

Tuscan Minestrone Soup

MAKES 6 SERVINGS

If your kids like vegetable soup and pasta, they'll love this veggie-packed Minestrone soup. The secret to mealtime success with this dish is to dice the zucchini and carrots into small, cute pieces so they go down with a smile along with the more familiar elbow pasta. And note, we use whole wheat blend pasta in this recipe, which is just as kid-pleasing as plain pasta, but is higher in fiber. Our soup can be a one-dish meal when served with a whole grain roll and sliced fruit on the side.

- 2 tablespoons extra virgin olive oil
- 2 medium zucchini (about 9 ounces each), unpeeled and cut into ½-inch dice
- 1 large carrot, peeled and cut into ¼-inch dice (1 cup)
- ½ small onion, cut into ¼-inch dice (½ cup)
- 2 cloves garlic, minced
- 1 teaspoon dried Italian seasoning
- 1 32-ounce carton all-natural chicken broth
- 1 15-ounce can tomato sauce
- 1 15-ounce can cannellini beans, drained and rinsed
- ½ cup dried whole wheat blend elbow pasta
- 3 fresh thyme sprigs
  Kosher salt and freshly ground black pepper
- ⅓ cup grated Parmesan cheese, optional

1 Heat the oil in a large Dutch oven or saucepan over medium heat. Add the zucchini, carrot, onion, garlic, and Italian seasoning and cook, stirring frequently, until the vegetables soften, about 12 minutes. Reduce the heat if the vegetables brown too quickly.

2 Stir in the broth and tomato sauce. Cover, raise the heat, and bring to a boil. Add the beans, pasta, and thyme, reduce the heat and cook at a low boil, uncovered, until the pasta is tender, about 10 minutes.

3 Remove the thyme sprigs, and season with salt and pepper to taste. Top each serving with the Parmesan cheese as desired.

PER SERVING (1 cup): 160 calories, 6g fat (0.5g saturated), 730mg sodium, 24g carbohydrate, 7g fiber, 7g protein, 60% vitamin A, 50% vitamin C, 10% iron

tip If you and your family enjoy the flavor of fresh basil, you can chop some up and sprinkle it over each steamy bowl.

mom's feedback When I served this soup, my 8-year old twins Megan and Molly said, "Can we have thirds?"

Yvette, mother of Megan and Molly, age 8 and Katie, age 10 ▪ Mason, OH

Piping-Hot Peanut Butter Soup

MAKES 6 TO 8 SERVINGS

The inspiration for this soup came from Janice's sister Lori, who got the recipe from one of her favorite restaurants in Olympia, Washington. Long story short, her husband and kids can't get enough of this soup, so we decided to take it on. After a few signature tweaks, we concocted one of the most flavorful, kid-friendly recipes in *Meal Makeover Moms'* history. It's hard to describe, but something truly magical happens when the flavors of the peanut butter, cumin, curry, and cinnamon hit the taste buds!

1 tablespoon canola oil

1 small onion, cut into ¼-inch dice (1 cup)

1 medium red or orange bell pepper, cut into ¼-inch dice (1½ cups)

2 cloves garlic, minced

1 32-ounce carton all-natural chicken broth

1 15-ounce can tomato sauce

½ teaspoon curry powder

½ teaspoon ground cumin

¼ teaspoon chili powder

¼ teaspoon ground cinnamon

¼ teaspoon celery salt or kosher salt

⅛ teaspoon black pepper

1 cup coarsely chopped cooked chicken (6 ounces)

¾ cup instant brown rice

⅔ cup creamy peanut butter

Roasted peanuts, chopped, optional

1 Heat the oil in a large Dutch oven or saucepan over medium heat. Add the onion and cook, stirring frequently, until softened, about 7 minutes. Raise the heat to medium-high, add the bell pepper and garlic and cook, stirring frequently, until the peppers soften, an additional 5 minutes.

2 Stir in the broth, tomato sauce, curry powder, cumin, chili powder, cinnamon, celery salt, and pepper. Cover, raise the heat, and bring to a boil. Reduce the heat and simmer, covered, until the flavors meld, about 45 minutes.

3 Add the chicken, rice, and peanut butter and stir well until the peanut butter melts into the soup. Cover, return to a simmer, and cook until the rice is tender, about 10 minutes. Top each serving with peanuts as desired.

PER SERVING (1 generous cup): 280 calories, 16g fat (3g saturated, 0.2g omega-3), 770mg sodium, 20g carbohydrate, 4g fiber, 14g protein, 30% vitamin A, 80% vitamin C

mom's feedback My family really loves the flavor and texture of this soup, and it's now the favorite in our home. Peter has declared this, "The best soup ever."

Deborah, mother of David, age 9, Peter, age 14 and Rachel, age 18 ▪ Belfast, Ireland

French Onion Soup du Jour

MAKES 5 SERVINGS

Snoop around most people's kitchens and chances are you'll find an onion or two lying around. Onions are certainly versatile, but did you know they're also nutritious? They're a good source of vitamin C and fiber, and they contain compounds that may lower the risk of heart disease and certain cancers. For this recipe, we caramelize the onions, which brings out their natural sweet flavor. We also add tiny bits of zucchini, another veggie rarely regarded as nutritious, but one that's brimming with lutein, an antioxidant that's good for eye health. Top this soup with crispy "croutons" and your kids will say, "Je t'aime."

- 2 tablespoons extra virgin olive oil
- 2 large sweet onions (1½ pounds), halved, peeled, and sliced into ⅛-inch-thick half moons (6 cups)
- 1 medium zucchini (about 9 ounces), unpeeled and cut into ¼-inch dice (1¾ cups)
- 1 teaspoon chopped fresh thyme or ½ teaspoon dried thyme
- ¼ teaspoon kosher salt
- 1 32-ounce carton all-natural vegetable broth
- 5 ¾-inch-thick slices French bread, lightly toasted and each cut into 6 croutons
- ¾ cup shredded Gruyère, Swiss, or part-skim mozzarella cheese

1 Heat the oil in a large Dutch oven or saucepan over medium heat. Add the onions, zucchini, thyme, and salt and cook, stirring every 3 to 5 minutes, until the onions are caramel colored and softened, about 40 minutes. If the vegetables start to brown too soon, reduce the heat, add a tablespoon of water, and scrape up any brown bits. Be patient — slow is the key when caramelizing onions.

2 Stir in the broth. Raise the heat and bring to a boil. Reduce the heat and simmer, uncovered, until the flavors meld, about 10 minutes. Remove from the heat and set aside.

3 Preheat the broiler to high. Place five oven-safe bowls or crocks on a large rimmed baking sheet. Ladle the soup into the bowls, place the French bread croutons on top, and sprinkle evenly with the cheese. Place the baking sheet under the broiler until the cheese melts, 30 to 60 seconds.

PER SERVING (1 cup): 290 calories, 12g fat (4g saturated, 0.2g omega-3), 680mg sodium, 34g carbohydrate, 3g fiber, 12g protein, 25% vitamin A, 40% vitamin C, 25% calcium, 10% iron

tip If you don't own oven-safe crocks or bowls, you can still enjoy this soup. Ladle the soup into regular soup bowls and top each with the croutons and a sprinkling of cheese. Heat in the microwave for 30 to 60 seconds until the cheese melts.

mom's feedback

I can't believe my kids ate all of these vegetables!

— Laura, mother of Sarah, age 3 and Rachel and Christopher, age 6 ▪ West Henrietta, NY

ABC Chicken Alphabet Soup

Chicken noodle soup is one of those quintessential kid favorites that moms serve again and again because, well, kids love it. We decided to add a fun twist to our version by using alphabet pasta. Check out the nutrition information below and you'll see that each serving provides over a day's worth of vitamin A, which promotes good vision. Unlike the few bits of carrot found floating in most canned soups, ours has just enough to make it super nutritious, but not so much that kids find it intimidating.

2 ounces dried alphabet pasta (⅓ cup)

1 tablespoon extra virgin olive oil

2 medium carrots, peeled, cut into quarters lengthwise, and sliced into ⅛-inch-thick pieces (1 cup)

1 stalk celery, trimmed, cut in half lengthwise, and sliced into ⅛-inch-thick pieces (⅓ cup)

1 boneless, skinless chicken breast (6 ounces), cut into ½-inch dice

1 32-ounce carton all-natural chicken broth

¼ teaspoon garlic powder

¼ teaspoon onion powder

1 Cook the pasta according to package directions. Drain and set aside.

2 While the pasta is cooking, heat the oil in a large Dutch oven or saucepan over medium heat. Add the carrots and celery and cook, stirring frequently, until the vegetables are softened, about 10 minutes.

3 Add the chicken and cook, stirring frequently, until no longer pink, about 3 minutes. Stir in the broth, garlic powder, and onion powder. Cover, raise the heat, and bring to a boil. Stir in the cooked pasta, heat through, and serve.

PER SERVING (1 cup): 150 calories, 4.5g fat (1g saturated), 490mg sodium, 13g carbohydrate, 2g fiber, 13g protein, 120% vitamin A

mom's **feed**back

This was wicked easy to make and yummy to eat! Simon loved picking out the letters.
Lizzie, mother of Sydney, age 15 months and Simon, age 3 ▪ Apex, NC

Cowboy Chili with Sweet Potatoes and Corn

MAKES 6 TO 8 SERVINGS

The *Halftime Taco Chili* from our first cookbook is Janice's go-to recipe when friends and family come over to watch Boston's best sports teams battle it out on TV. To see if we could top this tailgate favorite, we held a chili cookoff at *Meal Makeover Moms'* central (AKA, Janice's kitchen) and came up with a new recipe, made with lean ground turkey, small bits of sweet potato, fiber-filled pinto beans, and a medley of seasonings. We are thrilled to report that Janice's girls — her biggest fans — declared this new chili the best one ever. They like to eat it with warm corn bread served on the side.

1 tablespoon canola oil

2 cloves garlic, minced

1 small onion, cut into ¼-inch dice (1 cup)

1¼ pounds lean ground turkey

1 28-ounce can crushed tomatoes

1 15-ounce can pinto beans, drained and rinsed

1 medium sweet potato (about 12 ounces), peeled and cut into ¼-inch dice (2 cups)

1 cup water

1 cup frozen corn, thawed

1 tablespoon brown sugar

1 tablespoon chili powder

1 tablespoon ground cumin

½ teaspoon ground cinnamon

½ teaspoon kosher salt

Freshly ground black pepper

1 Heat the oil in a large Dutch oven or saucepan over medium heat. Add the garlic and cook, stirring frequently, until golden, 30 seconds to 1 minute. Add the onion and cook, stirring frequently, until softened, about 7 minutes.

2 Add the turkey and cook, breaking up the large pieces, until no longer pink, about 5 minutes. Drain excess fat.

3 Stir in the crushed tomatoes, pinto beans, sweet potato, water, corn, brown sugar, chili powder, cumin, cinnamon, and salt. Cover, raise the heat, and bring to a boil. Reduce the heat and cook at a low boil, covered, until the sweet potato is tender, about 45 minutes.

4 Season with additional salt and pepper to taste.

PER SERVING (about 1¼ cups): 290 calories, 7g fat (1.5g saturated, 0.2g omega-3), 260mg sodium, 37g carbohydrate, 9g fiber, 22g protein, 60% vitamin A, 25% vitamin C, 25% iron

tip You can add an array of optional toppings to this chili. We like light sour cream, shredded reduced-fat Cheddar cheese, crushed tortilla chips, and diced avocado.

mom's feedback

My family liked the subtle sweetness of this chili, and my 4-year old licked the bowl clean. I loved the flavor and the fact that each bowlful has three servings of veggies.

Jamie, mother of Bennett, age 2, Addy, age 4, Greyson, age 6 and Marin, age 8 ▪ Wenatchee, WA

Hooray for Hamburger Soup

MAKES 10 SERVINGS

When Liz first created this soup, she tested it out on Josh, her 15-year old son, and a group of his high school friends. Brimming with lots of nutritious vegetables, barley (a whole grain), and lean ground beef, the boys slurped it up like a swarm of locusts. To Liz, that was the ultimate compliment. Something else worth mentioning: We use a can of crushed tomatoes in this recipe instead of the chunkier, diced variety for a smoother texture.

1 tablespoon canola oil

1 medium onion, cut into ¼-inch dice (1½ cups)

8 ounces mushrooms, coarsely chopped

3 cloves garlic, minced

1 pound lean ground beef (90% or higher)

1 32-ounce carton all-natural beef broth

1 28-ounce can crushed tomatoes with basil

2 large carrots, peeled and cut into ¼-inch dice (2 cups)

½ cup barley

1 tablespoon Worcestershire sauce

1 teaspoon kosher salt

1 bay leaf

¾ teaspoon dried thyme

¾ teaspoon dried oregano

Freshly ground black pepper

Grated Parmesan cheese, optional

1 Heat the oil in a large Dutch oven or saucepan over medium heat. Add the onion and cook, stirring frequently, until softened, about 7 minutes. Raise the heat to medium-high, add the mushrooms and garlic, and cook, stirring frequently, until the mushrooms are softened, about 4 minutes.

2 Add the meat and cook, breaking up the large pieces, until no longer pink, about 5 minutes. Drain excess fat.

3 Stir in the broth, crushed tomatoes, carrots, barley, Worcestershire sauce, salt, bay leaf, thyme, and oregano. Cover, raise the heat, and bring to a boil. Reduce the heat and simmer, covered, until the carrots and barley are tender, about 1 hour.

4 Season with additional salt and pepper to taste. Remove the bay leaf and top each serving with grated Parmesan cheese as desired.

PER SERVING (1 cup): 170 calories, 5g fat (1.5g saturated), 490mg sodium, 19g carbohydrate, 4g fiber, 14g protein, 50% vitamin A, 20% vitamin C, 15% iron

mom's feedback

This stick-to-your-ribs soup reminds me of the soups my own mom made when I was growing up. Serve with some crusty Italian bread and a crisp salad, and it's a perfect winter dinner.

Lara, mother of Amanda, age 11 ▪ Los Gatos, CA

South-of-the-Border Tortilla Soup

MAKES 6 SERVINGS

There is no shortage of recipes for tortilla soup. What we like about this version is that it's a meal in a bowl, brimming with tomato sauce, protein-rich beans, and little corn kernels. And even though beans can be a tough sell with some kids, everyone who's ever tried this soup loves it — beans included. If you want our opinion, the crunchy corn chips on top really make the dish!

- 2 tablespoons canola oil, divided
- ½ small onion, cut into ¼-inch dice (½ cup)
- 2 cloves garlic, minced
- ¾ teaspoon ground cumin
- ½ teaspoon chili powder
- 1 32-ounce carton all-natural chicken broth
- 1 15-ounce can no-salt-added tomato sauce
- 1 15-ounce can black beans, drained and rinsed
- 1 cup frozen corn, thawed
- 10 6-inch corn tortillas, halved and sliced into ¼-inch-wide strips
- 1 tablespoon cornstarch
- 1 tablespoon cold water

Optional toppings: shredded reduced-fat cheese, diced avocado, chopped fresh cilantro, light sour cream

1 Heat 1 tablespoon of the oil in a large Dutch oven or saucepan over medium heat. Add the onion and cook, stirring frequently, until softened, about 7 minutes. Add the garlic, cumin, and chili powder and cook an additional 1 minute.

2 Stir in the broth, tomato sauce, black beans, and corn. Cover, raise the heat, and bring to a boil. Reduce the heat and simmer, uncovered, until the flavors meld, about 10 minutes.

3 While the soup is simmering, heat the oven to 400°F. Place the corn tortilla strips in a large bowl and toss with the remaining 1 tablespoon oil until well coated. Place on a rimmed baking sheet and cook until golden and crispy, stirring halfway through to ensure even cooking, 10 to 15 minutes.

4 Whisk together the cornstarch and water in a small bowl (this is called a slurry). Bring the soup back up to a boil, stir in the slurry, and cook, stirring constantly, until the mixture thickens slightly, about 3 minutes.

5 Top each serving with tortilla strips and the optional toppings as desired.

PER SERVING (1 generous cup): 220 calories, 6g fat (0g saturated), 540mg sodium, 36g carbohydrate, 7g fiber, 7g protein, 10% vitamin A, 10% vitamin C, 10% iron

mom's feedback

I've tried many versions of tortilla soup and this one was the best. It was easy, felt healthy, and was simply tastier. What I liked most was using tomato sauce. It made it rich and hearty (versus just basic chicken broth in my usual recipe). My 7-year old son sipped it up.

Vicky, mother of Aidan, age 7 ▪ Ft. Thomas, KY

**Chock-Full-O-Veggies
Lasagna**

CHAPTER 5

Pasta and Pizza Favorites

Getting whole grains and vegetables on to the family dinner table can be a challenge, to say the least. But when they're mixed in with kid faves like pasta and pizza, getting them down the hatch can be less of a fight. In this chapter, we use squiggly, curly, and tubular-shaped noodles along with flavorful pizzas as the vehicles for delivering better nutrition to your kids. Each and every recipe, from our *Garden Turkey Meatballs and Spaghetti* and *Mac & Cheese & Carrots* to our *Layers-of-Love Ravioli Lasagna* and *Buffalo Chicken Pizza Pies,* is familiar, satisfying, and newly nutritious.

Sous-chef, George and his mom, Valerie, assemble our veggie-filled lasagna. Dad joins in for the feast.

See more photos of our young cooks and moms cooking their favorite pasta and pizza recipes on Flickr
http://www.flickr.com/photos/mealmakeovermoms

Garden Turkey Meatballs and Spaghetti

If you subscribe to our monthly e-newsletter, you might remember that we once featured this recipe as a *Makeover Recipe of the Month*. Kids love meatballs, but they tend to be pretty high in fat and sodium. These are made with lean ground turkey to keep the saturated fat in check, grated carrots for a burst of vitamin A, Parmesan cheese for a boost of flavor, and oats and ground flaxseed for fiber. We suggest you serve them over whole wheat blend spaghetti, but the meatballs are also a kid pleaser wedged inside whole grain sub or hoagie rolls.

1 pound lean ground turkey

2 medium carrots (about 6 ounces), peeled and grated (⅔ cup)

1 large egg, beaten

½ cup quick-cooking oats

½ cup grated Parmesan cheese

2 tablespoons ground flaxseed or wheat germ

1 tablespoon dried Italian seasoning or dried basil

½ teaspoon garlic powder

½ teaspoon kosher salt

⅛ teaspoon black pepper

1 26-ounce jar pasta sauce

12 ounces dried whole wheat blend spaghetti

1 Preheat the oven to 400°F. Lightly oil or coat a large rimmed baking sheet with nonstick cooking spray and set aside.

2 Place the ground turkey, carrots, egg, oats, Parmesan cheese, flaxseed, Italian seasoning, garlic powder, salt, and pepper in a large bowl and mix until just combined. Shape the meat mixture into twenty-four 1½-inch balls. Place on the prepared baking sheet and cook until lightly browned, 10 minutes.

3 Meanwhile, place the pasta sauce in a large saucepan over medium heat. Cover and bring to a simmer. When the turkey meatballs come out of the oven, add them to the sauce, reduce the heat, and simmer, covered, until the meatballs are fully cooked and have absorbed some of the pasta sauce flavors, about 20 minutes.

4 While the sauce and meatballs are simmering, cook the pasta according to package directions. Drain, transfer to a large bowl or platter, and serve with the sauce and meatballs on top.

PER SERVING (4 meatballs & 2 ounces pasta): 440 calories, 10g fat (2.5g saturated, 0.5g omega-3), 650mg sodium, 56g carbohydrate, 8g fiber, 32g protein, 60% vitamin A, 10% vitamin C, 15% calcium, 15% iron

mom's feedback
This recipe was so easy! And I liked that the carrots added an extra serving of veggies to the meal.

— Desiree, mother of Zy, age 1 and Matt, age 11 ■ Calgary, Alberta, Canada

Cheesy Penne with Chicken and Broccoli

MAKES 5 SERVINGS

Most kids love mac & cheese, and we don't know too many who would turn their noses up to chicken fingers, so we tossed them together with a bunch of crisp broccoli florets for a nutritious comfort food dinner. We call for whole wheat blend penne in this recipe, but if you can't find it, feel free to use regular pasta. You'll still be getting plenty of vitamin C from the broccoli, calcium from the cheese sauce (reduced-fat, of course), and high-quality protein from the chicken.

- 8 ounces dried whole wheat blend penne pasta (about 2½ cups)
- 5 cups medium-size broccoli florets
- 1 pound skinless, boneless chicken breast halves, cut into ¾-inch x 2-inch strips
- ⅓ cup seasoned dried bread crumbs
- 1 tablespoon canola oil
- 1 tablespoon butter
- 2 tablespoons all-purpose flour
- 1 cup 1% low-fat milk
- 1 cup all-natural chicken broth
- 1 cup shredded reduced-fat Cheddar cheese
- Kosher salt and freshly ground black pepper

1 Preheat the oven to 350°F. Cook the pasta according to package directions. Two to 4 minutes before the pasta is done (depending on how crisp you like the broccoli), add the florets, bring back to a boil, and continue to cook until the pasta and broccoli are done. Drain and return to the pan.

2 While the pasta is cooking, coat the chicken in the bread crumbs. Place on a baking sheet and cook until golden and no longer pink in the middle, about 12 minutes.

3 While the pasta is cooking and the chicken is in the oven, heat the canola oil and butter in a saucepan over medium heat until the butter melts. Add the flour and whisk constantly until smooth, about 2 minutes.

4 Whisk the milk and broth slowly into the flour mixture. Raise the heat and bring to a low boil, stirring constantly. Reduce the heat and continue to simmer and stir gently until the mixture thickens, about 3 minutes. Remove from the heat, stir in the cheese until it melts, and season with salt and pepper to taste.

5 Place the cooked pasta, broccoli, and chicken in a large serving bowl. Pour the sauce on top and serve.

PER SERVING 450 calories, 13g fat (5g saturated, 0.6g omega-3), 530mg sodium, 47g carbohydrate, 6g fiber, 38g protein, 35% vitamin A, 80% vitamin C, 25% calcium, 10% iron

mom's feedback

Everyone liked the taste and different textures of this dish. They also thought the cheese sauce was great because it wasn't overpowering. Maggie said the noodles were the best she ever had and Theo asked if we could have it again!

Carey, mother of Maggie, age 3, Theo, age 8 and Tim, age 12 ▪ New Brighton, MN

Hidden Treasure Shells and Shrimp

We're crazy about shrimp. And so are lots of kids. Although shrimp is relatively high in cholesterol — a 3-ounce serving has over 100 milligrams, which is more than you'd find in lean beef — it's low in total fat and saturated fat, and it's a good source of heart-healthy omega-3 fats. Interestingly, studies show that eating shrimp (excluding deep-fat fried) doesn't raise your blood cholesterol level. Something else we like about shrimp: it contains a respectable amount of vitamin D, a nutrient important for strong bones and immunity. The hidden treasure in this dish is the edamame (shelled soybeans) which sneak their way inside the pasta shells.

8 ounces dried medium pasta shells (about 3 cups)

1 cup frozen shelled edamame, thawed

1½ cups all-natural chicken broth

¼ cup lemon juice

2 tablespoons cornstarch

1 teaspoon lemon zest, optional

½ teaspoon reduced-sodium Old Bay Seasoning

1 tablespoon extra virgin olive oil

1 tablespoon butter

2 cloves garlic, minced

1 pound frozen shelled and deveined cooked shrimp (small or medium), thawed

½ cup grated Parmesan cheese

2 teaspoons chopped fresh dill or ½ teaspoon dried dill

Kosher salt and freshly ground black pepper

1 Cook the pasta according to package directions. Add the edamame at the beginning (or halfway through if you like them a bit crunchier), and cook along with the pasta. When the pasta and edamame are done, drain and return to the pan.

2 While the pasta is cooking, whisk together the broth, lemon juice, cornstarch, lemon zest as desired, and Old Bay Seasoning in a bowl until well blended. Set aside.

3 Heat the oil and butter in a large nonstick skillet over medium heat. Add the garlic and cook, stirring frequently, until golden, 30 seconds to 1 minute. Add the shrimp, and warm through, about 1 minute.

4 Re-whisk the cornstarch mixture to make sure the cornstarch is well incorporated, stir into the skillet, raise the heat, and bring to a low boil, stirring frequently. Lower the heat and continue to simmer, stirring constantly, until the sauce thickens, about 2 minutes.

5 Stir the cooked pasta, edamane, Parmesan cheese, and dill into the shrimp mixture until well combined. Season with salt and pepper to taste.

PER SERVING (1⅓ cups): 390 calories, 11g fat (3g saturated, 0.5g omega-3), 470mg sodium, 42g carbohydrate, 3g fiber, 31g protein, 20% vitamin C, 15% calcium, 25% iron

tip If using raw shrimp, cook about 3 minutes, until partially cooked, before adding the broth.

mom's feedback My daughter, Izzy, loved the hint of lemon flavor in the dish. This is a keeper and something new to add to our list of family recipes.

Michelle, mother of Gabe, age 2, Abby, age 4 and Izzy, age 5 ▪ Shawnee, KS

Spaghetti Zucchini Pie

MAKES 5 TO 6 SERVINGS

Never in our wildest dreams would we challenge a master chef like Emeril Lagasse to a cook-off, but when a *Meal Makeover Moms' Kitchen* blog reader sent us Emeril's spaghetti pie recipe and asked us to "kick it up a few nutritional notches," we couldn't resist her challenge. Emeril's recipe is made with spaghetti, cheese, whole milk, eggs, and lots of pepperoni, and it also calls for green bell peppers — nutritious, yes, but not always a kid favorite. To slim down the calories and sodium, boost the fiber, and cut the saturated fat in half, we use a whole wheat blend spaghetti, switch to part-skim mozzarella cheese, opt for turkey pepperoni, and choose mild, shredded zucchini as our star vegetable (which, by the way, blends right in with the squiggly spaghetti).

8 ounces dried whole wheat blend spaghetti, broken in half

1 cup pasta sauce

1 tablespoon extra virgin olive oil

2 cloves garlic, minced

1 large zucchini (about 12 ounces), unpeeled and shredded (2 cups)

½ teaspoon dried basil

Kosher salt and freshly ground black pepper

1 cup shredded part-skim mozzarella cheese

1 ounce sliced turkey pepperoni (about 10 slices), coarsely chopped, optional

4 large eggs

½ cup 1% low-fat milk

¼ cup grated Parmesan cheese

1 Preheat the oven to 375°F. Lightly oil or coat a 2-quart baking dish with nonstick cooking spray and set aside. Cook the pasta according to package directions. Drain and return to the pan. Stir in the pasta sauce and set aside.

2 While the pasta is cooking, heat the oil in a large nonstick skillet over medium heat. Add the garlic and cook, stirring frequently, until golden, 30 seconds to 1 minute. Add the zucchini and basil and cook, stirring occasionally, until the zucchini is tender, about 8 minutes. Season with salt and pepper to taste.

3 Stir the cooked zucchini, mozzarella cheese, and pepperoni as desired into the pasta until well combined. Transfer the mixture to the prepared dish.

4 Meanwhile, whisk together the eggs and milk in a bowl. Pour the egg mixture evenly over the top of the spaghetti, and sprinkle with the Parmesan cheese.

5 Bake until bubbly and golden brown on top, 25 to 30 minutes. Let stand about 5 minutes before slicing and serving.

PER SERVING (1 piece): 310 calories, 11g fat (4g saturated, 0.4g omega-3), 430mg sodium, 33g carbohydrate, 4g fiber, 21g protein, 15% vitamin A, 35% vitamin C, 25% calcium, 10% iron

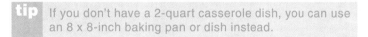

tip If you don't have a 2-quart casserole dish, you can use an 8 x 8-inch baking pan or dish instead.

mom's feedback

The pepperoni gave the dish a lot of flavor, and shredding the zucchini made it disappear in the dish. I was amazed when my extremely picky 4-year old said, "I want to eat this tomorrow night too."

— Andrea, mother of Avery, age 1, Allyson, age 4 and Emily, age 6 ▪ Shrewsbury, MA

One-Pot Pasta and Beef Dinner

MAKES 5 TO 6 SERVINGS

Pasta with meat sauce is super easy to make … and it's a pretty easy sell with kids too. Toss in a vegetable, however, and you could have a mutiny on your hands. Since keeping our kids and yours happy and well fed is our goal, we take a few baby steps toward improving this classic dish. For starters, we add a finely diced red bell pepper which we first sauté until soft and caramelized (to bring out its natural sweetness). We choose a red pepper versus green not only because it's less conspicuous when mixed into the sauce, but it's richer in vitamins A and C (extra ripening time on the vine has its benefits!). By using a whole wheat blend pasta we up the fiber, and by switching to lean ground beef and part-skim cheese, we cut down on the unhealthy saturated fat.

1   teaspoon canola oil

1   medium red bell pepper, cut into ¼-inch dice (1½ cups)

1   pound lean ground beef (90% or higher)

1   26-ounce jar pasta sauce

2   cups water

8   ounces dried whole wheat blend rotini pasta (about 3 cups)

1   cup shredded part-skim mozzarella cheese

¼   cup grated Parmesan cheese, optional

1 Heat the oil in a large Dutch oven or saucepan over medium-high heat. Add the bell pepper and cook, stirring frequently, until tender, about 5 minutes.

2 Add the meat and cook, breaking up the large pieces, until no longer pink, about 5 minutes. Drain excess fat.

3 Stir in the pasta sauce and water, raise the heat to high, and bring to a boil. Stir in the pasta and return to a boil. Reduce the heat and cook at a low boil, covered, stirring occasionally, until the pasta is tender, about 15 minutes.

4 Remove from the heat and stir in the mozzarella cheese. Cover and let stand until the cheese melts. Sprinkle with Parmesan cheese as desired.

PER SERVING 410 calories, 12g fat (4.5g saturated, 0.3g omega-3), 570mg sodium, 43g carbohydrate, 6g fiber, 32g protein, 40% vitamin A, 100% vitamin C, 20% calcium, 20% iron

mom's feedback
Everyone liked this dish. In fact, I may even add some chopped spinach or broccoli along with the bell pepper to make it even healthier!

Darcey, mother of Michael, age 3 and Sarah and Phillip, age 5 ▪ Port Jervis, NY

Mac & Cheese & Carrots

MAKES 5 SERVINGS

The nutritional merits of mac & cheese — which is typically made with white pasta, milk, butter, and a packet of artificially-colored orange powdered cheese — are rarely stellar. So for our made-from-scratch version, we use a whole wheat blend pasta for extra fiber, tiny bits of carrot for vitamin A (and a natural hit of orange color), and real cheese for a kick of bone-building calcium. The honey and carrots add a nice hint of sweetness to the dish.

- 8 ounces dried whole wheat blend elbow pasta (about 2 cups)
- 1 large carrot, peeled and cut into ¼-inch dice (about ¾ cup)
- 1 tablespoon canola oil
- 1 tablespoon butter
- 2 tablespoons all-purpose flour
- 1 cup 1% low-fat milk
- 1 cup all-natural chicken broth
- 1 cup shredded reduced-fat Cheddar cheese
- ¼ cup grated Parmesan cheese
- 1 tablespoon honey
- Kosher salt and freshly ground black pepper

1 Cook the pasta according to package directions. Add the carrot at the beginning, and cook along with the pasta. When the pasta and carrot are done, drain and set aside.

2 In the same saucepan, heat the canola oil and butter over medium heat until the butter melts. Add the flour and whisk constantly until smooth, about 2 minutes.

3 Whisk the milk and broth slowly into the flour mixture. Raise the heat and bring to a low boil, stirring constantly. Reduce the heat and continue to simmer and stir gently until the mixture thickens, about 3 minutes.

4 Remove from the heat and stir in the Cheddar cheese, Parmesan cheese, and honey until the cheese melts. Stir in the cooked pasta and carrot, and season with salt and pepper to taste. Reheat if necessary and serve.

PER SERVING (1 cup): 340 calories, 11g fat (5g saturated, 0.4g omega-3), 370mg sodium, 43g carbohydrate, 4g fiber, 19g protein, 80% vitamin A, 30% calcium

tip One 2-ounce standard serving of white pasta has less than 2 grams of fiber. The same amount of whole wheat blend pasta has 4 grams of fiber; and whole wheat pasta has 5 grams. You can see why we usually recommend the whole grain options. Our recipes are flexible, so any type of pasta will work.

mom's feedback Everyone liked the flavor of this mac & cheese, and the addition of the carrot didn't seem to bother anyone.

Jill, mother of TJ, age 10 and Hayley, age 12 ▪ Bedford, MA

Layers-of-Love Ravioli Lasagna

MAKES 4 TO 5 SERVINGS

We don't play favorites with vegetables. But if we had to pick one vegetable out of the crowd, we might choose Swiss chard. Packed with vitamin A — good for eyes and an immune-boosting powerhouse — and vitamin K — a big-time bone builder — this green leafy vegetable is considered one of the most nutritious in the produce aisle. We would be remiss if we didn't include it in at least one recipe in the book. For this oh-so-simple dish, we sauté Swiss chard until it's nice and tender, spread it between layers of pasta sauce, frozen ravioli, and cheese, and bake until the ravioli are cooked through. And no boiling water required!

1 large bunch Swiss chard (or one 5-ounce bag baby spinach, coarsely chopped)

1 tablespoon extra virgin olive oil

1 clove garlic, minced

Kosher salt and freshly ground black pepper

1½ cups pasta sauce

1 16-ounce bag medium-size frozen cheese ravioli, preferably whole wheat

1 cup shredded part-skim mozzarella cheese

1 Preheat the oven to 375°F. Rinse the chard well under running water until all the dirt is removed. Remove stems and center ribs, and coarsely chop the leaves.

2 Heat the oil in a large nonstick skillet over medium heat. Add the garlic and cook, stirring frequently, until golden, 30 seconds to 1 minute.

3 Raise the heat to medium-high, add the chard, and cook, stirring occasionally, until tender, about 5 minutes. Season with salt and pepper to taste.

4 Lightly oil or coat an 8 x 8-inch baking pan or dish with nonstick cooking spray. Spread ¼ cup of the sauce in the pan. Arrange half the ravioli (about 16 pieces) evenly on top of the sauce. Spread the chard over the ravioli, then top with ½ cup cheese and ½ cup sauce. Cover evenly with the remaining ravioli, ¾ cup sauce, and ½ cup cheese.

5 Cover with aluminum foil and bake until bubbly, 35 to 40 minutes. Remove the foil and bake until the cheese completely melts, an additional 5 minutes. Let stand about 5 minutes before slicing and serving.

PER SERVING 340 calories, 11g fat (3.5g saturated), 680mg sodium, 43g carbohydrate, 8g fiber, 18g protein, 120% vitamin A, 35% vitamin C, 30% calcium, 25% iron

mom's feedback The kids ate all of the Swiss chard and never tried to pick it out. Eric actually said the Swiss chard was the best part about the dish.

Lucy, mother of Ethan, age 6 and Eric, age 8 ▪ Midland, TX

Chock-Full-O-Veggies Lasagna

MAKES 8 SERVINGS

Liz's boys are adventurous eaters — willing to try new foods and give "I hate it" dishes a second or third chance. But it took umpteen failed attempts before Liz realized the ricotta cheese in her veggie lasagna was grossing the boys out! To replace it, she creates a white sauce (known as a béchamel sauce) with low-fat milk, flour, and olive oil instead of butter. Josh and Simon now eat every bite.

4   tablespoons extra virgin olive oil, divided

½   small onion, cut into ¼-inch dice (½ cup)

4   cloves garlic, minced

8   ounces mushrooms, coarsely chopped

1   small zucchini (about 6 ounces), unpeeled and shredded (1 cup)

1   medium carrot, peeled and shredded (½ cup)

    Kosher salt and freshly ground black pepper

1   pound lean ground turkey

2   teaspoons chopped fresh thyme

1   26-ounce jar pasta sauce

3   tablespoons all-purpose flour

2½ cups 1% low-fat milk

¼   teaspoon ground nutmeg

1   9-ounce box dried no-boil lasagna noodles (16 sheets)

½   cup grated Parmesan cheese

1   cup shredded part-skim mozzarella cheese

1 Preheat the oven to 375°F. Heat 1 tablespoon of the oil in a large Dutch oven or saucepan over medium heat. Add the onion and cook, stirring frequently, until softened, about 7 minutes. Add the garlic and cook an additional 1 minute.

2 Raise the heat to medium–high, stir in the mushrooms, zucchini, carrot, and salt and pepper to taste and cook, stirring frequently, until the vegetables are softened, about 8 minutes. Add the turkey and thyme and cook until no longer pink, about 5 minutes. Stir in the pasta sauce, heat through, and set aside.

3 Heat the remaining oil in a medium saucepan over medium heat. Add the flour and whisk until smooth, about 2 minutes. Whisk the milk and nutmeg slowly into the flour mixture. Raise the heat and bring to a low boil, stirring constantly. Reduce heat, simmer, and stir until the mixture thickens, about 3 minutes.

4 To assemble, lightly oil or coat a 9 x 13-inch baking pan or dish with nonstick cooking spray. Spread 1 cup meat mixture on the bottom. Lay 5 noodles on top, allowing them to overlap. Break the fifth noodle into a few pieces and fill in empty spaces. Top with ¾ cup béchamel sauce, ¼ cup Parmesan, 2 cups meat mixture, and ¼ cup mozzarella. Repeat with a second layer of 6 noodles (overlapping and two broken), ¾ cup sauce, ¼ cup Parmesan, the remaining meat, and ¼ cup mozzarella.

5 Top with the remaining noodles, béchamel sauce, and cheese. Cover loosely with foil and bake until bubbly, about 50 minutes. Remove the foil and bake until the cheese melts, 5 minutes.

PER SERVING 440 calories, 19g fat (5g saturated), 710mg sodium, 41g carbohydrate, 4g fiber, 28g protein, 35% vitamin A, 15% vitamin C, 30% calcium, 15% iron

mom's feedback

I liked the fact that the béchamel sauce was low in fat and still brought a rich taste to the dish. For more of a kick, I might add some crushed red pepper flakes to the meat mixture.

— Valerie, mother of George, age 4 ▪ Waipahu, HI

Sausage, Mushroom and Cannellini Pesto Pizza

MAKES 10 SERVINGS

One slice of pizza parlor sausage pizza can have upwards of 500 calories and 10 grams of bad-for-you saturated fat. To lighten things up, we make ours with lean chicken sausage … but we don't stop there. We also toss in some coarsely chopped mushrooms and an admittedly weird, but wonderfully delicious concoction made with pesto and cannellini beans, which we use instead of pasta sauce. It's an unlikely combination of ingredients, but they all come together for a mouth-watering pizza all of our kids love.

- 1 15-ounce can cannellini beans, drained and rinsed
- 2 tablespoons prepared basil pesto
- 1 tablespoon lemon juice
- 1 tablespoon water
  Kosher salt and freshly ground black pepper
- 1 tablespoon extra virgin olive oil
- 8 ounces mushrooms, coarsely chopped
- 1 12-ounce package chicken sausage (use your favorite flavor), casings removed and the meat crumbled
- 2 12-inch premade pizza crusts
- 2 cups shredded part-skim mozzarella cheese

1 Place the beans, pesto, lemon juice, and water in the bowl of a food processor and process until smooth and creamy. Season with salt and pepper to taste and set aside.

2 Preheat the oven to 450°F (or the temperature indicated on your prepared pizza crust package).

3 Heat the oil in a large nonstick skillet over medium heat. Add the mushrooms and cook, stirring frequently, until softened, about 7 minutes. Add the crumbled sausage and cook until fully cooked, about 5 minutes (the time may vary depending on whether the sausage was precooked or not).

4 Spread the bean puree evenly over the 2 pizza crusts. Top each with the mushroom and sausage mixture. Top evenly with the cheese (1 cup per pizza crust).

5 Bake according to pizza crust package directions and until the cheese melts. Cut each pizza into 5 slices and serve.

PER SERVING (1 slice): 320 calories, 12g fat (4.5g saturated), 600mg sodium, 33g carbohydrate, 3g fiber, 20g protein, 25% calcium, 15% iron

 tip The bean puree and mushroom/sausage mixture can be refrigerated or frozen for later use if you only want to make one pizza at a time.

 **mom's feedback** We liked the sausage and mushroom combo, and the next time I make this, I may add more pesto for even more flavor.

Sarah, mother of Elijah, age 2 and Aidan, age 3 ▪ Indianapolis, IN

Buffalo Chicken Pizza Pies

MAKES 6 SERVINGS

Every Tuesday is buy-one-get-one-free night at a pizza place near Janice's house, and since she can't resist a bargain, she occasionally succumbs to her daughters' pleas for pies. Their favorite is the *Buffalo Chicken Specialty Pizza* topped with roasted red peppers, a hefty helping of blue cheese dressing, and a gooey layer of cheese. As you can well imagine, this is an occasional indulgence, and Janice always serves a big green salad on the side! Since Leah and Carolyn can't seem to get enough of their favorite buffalo chicken pizza, we decided to create a healthier, nutrient-rich homemade version. For our pizzas, we use whole wheat English muffins as the base and top them with sautéed chicken and diced bell pepper, part-skim cheese, and just enough buffalo sauce and blue cheese dressing to add that familiar zing.

1 12-ounce package whole wheat English muffins (6 muffins)

1 medium orange bell pepper, cut into ¼-inch dice (1½ cups)

1 tablespoon canola oil

12 ounces boneless, skinless chicken breast halves, cut into ½-inch dice

½ cup pasta sauce

1 tablespoon Buffalo sauce

1 tablespoon blue cheese dressing

1½ cups shredded part-skim mozzarella cheese

1 Preheat the oven to 400°F. Slice the English muffins in half and place on a large baking sheet. Toast in the oven for about 5 minutes. Remove and set aside.

2 Heat the oil in a large nonstick skillet over medium-high heat. Add the bell pepper and cook, stirring frequently, until softened, about 5 minutes.

3 Add the chicken and cook until no longer pink, 3 to 4 minutes. Stir in the pasta sauce, Buffalo sauce, and blue cheese dressing and mix well.

4 To assemble the pizzas, top each muffin half evenly with the chicken mixture, and sprinkle evenly with the cheese. Bake until the cheese melts, about 5 minutes.

PER SERVING (2 halves): 310 calories, 11g fat (3.5g saturated), 550mg sodium, 28g carbohydrate, 4g fiber, 26g protein, 30% vitamin A, 80% vitamin C, 30% calcium

mom's feedback

These pizzas were a cinch. I like that they have a kick ... but not too much. I would add more Buffalo sauce for my husband but keep it where it is for the kids.

Laura, mother of Mia, age 9, Gianna, age 11 and Allison, age 13 ▪ Melrose, MA

Green Eggs and Bacon Pizza

MAKES 5 SERVINGS

There's a back story to most of the recipes in our book, and the one behind this dish begins with a trip to Napa, CA for the annual *Manic Mommies Escape* (the *Manic Mommies* host a weekly radio podcast and they invited us to speak and cook at their conference). On our last day in wine country, we had breakfast at the Boon Fly Café before heading back to San Francisco to catch our flight to Boston. Not knowing when our next meal would come, Janice (who, if you don't know this already, is always hungry) ordered their *Flatbread with Two Fried Eggs, Bacon, Caramelized Onions, and Mozzarella*. It was so amazing — though we shudder to guess the fat and calories in each slice — that we decided to create a breakfast pizza of our own. Our *Green Eggs and Bacon Pizza* is definitely family-friendly, and it certainly doesn't have to be limited to breakfast. Topped with sautéed baby spinach, chopped bacon, and a sprinkling of cheese, this pizza isn't as decadent as the Boon Fly's, but it's (almost) as delicious.

- 1 12-inch premade pizza crust
- 1 teaspoon extra virgin olive oil
- 1 clove garlic, minced
- 2 packed cups baby spinach (about 3 ounces), coarsely chopped
- 5 large eggs, beaten
- 4 slices nitrite-free bacon, cooked and coarsely chopped
- 1 cup shredded reduced-fat Italian blend or reduced-fat Cheddar cheese

1 Preheat the oven to 450°F (or the temperature indicated on your prepared pizza crust package). Bake the pizza crust according to package directions.

2 While the crust is cooking, heat the oil in a large nonstick skillet over medium heat. Add the garlic and cook, stirring frequently, until golden, 30 seconds to 1 minute.

3 Raise the heat to medium-high. Add the spinach and cook, stirring frequently, until wilted, about 3 minutes. Add the eggs and bacon and scramble until the eggs are set, about 3 minutes.

4 Remove the cooked crust from the oven. Top evenly with the egg and spinach mixture and the shredded cheese. Place back in the oven and cook until the cheese melts, another 2 minutes.

PER SERVING (1 slice): 320 calories, 13g fat (5g saturated, 0.2g omega-3), 650mg sodium, 27g carbohydrate, 2g fiber, 20g protein, 20% vitamin A, 25% calcium, 15% iron

mom's feedback

Baby Quinn ate a whole piece! Will said, "I could eat a thousand of these pizzas!" The next time I make it, I may add sautéed onions or mushrooms too.

Teresa, mother of Quinn, age 1, Will, age 9 and Zan, age 12 ▪ Vancouver, WA

Stuffed Spinach and Cheese Pizza

MAKES 5 SERVINGS

Making your own pizza from scratch can actually save time (after all, you don't have to call the pizza delivery man), money, and it can certainly be more nutritious since you get to control what goes on top. In this recipe, you also get to control what goes in the middle. It starts with a whole wheat pizza dough, or a regular dough if you can't find the whole wheat kind, and a filling made with inexpensive frozen chopped spinach, turkey pepperoni (it's a lot lower in saturated fat than regular pepperoni), and part-skim mozzarella cheese. All the stretching, squishing, stirring, and spreading in this recipe make it a good one for cooking with pint-size helpers.

1 10-ounce package frozen chopped spinach, thawed

1 tablespoon extra virgin olive oil, divided

1 16-ounce whole wheat pizza dough (or one 13.8-ounce tube refrigerated pizza dough)

1 cup shredded part-skim mozzarella cheese

¼ cup grated Parmesan cheese

¼ cup crumbled feta cheese, optional

1 ounce turkey pepperoni (about 10 slices), coarsely chopped, optional

¼ teaspoon garlic powder

Freshly ground black pepper

1 Preheat the oven to 425°F. Drain the spinach in a colander. Press with the back of a large spoon and pat with paper towels to remove excess moisture. Set aside.

2 Place 2 teaspoons of the oil in the center of a large, rimmed baking sheet. Roll the dough in the oil until it's completely coated. Use your fingers to gently stretch the dough (or unroll it) until it covers the entire baking sheet. It's okay if it extends slightly over the baking sheet. Your pizza should resemble a large rectangle at this point. Use your fingers to pinch together any tears in the dough.

3 In a bowl, stir together the spinach, mozzarella cheese, Parmesan cheese, feta cheese as desired, pepperoni as desired, garlic powder, and a few cranks of pepper until well combined.

4 Spread the spinach mixture evenly over the wider bottom half of the crust, leaving a ½-inch border. Carefully fold the top part of the dough over the filling. Use a fork (tines facing towards you and away from the pizza) to press the edges together. Brush the remaining 1 teaspoon olive oil over the top of the pizza. Make three 1-inch cuts across the top to allow steam to escape.

5 Bake until the crust is golden brown, about 15 minutes. Slice into 5 stuffed pizza pieces and serve.

PER SERVING (1 slice): 360 calories, 14g fat (4g saturated), 650mg sodium, 43g carbohydrate, 3g fiber, 18g protein, 140% vitamin A, 10% vitamin C, 30% calcium, 15% iron

mom's feedback

My daughter will eat just about anything, but if I tell her it's "spinach" or "broccoli," she'll say, "Eeeeew." But even with the spinach, she certainly enjoyed this pizza.

— Ashley, mother of Jane, age 2 ▪ La Mesa, CA

Polynesian Shrimp Tacos

CHAPTER 6

Make 'em Again Dinners

When the dinner hour rolls around, do you find yourself making the same meals over and over again? This chapter is designed to shake things up with a dozen new recipes, all with fun, kid-friendly twists. Tired of meat loaf? Try our playful mini loaves instead. Looking for new ways to add more seafood into your family's diet? Serve up some *Polynesian Shrimp Tacos*. Bored with the same-old, same-old chicken? Our *Chicken Pot Pie Bundles* have it all! In short, we hope these recipes will inspire you to expand both your repertoire of family dinners and your kids' taste buds.

Benjamin makes our tasty *Polynesian Shrimp Tacos* for dinner. His dad, Robert, serves 'em up with a smile.

See more photos of our young cooks and moms cooking their favorite dinner recipes on Flickr http://www.flickr.com/photos/mealmakeovermoms

Coconut Chicken Fingers

MAKES 4 SERVINGS

We have never met a child who didn't love chicken fingers or nuggets (although we know there are a few out there)! However, their less-than-stellar reputation comes from the fact that many are made with processed chicken "parts," and a thick layer of breading using ingredients that are hard to pronounce. We make ours from scratch with real chicken breast meat, rich in high-quality protein (almost double the protein of some store-bought frozen brands). Our coating is made with crunchy panko bread crumbs, sweet shredded coconut, and ginger, and the chicken is cooked in a healthy oil. What we end up with are home-style chicken fingers that are as finger lickin' good as they are good for you.

1 pound skinless, boneless chicken breast halves

½ cup sweetened shredded coconut

½ cup panko bread crumbs

½ teaspoon kosher salt

½ teaspoon ground ginger

¼ teaspoon garlic powder

1 large egg, beaten

3 tablespoons all-purpose flour

4 teaspoons canola or peanut oil, divided

1 Place the chicken on a cutting board and slice each breast into ½-inch-thick by 4-inch-long strips (to yield about 7 strips per breast).

2 Place the coconut, bread crumbs, salt, ginger, and garlic powder in a medium bowl and stir to combine. Use a fork or your fingers to break up any clumps of coconut.

3 Place the egg in another bowl and the flour on a plate. To bread the chicken, coat both sides with the flour and shake off excess. Dip in the egg and then coat evenly with the coconut mixture.

4 Heat 2 teaspoons of the oil in a large nonstick skillet over medium-high heat. Add the chicken and cook until the bottoms are golden brown, 4 to 5 minutes. Reduce the heat if the coconut browns too quickly. Flip the chicken strips, add the remaining oil, and cook until the meat is no longer pink and the bottoms are golden brown, about 4 minutes.

PER SERVING (3 to 4 chicken fingers): 290 calories, 12g fat (4.5g saturated, 0.5g omega-3), 270mg sodium, 19g carbohydrate, 1g fiber, 26g protein, 10% iron

tip If the chicken breast halves are thick at one end, use a meat mallet or the bottom of a heavy saucepan to pound the chicken to a uniform thickness before slicing.

mom's feedback My 2-year old kept on saying, "More, please." My 5-year old said they were much nicer than regular chicken nuggets, and, "Could we always have these, please?"

— Helen, mother of Annabelle, age 2 and Charlotte, age 5 ▪ Elmesthorpe, England

Cheesy Chicken Parmesan

MAKES 4 SERVINGS

We often hear from parents that the best way to get kids to try a new food is to order it at a restaurant first. There's something about having someone else do the cooking that motivates kids to pick up their forks and take that very first bite. However, compared to home-cooked meals, restaurant food is often a lot higher in fat and sodium. Chicken Parmesan is a prime example. The cutlets are usually breaded and deep-fat fried, and we suspect the cheese on top is the full-fat kind (and there's always lots of it). For our homemade version, the breading is made with panko bread crumbs and omega-3-rich ground flaxseed; we then sauté the cutlets in olive oil and top with pasta sauce and part-skim cheese. Our kids say it's just as satisfying, and we know it's a whole lot healthier.

4 5-ounce boneless, skinless chicken breast halves

Kosher salt and freshly ground black pepper

¾ cup panko bread crumbs

¼ cup grated Parmesan cheese

1 tablespoon ground flaxseed or wheat germ

1 large egg

1 tablespoon water

¼ cup all-purpose flour

2 tablespoons extra virgin olive oil, divided

1 cup pasta sauce

¾ cup part-skim shredded mozzarella cheese

2 tablespoons chopped fresh basil, optional

1 Wrap the chicken breast halves between wax paper or plastic wrap. Place on a cutting board and pound into ¼-inch-thickness using a meat mallet or the bottom of a heavy saucepan. Season both sides of the chicken with salt and pepper.

2 Preheat the oven to 375°F. Place the bread crumbs, Parmesan cheese, and flaxseed in a medium bowl and stir to combine. Whisk together the egg and water in another bowl, and place the flour on a large plate.

3 To bread the chicken, coat both sides with the flour and shake off excess. Dip in the egg and then coat evenly with the bread crumb mixture.

4 Heat 1 tablespoon of the oil in a large nonstick skillet over medium-high heat. Cook the chicken until the bottoms are golden brown, about 2 minutes. Add the remaining oil, flip the chicken, and cook an additional 2 minutes. Work in batches if necessary.

5 Arrange the chicken on a baking sheet and top evenly with the pasta sauce and shredded cheese. Bake until the chicken is cooked through and the cheese melts, about 7 minutes. Top with the chopped basil as desired.

PER SERVING (1 cutlet): 450 calories, 18g fat (5g saturated), 500mg sodium, 27g carbohydrate, 2g fiber, 41g protein, 10% vitamin A, 25% calcium, 15% iron

mom's feedback

The chicken was full of flavor and stayed moist even after I baked it. The recipe was a nice way to give chicken some pizzazz and to get more fiber (from the flaxseed) into my family's diet.

Sarah, mother of Zane, age 1 ▪ Middletown, OH

Chicken Pot Pie Bundles

MAKES 6 SERVINGS

This may be hard to digest, but a typical chicken pot pie made with a shortening-laden crust can have a staggering 10 grams of trans fat and 20 grams of saturated fat — both culprits in heart disease. To slash the unhealthy fats, we create a crustless pot pie using egg roll wraps to hold the savory filling. Our new twist on this pie is a bundle of fun to eat. In fact, we suggest that you let your kids eat the bundles with their hands and use a spoon only to pick up the bits of chicken and veggies that escape.

1½ tablespoons canola oil, divided

1 large carrot, peeled and cut into ¼-inch dice (1 cup)

½ small onion, cut into ¼-inch dice (½ cup)

2 cloves garlic, minced

1 pound boneless, skinless chicken breast halves, cut into ½-inch dice

2 teaspoons chopped fresh tarragon or ½ teaspoon dried tarragon

½ teaspoon kosher salt

1 pinch black pepper

1 cup all-natural chicken broth

4 teaspoons cornstarch

¾ cup frozen petite peas, thawed

¾ cup frozen corn, thawed

2 tablespoons grated Parmesan cheese

12 egg roll wraps (**not** the smaller wonton wraps)

1 Preheat the oven to 350°F. Heat 1 tablespoon of the oil in a large nonstick skillet over medium-high heat. Add the carrot and onion and cook, stirring frequently, until softened, about 5 minutes. Add the garlic, and cook an additional 1 minute.

2 Stir in the chicken, tarragon, salt, and pepper. Cook until the chicken is no longer pink, about 5 minutes.

3 Place the broth and cornstarch in a bowl and whisk until well combined. Add to the skillet along with the peas and corn, and bring the liquid to a simmer, stirring constantly. Continue to simmer and stir gently until the sauce thickens, about 2 minutes.

4 To prepare the bundles, use a muffin pan with 12 medium-size cups (do not coat with nonstick cooking spray). Gently place 1 egg roll wrap into each cup, letting it extend over the sides.

5 Place a generous ¼ cup of the chicken mixture into each wrap, and sprinkle the Parmesan cheese on top. Fold the corners up and over the top of the filling and press to seal the edges together. Brush the remaining oil on top of each bundle.

6 Bake until golden and crispy on top, 12 to 15 minutes. Cool slightly before eating.

PER SERVING (2 bundles): 360 calories, 7g fat (1g saturated, 0.4g omega-3), 680mg sodium, 48g carbohydrate, 3g fiber, 24g protein, 70% vitamin A, 15% iron

mom's feedback

We loved the flavor of the tarragon, and the size of the chicken pieces was just right. Maya thought they were amazing, and we talked about using different fillings next time — like beef stew or apple pie filling.

— Rachel, mother of Maya, age 12 and Gabi, age 16 ▪ Lexington, MA

Quick Apple Sausage Quesadillas

MAKES 5 SERVINGS

As family nutrition experts, we're often asked to give cooking demonstrations and lectures to groups of moms. From preschool playgroups to parent teacher organizations, we welcome the opportunity to meet fellow moms (and dads) and to dish about our favorite topic: preparing healthy, nutrient-packed meals for kids. The recipe we find ourselves making most often is this one for apple sausage quesadillas. Our electric burner, nonstick skillet, and glass bowls are always ready for action. This recipe comes together quickly, and it demonstrates how easy it is to get nutritious meals on the table that everyone can — and will — eat.

2 tablespoons canola oil, divided

1 medium red bell pepper, cut into ¼-inch dice (1½ cups)

2 fully cooked apple chicken sausages, casings removed and meat coarsely chopped

1 cup reduced-fat shredded Cheddar cheese

½ cup frozen corn, thawed

2 tablespoons barbecue sauce

5 8-inch flour tortillas, preferably whole wheat

1 Heat 1 tablespoon of the oil in a large nonstick skillet over medium-high heat. Add the bell pepper and cook, stirring frequently, until softened, about 7 minutes. Stir in the sausage, reduce the heat to medium, and cook until heated through, 2 to 3 minutes.

2 In a bowl, stir together the cooked bell pepper and sausage, cheese, corn, and barbecue sauce. Spread the mixture evenly over half of each tortilla. Fold over, press down gently, and set aside.

3 Heat 1 teaspoon of the oil in the skillet over medium-high heat (you may want to wipe out the skillet first). Add 2 of the quesadillas and cook, pressing down occasionally with a spatula, until the bottoms are crisp and golden, about 3 minutes. Flip them, and cook until the other sides are golden, about 2 minutes.

4 Repeat with the remaining oil and quesadillas. Cut into halves or quarters and serve.

PER SERVING (1 quesadilla): 320 calories, 15g fat (3.5g saturated, 0.5g omega-3), 710mg sodium, 30g carbohydrate, 3g fiber, 17g protein, 35% vitamin A, 100% vitamin C, 20% calcium

tip These quesadillas are versatile: You can swap the slightly sweet chicken apple sausage for something more spicy or savory, and if you're not a fan of bell pepper, you can use sautéed spinach, shredded carrot, or pinto beans instead.

mom's feedback My husband and I added a spicy barbecue sauce to the ones we ate, and we used a sweeter BBQ sauce for my daughter.

— Sharon, mother of Zachary, age 3 weeks and Melina, age 4 ▪ Sonoma, CA

Almond-Crusted Tilapia

MAKES 6 SERVINGS

The recommendation to eat two fish meals a week can seem daunting if your kids don't like seafood. That's one reason we often turn to tilapia. This farm-raised white fish is more likely to go down the hatch without a hitch because it's so mild. In fact, when Liz's boys were younger, they often thought they were eating chicken when this dish was served. Offer up some ketchup on the side for dipping and your crew may discover they actually like fish.

1½ pounds tilapia (4 to 6 fillets)

1 cup sliced or slivered unsalted almonds, finely chopped

3 tablespoons plain dried bread crumbs

2 tablespoons brown sugar

¾ teaspoon reduced-sodium Old Bay Seasoning

½ teaspoon kosher salt

¼ teaspoon ground cinnamon

⅛ teaspoon black pepper

1 large egg

1 tablespoon water

¼ cup all-purpose flour

1 Preheat the oven to 425°F. Place the tilapia on a cutting board and slice each fillet down the center where the fish connects to create 2 smaller fillets. Season both sides of the fish with salt and pepper and set aside.

2 Lightly oil or coat a large baking sheet with nonstick cooking spray and set aside. Combine the almonds, bread crumbs, brown sugar, Old Bay Seasoning, salt, cinnamon, and pepper in a shallow bowl. Whisk together the egg and water in another bowl, and place the flour on a large plate.

3 To bread the fish, coat both sides with the flour and shake off excess. Dip in the egg and then coat evenly with the nut mixture. Place the fish on the baking sheet, mist with nonstick cooking spray, and bake until golden brown and the fish is cooked through, about 15 minutes.

PER SERVING (2 fillet halves): 380 calories, 16g fat (2.5g saturated, 0.3g omega-3), 360mg sodium, 19g carbohydrate, 3g fiber, 42g protein, 10% calcium, 15% iron

 tip You can also use catfish or barramundi in this recipe. Both are mild in flavor and are raised sustainably in the USA.

 **mom's feed**back

Most of us are not fish lovers so I was surprised when Austen said, "I don't like fish at all, but this is really good," and when Jack said, "I'm going to eat all of this." I'm glad we've found a way to add more fish to our diet.

Kelli, mother of Jack, age 4, Hayden, age 9 and Austen, age 11 ▪ Windermere, FL

You Can't "Foil" Me Salmon

MAKES 4 SERVINGS

When it comes to omega-3-rich foods, salmon is the hands-down king of the sea. Getting your kids to eat it, however, may be another story. The key to this recipe is the blanket of slightly sweet teriyaki-brown sugar sauce that seasons both the salmon and the tender-crisp veggies as they cook. This dish is easy to assemble and doesn't even dirty a pan! Serve over a sweet rice such as Jasmine.

¼ cup reduced-sodium teriyaki sauce

1 tablespoon brown sugar

1 teaspoon toasted sesame oil

1 teaspoon minced fresh ginger or ¼ teaspoon ground ginger

1 teaspoon cornstarch

1½ cups snow pea pods (about 4 ounces), trimmed

1 large carrot, cut into 2-inch-long matchsticks (1 cup)

4 5-ounce skinless salmon fillets

Kosher salt and freshly ground black pepper

1 tablespoon toasted sesame seeds, optional

1 Preheat the oven to 400°F. Cut four 14-inch square pieces of aluminum foil and set aside.

2 Whisk together the teriyaki sauce, brown sugar, sesame oil, ginger, and cornstarch in a small bowl until well blended.

3 Lay the snow peas and carrots in the center of each piece of foil. Lay the salmon on top and season with salt and pepper. Spoon the teriyaki mixture evenly over each salmon fillet. Seal the packets by bringing up the sides and folding the top edge over twice. Seal the sides in the same way.

4 Place the packets on a baking sheet and bake until the fish is cooked through and the vegetables are crisp-tender, about 18 minutes. Open the packets (be careful of the steam!), place the salmon on individual plates, and top with the vegetables and sauce. Sprinkle with toasted sesame seeds as desired.

PER SERVING 230 calories, 7g fat (1g saturated, 1.6 omega-3), 440mg sodium, 9g carbohydrate, 1g fiber, 33g protein, 60% vitamin A, 20% vitamin C, 10% iron

tip You can use bottled minced ginger or frozen minced ginger cubes instead of fresh or ground.

mom's feedback

My son requested "more meat" from daddy's plate, and my daughter ate all her veggies and took three bites of the salmon ... which is good for her because she's not a big meat/fish eater. This was easy to prepare and very tasty.

Nancy, mother of Natalie and Myles, age 2 ▪ Winkler, Manitoba, Canada

Grilled Salmon with Avocado Tarragon Sauce

MAKES 6 SERVING

There are lots of sauces out there that kids love — ketchup, mustard, barbecue sauce, and salsa — but our green avocado tarragon sauce may be a bit of a culinary stretch. That said, the slightly tangy flavor of this sauce is the perfect accompaniment to the smoky flavor of grilled salmon. On several occasions, we've been known to serve this sauce like guacamole, with a bowl of tortilla chips on the side.

1 medium ripe avocado (about 8 ounces), halved and pitted

⅓ cup 0%-fat plain Greek or regular yogurt

2 tablespoons lemon juice

2 tablespoons extra virgin olive oil

2 tablespoons fresh tarragon leaves

½ small clove garlic

½ teaspoon kosher salt

Freshly ground black pepper

6 5-ounce skinless salmon fillets

1 tablespoon extra virgin olive oil

1 tablespoon honey

1 Slice the avocado halves in half again, peel away the skin, and place the avocado, yogurt, lemon juice, olive oil, tarragon, garlic, salt, and a few cranks of pepper in the bowl of a food processor, and process until smooth. Scrape down the sides as necessary, and set aside.

2 Preheat the grill to medium–high and lightly oil the grate. Combine the olive oil and honey and brush on both sides of the salmon. Sprinkle with salt and pepper. Place the salmon on the prepared grill and cook until easily flaked with a fork, 4 to 5 minutes per side.

3 Top each salmon fillet with the avocado sauce and serve.

PER SERVING (1 fillet and 2 tablespoons sauce): 320 calories, 17g fat (2.5g saturated, 1.7g omega-3), 200mg sodium, 7g carbohydrate, 2g fiber, 33g protein, 10% vitamin C

tip Avocados don't ripen on the tree. Once harvested, it can take 2 to 7 days to ripen at room temperature. To check for ripeness, do the "squeeze" test. Gently squeeze the avocado in the palm of your hand, and when it yields to gentle pressure, it's ready to enjoy.

mom's feedback We loved the flavor. I'm always trying to fit more fish into our diet and this was a very tasty way to do it.

— Lori, mother of Cameron Hunter, age 4 ▪ Carmel, NY

Corny Salmon Cakes

MAKES 4 SERVINGS

With a well stocked pantry, you can whip up healthy, last-minute meals, even when you walk in the door at 5 PM and wonder, "What's for dinner tonight?" One ingredient we always keep on hand is boneless, skinless pink salmon. It's mild in flavor, rich in heart-healthy omega-3 fats, and appears as the star ingredient in many of our favorite recipes — everything from *Scoop-It-Up-Salmon Salad* (page 38) and *Silly Salmon Noodle Bake* (page 127) to these easy-does-it salmon cakes. To keep the health factor high, we add other pantry staples including frozen corn kernels and shredded reduced-fat cheese, and we cook them in canola oil.

2 5-ounce cans boneless, skinless pink salmon, drained and finely flaked

¾ cup plain dried bread crumbs, divided

⅔ cup shredded reduced-fat Cheddar cheese

⅔ cup frozen corn, thawed

¼ cup light mayonnaise

1 large egg, beaten

1 tablespoon Dijon mustard

¼ teaspoon reduced-sodium Old Bay Seasoning

1 tablespoon canola oil

1 Combine the salmon, ½ cup bread crumbs, cheese, corn, mayonnaise, egg, mustard, and Old Bay Seasoning in a bowl and mix until well combined.

2 Shape the mixture into 8 patties (a generous ¼ cup each) and coat with the remaining ¼ cup bread crumbs.

3 Heat ½ tablespoon of the oil in a large nonstick skillet over medium-high heat. Cook the patties until the bottoms are golden brown, 5 minutes. Flip the patties, add the remaining oil, and cook until the other sides are golden brown, an additional 4 to 5 minutes.

PER SERVING (2 cakes): 340 calories, 16g fat (3g saturated, 1.5g omega-3), 800mg sodium, 22g carbohydrate, 2g fiber, 28g protein, 15% calcium, 10% iron

I was happy that the entire family ate the same meal, because this never happens! Brian said, "Yummy. I'm eating just like daddy."

— Wendy, mother of Brian, age 4 ▪ San Jose, CA

Polynesian Shrimp Tacos

MAKES 6 SERVINGS

Taco filling is typically made with ground meat — but it doesn't have to be. For this recipe, we combine the convenience of frozen shrimp with the usual taco seasonings: chili powder, cumin, garlic, and salsa. Then we add in some unlikely ingredients: black beans and crushed pineapple. Depending on the ages of your children and the number of front teeth they're missing, you may want to switch from the crunchy taco shells to soft flour or corn tortillas.

12 taco shells

 1 tablespoon canola oil

 1 pound frozen small cooked shrimp, thawed

 1 teaspoon ground cumin

 1 teaspoon chili powder

 ½ teaspoon garlic powder

 1 15-ounce can black beans, drained and rinsed

1½ cups frozen corn, thawed

 1 8-ounce can crushed pineapple, drained

 ½ cup salsa

 1 cup shredded reduced-fat Cheddar cheese

    Kosher salt and freshly ground black pepper

Optional toppings: diced avocado, chopped tomato, light sour cream, shredded lettuce

1 Preheat the oven to 350°F. Bake the taco shells according to package directions and set aside.

2 While the shells are baking, heat the oil in a large non-stick skillet over medium-high heat. Add the shrimp, cumin, chili powder, and garlic powder and cook until the shrimp are warmed through, about 1 minute (if using fresh shrimp, cook an additional 2 to 3 minutes).

3 Stir in the beans, corn, pineapple, and salsa and heat through, about 2 minutes. Add the cheese and heat until it melts. Season with salt and pepper to taste.

4 Using a slotted spoon to remove any excess liquid, place a generous ⅓ cup of the shrimp mixture into each taco shell. Serve with optional toppings.

PER SERVING (2 tacos): 380 calories, 13g fat (3g saturated, 0.5g omega-3), 540mg sodium, 41g carbohydrate, 6g fiber, 27g protein, 10% vitamin A, 15% vitamin C, 20% calcium, 20% iron

mom's feedback My husband said he could eat this once a week, and my son thought it was great. They were surprised there was pineapple in the recipe.

Charlotte, mother of Benjamin, age 11 and Jessica, age 15 ▪ New Orleans, LA

Turkey Tortilla Pie

MAKES 6 SERVINGS

Tell your family they're having pie for dinner and you'll win the Mother-of-the-Year award. They may be initially disappointed when they see the pie is savory, not sweet, but trust us, it's just as satisfying. Made with layers of lean ground turkey, nutrient-rich black beans, salsa, corn, reduced-fat cheese, and flour tortillas, there's nothing not to like about it! And with 5 grams of fiber and 35% calcium in each slice, you'll be happy to serve them a second piece.

4 10-inch flour tortillas

1 pound lean ground turkey or beef (90% or higher)

1 15-ounce can black beans, drained and rinsed

½ cup salsa

½ cup frozen corn, thawed

1½ teaspoons ground cumin

1 teaspoon chili powder

½ teaspoon garlic powder

2 cups shredded reduced-fat Cheddar or Mexican blend cheese

¼ cup sliced black olives, optional

Optional toppings: light sour cream, guacamole, salsa

1 Preheat the oven to 400°F. Trim the tortillas with kitchen scissors or a paring knife to fit a 9-inch springform pan, using the removable bottom of the pan as a guide (if you own a 10-inch springform, don't bother with this step). Lightly oil or coat the bottom and sides with nonstick cooking spray and set aside.

2 Cook the turkey in a large nonstick skillet over medium-high heat, breaking up the large pieces until no longer pink, about 5 minutes. Drain excess fat. Add the beans, salsa, corn, cumin, chili powder, and garlic powder and stir to combine.

3 Place one tortilla in the bottom of the prepared pan. Spread with a third of the turkey mixture and top with ½ cup cheese. Repeat with 2 more layers. Top with the last tortilla, and sprinkle with the remaining ½ cup cheese and the olives as desired.

4 Bake until the top is golden and the cheese melts, about 15 minutes. Run a knife around the inside edge of the pan, and remove the sides. Cut into wedges using a serrated knife and serve.

PER SERVING (1 slice): 370 calories, 14g fat (6g saturated), 770mg sodium, 35g carbohydrate, 5g fiber, 32g protein, 10% vitamin A, 35% calcium, 20% iron

mom's feedback

At first, Jack was hesitant, but once he ate it, he said it was "super yummy." I think the cheese was the biggest hit.

Lee, mother of Lachlan, age 3 and Jack, age 6 ▪ Aurora, IL

Mini Meat Loaf Muffins

MAKES 6 SERVINGS

If you and your family are meat loaf fans, but you don't have an hour to spare while it cooks, give our mini meat loaves a try. Each adorable "muffin" is made with a mixture of lean ground beef to keep the saturated fat in check, tomato sauce, and various seasonings. For an added bonus, we blend in oatmeal (instead of the usual bread crumbs), grated carrot, and Parmesan cheese for flavor. The small size and cupcake shape of our mini muffins make them hard for any kid to resist.

2 large eggs

1 8-ounce can tomato sauce, divided

1 teaspoon dried Italian seasoning

½ teaspoon kosher salt

¼ teaspoon black pepper

¼ teaspoon onion powder

¼ teaspoon garlic powder

1 cup quick-cooking oats

1 medium carrot, grated (⅓ cup)

⅓ cup grated Parmesan cheese

1¼ pounds lean ground beef (90% or higher)

1 Heat the oven to 375°F. Lightly oil or coat 12 muffin cups with nonstick cooking spray and set aside.

2 Whisk together the eggs, tomato sauce (save 3 tablespoons to use for the topping), Italian seasoning, salt, pepper, onion powder, and garlic powder in a large bowl until well blended. Stir in the oats, carrot, and Parmesan cheese.

3 Using your clean hands, mix the ground meat into the oat mixture until just combined. Divide the meat mixture evenly among the muffin cups and spread the reserved tomato sauce evenly on top of each one.

4 Bake until an instant-read meat thermometer registers 160°F, 25 to 30 minutes.

PER SERVING (2 muffins): 250 calories, 10g fat (3.5g saturated), 390mg sodium, 12g carbohydrate, 2g fiber, 24g protein, 25% vitamin A, 20% iron

mom's feedback The loaves were moist and flavorful and we loved the cute shapes. Andrea asked to have them instead of steak.

Amy, mother of Andrea, age 14 ▪ Weston, CT

Grilled Pork with Pineapple Pizzazz

MAKES 4 SERVINGS

They don't call pork "the other white meat" for no reason. A 3-ounce serving of pork tenderloin, our favorite cut, is comparable to skinless chicken breast with 120 calories, 3 grams fat, and 1 gram of saturated fat. Pork is rich in the B vitamins, thiamin and B6, important for converting food into energy, and when it comes to grilling, it's super easy. For this recipe, we pair it with grilled slices of sweet pineapple. But don't stop there! While you're at it, fill your grill with an array of veggies — zucchini, bell peppers, Portobello mushrooms, and onion. Your kids will think they're at a luau.

- 2 tablespoons reduced-sodium soy sauce
- 2 tablespoons honey
- 2 tablespoons lime juice
- 1 tablespoon toasted sesame oil
- 1 small clove garlic, minced
- 1 teaspoon curry powder
- ½ teaspoon ground ginger
- ⅛ teaspoon black pepper
- 1¼ pounds pork tenderloin
- 1 20-ounce can pineapple slices in juice, drained

1 Whisk together the soy sauce, honey, lime juice, sesame oil, garlic, curry powder, ginger, and black pepper in a small bowl until well blended. Pour into a large zip-top bag and add the pork tenderloin. Place in the refrigerator and marinate at least 1 hour and up to overnight.

2 Preheat the grill to medium and lightly oil the grate. Grill the tenderloin, turning halfway through, until an instant-read meat thermometer registers 155°F, 20 to 25 minutes. The pork should still be slightly pink in the center. Remove from the grill, cover with foil, and let stand before slicing, about 5 minutes.

3 While the pork is resting, spray the pineapple slices lightly with nonstick cooking spray and grill until grill marks appear, 1 to 2 minutes per side.

4 Serve the sliced pork with the grilled pineapple.

PER SERVING (4 ounces pork & 2½ pineapple rings): 270 calories, 5g fat (1.5g saturated), 140mg sodium, 25g carbohydrate, 1g fiber, 30g protein, 25% vitamin C, 10% iron

mom's **feed**back

This was extremely easy to make, and while it was kid friendly, we adults felt like we were eating something with sophisticated flavors. Liam said, "Wow, that lime flavor is amazing."

— Anne, mother of Liam, age 11 and Hannah, age 16 ▪ Melrose, MA

Slow Cooked Barbecue Beef

CHAPTER 7

Slow Cooker Creations

What we love about the slow cooker is the way it lets you make a feast without the fuss. What could be easier than prepping a few ingredients, tossing them in the slow cooker, and then walking away while dinner practically cooks itself? As you read our recipes, you'll notice that most require no pre-cooking (browning meats or sautéing vegetables), so they're super easy, and bursting with nutrition. From *Pulled Pork Primavera* and *Chicken and Sweet Potato Enchilada Casserole* to our *Mile-High Spinach Lasagna*, we go heavy on the veggies and big on the flavor.

Mom, Sari, makes our *Slow Cooked Barbecue Beef* with help from her pint-size kitchen assistants, Benjamin and Warren.

See more photos of our young cooks and moms cooking their favorite slow cooker recipes on Flickr http://www.flickr.com/photos/mealmakeovermoms

Luau Chicken with Pineapple and Carrots

MAKES 8 SERVINGS

The idea for this recipe came from a Facebook fan whose teriyaki chicken called for so much soy sauce that it was swimming in sodium. We played around with the recipe and finally decided to use reduced-sodium teriyaki to keep the flavor big and the sodium in check. The "luau" part of this dish comes from the crushed pineapple that we stir in at the end. If you think it's too weird for your kids' palates, consider Liz's son, Simon, who is not a pineapple fan but still loves this dish. Serve over noodles or rice — preferably brown rice — to sop up all the delicious juices (feel free to use Liz's favorite shortcut of frozen rice which takes just three minutes in the microwave).

3 pounds boneless, skinless chicken thighs, trimmed of fat

8 ounces baby carrots (half a bag)

½ cup reduced-sodium teriyaki sauce

1 clove garlic, minced

½ teaspoon ground ginger

2 tablespoons cornstarch

1 8-ounce can crushed pineapple packed in juice, drained with liquid reserved

1 Add the chicken, carrots, teriyaki sauce, garlic, and ginger to a 5- or 6-quart slow cooker, and stir to combine. Cover and cook on low until the chicken is cooked through and the carrots are tender, about 4 hours.

2 When done, maintain the slow cooker on low heat. In a bowl, whisk together the cornstarch and the reserved pineapple juice until well combined. Carefully remove the chicken and carrots and place in a large bowl. Cover with aluminum foil to keep warm. Gently stir the cornstarch mixture and the crushed pineapple into the slow cooker and cover until the liquid thickens, about 5 minutes.

3 Pour the sauce over the chicken and carrots, or gently stir the chicken and carrots back into the slow cooker and serve directly from there.

PER SERVING 300 calories, 13g fat (3.5g saturated, 0.2g omega-3), 440mg sodium, 12g carbohydrate, 1g fiber, 32g protein, 90% vitamin A, 10% iron

mom's **feed**back

My son loves pineapple and carrots. He ate this dish happily, but he didn't really talk much because he's only 18 months old!

Ann, mother of Cameron, age 18 months ▪ Marietta, GA

Chicken and Sweet Potato Enchilada Casserole

MAKES 6 TO 8 SERVINGS

Mexican dishes tend to go over big with kids, which may explain why this dish is a staple with our families. The naturally-sweet sweet potatoes are the perfect complement to the slightly spicy sauce, and the chicken absorbs all the great flavors. Chicken doesn't need a whole lot of time in the slow cooker, so you can pull the plug after three or four hours. Serve over rice or wrap the mixture inside flour tortillas, and enjoy a whopping 210 percent of vitamin A per serving!

2 pounds skinless, boneless chicken breast halves, cut into 1-inch dice

1 large sweet potato (about 1¼ pounds), peeled and cut into ½-inch dice (3 cups)

1 small onion, cut into ¼-inch dice (1 cup)

1 15-ounce can enchilada sauce

1½ teaspoons ground cumin

½ teaspoon chili powder

½ teaspoon garlic powder

1 cup frozen corn, thawed

1 cup shredded reduced-fat Cheddar cheese

1 Add the chicken, sweet potato, onion, enchilada sauce, cumin, chili powder, and garlic powder to a 5- or 6-quart slow cooker and stir to combine. Cover and cook on low until the sweet potato is tender and the chicken is cooked through, about 4 hours.

2 Stir in the corn and cheese until the cheese melts and the corn is heated through.

PER SERVING (1 generous cup): 290 calories, 7g fat (2.5g saturated), 460mg sodium, 23g carbohydrate, 3g fiber, 33g protein, 210% vitamin A, 10% vitamin C, 15% calcium

tip For even more flavor, sprinkle some smokey-flavored chili chipotle powder over the chicken and stir to combine. Taste as you go.

mom's feedback The simplicity, the basic flavor combinations, and the balanced nutrition appealed to me. Kai ate it and gave us a few smiles and spontaneous clapping!

— Kari, mother of Kai, age 11 months ▪ St. Paul, MN

Greek Chicken and Chickpea Stew

MAKES 6 TO 8 SERVINGS

Chickpeas — also known as garbanzo beans — are considered a legume, a plant with seed pods that split along both sides when ripe. Lentils, peanuts, peas, beans, and soybeans are also legumes and they all provide a boatload of nutrients including fiber, protein, B vitamins, and disease-fighting antioxidants. The best thing about chickpeas is that they are mild in flavor and even little kids can pick them up and eat them. For this recipe, we combine the chickpeas with olives, oregano, orzo, and feta cheese for a Greek-inspired dish meant to entice kids to try something new.

2 pounds skinless, boneless chicken breast halves, cut into 12 pieces

1 15-ounce can chickpeas, drained and rinsed

1 15-ounce can tomato sauce

1 small onion, cut into ¼-inch dice (1 cup)

¼ cup coarsely chopped pitted kalamata or black olives

1 tablespoon chopped fresh oregano or 1 teaspoon dried oregano

1 clove garlic, minced

¼ teaspoon black pepper

12 ounces dried orzo pasta (2 cups)

6 tablespoons crumbled feta cheese

1 Add the chicken, chickpeas, tomato sauce, onion, olives, oregano, garlic, and pepper to a 5- or 6-quart slow cooker and stir to combine. Cover and cook on low until the chicken is tender, about 4 hours.

2 A few minutes before the stew is done, cook the orzo according to package directions. Drain and set aside.

3 Serve the stew over the orzo and top each serving with feta cheese. Garnish with a sprig of fresh oregano as desired.

PER SERVING (about 1 cup stew & ⅔ cup pasta): 450 calories, 7g fat (2.5 saturated), 550mg sodium, 56g carbohydrate, 5g fiber, 39g protein, 15% vitamin C, 10% calcium, 20% iron

mom's feedback This was the first time my oldest daughter tried feta cheese, and she asked for more. My 4-year old was willing to try the dish because she heard everyone exclaim over the flavor. She said, "This looks yucky but tastes yummy!"

— Ashley, mother of Madelyn, age 4 and Emma, age 7 ▪ Tallahassee, FL

Pulled Pork Primavera

MAKES 8 SERVINGS

There is certainly no shortage of slow cooker pulled pork recipes. In fact, when we "Googled" it, we came up with a staggering two hundred thousand! To set our recipe apart from the crowd, we use classic ingredients — onion and barbecue sauce — but we also toss in carrot and bell pepper for added color and vitamins A and C. By using a lean cut of pork (tenderloin or loin), we keep the saturated fat to a reasonable 3½ grams per serving. The flavor and kid appeal are out of this world. When Liz's boys first tried it, they said, "We could eat this meal every day for the rest of our lives." How's that for an endorsement? Serve with our easy *Cranberry Coleslaw* (see tip below).

2½ pounds pork loin, trimmed of fat and cut into 3 pieces

1 large carrot, peeled and shredded (1 cup)

1 large red bell pepper, cut into ½-inch dice (2 cups)

1 medium onion, cut in half and sliced into ½-inch wedges

1 12-ounce jar barbecue sauce

8 whole wheat hamburger buns, lightly toasted

1 Add the pork, carrot, bell pepper, onion, and barbecue sauce to a 5- or 6-quart slow cooker, and stir to combine (you can also add half the barbecue sauce now and stir in the rest when the dish is done). Cover and cook on low until the pork is tender, 6 to 8 hours.

2 When the meat is done, remove from the slow cooker and place on a cutting board. Use two forks to pull the meat into shredded pieces.

3 Stir the meat back into the slow cooker until it is well combined with the sauce (the vegetables virtually disappear). Divide the pork mixture evenly between the hamburger buns and serve.

PER SERVING (1 sandwich): 400 calories, 11g fat (3.5g saturated), 570mg sodium, 46g carbohydrate, 4g fiber, 30g protein, 60% vitamin A, 50% vitamin C, 15% iron

tip Coleslaw is the perfect accompaniment to these rib-sticking sandwiches. To make our Cranberry Coleslaw, stir together ⅓ cup light mayonnaise, 3 tablespoons cider vinegar, 3 tablespoons pure maple syrup, and ½ teaspoon kosher salt in a large bowl. Add one, 16-ounce package coleslaw and ½ cup dried cranberries and stir until well combined. Serve right away or refrigerate and serve chilled.

mom's feedback I loved the ease of the preparation and the way the cranberry coleslaw complemented the pork. Overall, this combination is a winner!

— Elizabeth, mother of Emma, age 11, Hannah, age 14 and Hayley, age 15 ▪ Reading, MA

Coconut Curry Pork

If you're a fan of Indian cuisine, this is the dish for you. If your family has never tried it … now's your chance. After six long hours simmering in the slow cooker, the curry, garlic, ginger, and coconut milk come together for a fragrant dish that's slightly sweet but not too spicy. Thanks to the lean pork loin and the light coconut milk, it's surprisingly low in saturated fat. Serve over aromatic rice — Jasmine or basmati are especially nice — or egg noodles.

2½ pounds pork loin, trimmed of fat and cut into 1½-inch pieces

1 large red bell pepper, cut into 1-inch pieces

1 small onion, cut into ¼-inch dice (1 cup)

1 14-ounce can light coconut milk

3 cloves garlic, chopped

2 tablespoons brown sugar

1 tablespoon curry powder

1 teaspoon ground ginger

1 teaspoon kosher salt

½ teaspoon black pepper

3 tablespoons cornstarch

2 tablespoons lime juice

¾ cup frozen petite peas, thawed

 Add the pork, bell pepper, onion, coconut milk, garlic, brown sugar, curry, ginger, salt, and pepper to a 5-or 6-quart slow cooker and stir to combine. Cover and cook on low until the pork is tender, about 6 hours.

2 When done, maintain the slow cooker on low heat. In a bowl, whisk together the cornstarch and lime juice until well combined. Gently stir the cornstarch mixture and the peas into the slow cooker and cover until the liquid thickens and the peas warm through, about 5 minutes. Season with additional salt and pepper to taste.

PER SERVING (about 1 cup): 310 calories, 10g fat (4.5g saturated), 300mg sodium, 14g carbohydrate, 2g fiber, 38g protein, 15% vitamin A, 60% vitamin C

tip If you have Thai curry paste on hand, you can use a tablespoon in place of the curry powder.

mom's **feed**back This tasted like a curried stroganoff. It was a one-pot healthy dinner, and it was easy to prepare.

— Heather, mother of Ashley, age 4 months and Ava, age 2 ▪ London, England

Sweet and Hearty Beef Stew

MAKES 6 SERVINGS

A few years back, the editors of *Baby Talk* magazine asked us to write an article featuring easy and nutritious 5-Minute Meals for new moms, and this *Sweet and Hearty Beef Stew* made the cut. Even though it takes six or seven hours to cook, the prep time is literally just five short minutes. We use several speedy ingredients — presliced mushrooms, baby carrots, stew meat, and frozen peas — for a simple dish that any mom (new or otherwise) will appreciate. The maple syrup adds an extra kid-friendly touch. Serve with whole grain dinner rolls, mashed potatoes, or rice to round out the meal.

8 ounces presliced mushrooms

2 pounds lean stew meat, trimmed of fat

1 16-ounce bag baby carrots

1 8-ounce can tomato sauce

⅓ cup pure maple syrup

2 tablespoons cider vinegar

½ teaspoon kosher salt

3 tablespoons cornstarch

3 tablespoons cold water

1 cup frozen petite peas, thawed

1 Place the mushrooms in a 5- or 6-quart slow cooker. Top with the stew meat and carrots. In a bowl, mix together the tomato sauce, maple syrup, vinegar, and salt and pour evenly over the meat and vegetables. Cover and cook on low until the meat and carrots are tender, 6 to 7 hours.

2 When done, maintain the slow cooker on low heat. In a bowl, whisk together the cornstarch and water until well combined. Gently stir the cornstarch mixture and the peas into the slow cooker and cover until the liquid thickens and the peas heat through, about 5 minutes.

PER SERVING 350 calories, 11g fat (4g saturated), 420mg sodium, 29g carbohydrate, 4g fiber, 32g protein, 220% vitamin A, 15% vitamin C, 25% iron

mom's feedback

I liked that it wasn't too sweet and that the meat turned out very tender. My kids like potatoes, so I may add some to the slow cooker when I make this again.

— Lisa, mother of Taylor, age 3, Jackson, age 5 and Anthony, age 8 ▪ Marana, AZ

Slow Cooked Barbecue Beef

MAKES 10 SERVINGS

Tell your kids they're having prunes for dinner and we're pretty sure they'll balk. You might have more luck if you call them "dried plums." To set you at ease, we promise that (a) no one in your family will know they're eating prunes, and (b) the flavor is so awesome, your kids will ask for seconds. Believe it or not, when prunes are paired with lean chunks of stew meat and then cooked all day in your favorite barbecue sauce, the result is a sweet, protein- and iron-rich mixture your family will gobble up. Prunes are also good for digestion, so if you have tummy issues in your household, this dish may be just what the doctor ordered.

2 pounds lean stew meat, trimmed of fat

1 medium onion, cut into ½-inch dice (1½ cups)

1 cup pitted prunes

1 cup barbecue sauce

10 whole wheat hamburger buns, lightly toasted

1 Add the meat, onion, prunes, and barbecue sauce to a 5-or 6-quart slow cooker and stir to combine. Cover and cook on low until the meat is tender, 6 to 8 hours.

2 When the meat is done, use two forks to pull the meat and prunes into shredded pieces (there's no need to take the meat out; you can do this right in the slow cooker). Divide the mixture evenly between the hamburger buns and serve.

PER SERVING (1 bun with ½ cup filling): 330 calories, 8g fat (2.5g saturated), 510mg sodium, 43g carbohydrate, 4g fiber, 22g protein, 20% iron

mom's feedback

The prunes — our little secret (wink, wink) — added just the right amount of sweetness. I used an all-natural barbecue sauce without high fructose corn syrup and it was still tasty.

Sari, mother of Warren, age 4 and Benjamin, age 8 ▪ Garnet Valley, PA

Sunday Dinner Brisket

MAKES 8 SERVINGS

Lean cuts of meat like brisket love the slow cooker. Cooked all day — low and slow — results in a meat that's so moist and tender, it literally melts in your mouth. This is one of Janice's go-to recipes when she has friends and family over for Sunday dinner. Before she heads off to church, she loads the slow cooker with simple ingredients — brisket, potatoes, and carrots — and tops it off with a slightly sweet tomato-based sauce. Our brisket dinner is a definite crowd pleaser, and any leftover meat gets turned into sandwiches the next day.

2 pounds fingerling or baby Yukon gold potatoes

1 3-pound beef brisket, trimmed of fat

1 medium onion, cut into ½-inch dice (1½ cups)

1 16-ounce bag carrots, peeled and cut into 1-inch pieces

1 8-ounce can tomato sauce

¼ cup brown sugar

2 tablespoons cider vinegar

1 tablespoon Worcestershire sauce

½ teaspoon celery salt or kosher salt

¼ teaspoon black pepper

1 bay leaf

3 tablespoons cornstarch

3 tablespoons cold water

1 Place the potatoes in a 6-quart (or larger) slow cooker. Top with the brisket, onion, and carrots.

2 Whisk together the tomato sauce, brown sugar, vinegar, Worcestershire sauce, celery salt, pepper, and bay leaf in a medium bowl, and pour evenly over the meat and vegetables. Cover and cook on low until the meat and vegetables are tender, about 8 hours.

3 When done, maintain the slow cooker on low heat and remove the meat only to a cutting board. Discard the bay leaf. In a bowl, whisk together the cornstarch and water until well combined. Gently stir the cornstarch mixture into the slow cooker and cover until the liquid thickens, about 5 minutes.

4 Slice the meat against the grain, on the diagonal, into thin slices. Transfer to a large platter and top with the vegetables and sauce, or place the meat back into the slow cooker and serve directly from there.

PER SERVING 410 calories, 9g fat (3.5g saturated), 330 sodium, 38g carbohydrate, 4g fiber, 47g protein, 190% vitamin A, 45% vitamin C, 25% iron

mom's feedback I liked that the meat was moist and had good flavor. My son ate two helpings. It was a whole meal in one!

— Amanda, mother of Xavier, age 2 ▪ Arnold, MO

Lazy Day Beef and Veggie Soup

MAKES 8 SERVINGS

If you made this recipe stovetop, it would take hours for the meat to turn tender, and you'd be tethered to your kitchen all day, hovering, stirring, and making sure the soup is kept at a low simmer. With our version, you're free to walk away while the slow cooker does the work for you. This soup hits the spot on chilly days because it's hearty as well as healthy, with nutritious chickpeas and small bits of corn, peas, and carrots (or whatever else comes in your frozen mixed veggie medley). If you can't find ditalini pasta at your local market, look for small shells or orzo.

2½ pounds lean stew meat, trimmed of fat and cut into ¾-inch pieces

1 32-ounce carton all-natural beef broth

1 15-ounce can tomato sauce

1 teaspoon dried Italian seasoning

1 large clove garlic, peeled and thinly sliced

¼ teaspoon black pepper

2 cups frozen mixed vegetables, thawed

1 7 ¾-ounce can chickpeas, drained and rinsed (about 1 cup)

½ cup dried ditalini or other small pasta

2 tablespoons chopped fresh basil, optional

1 Place the beef, broth, tomato sauce, Italian seasoning, garlic, and pepper in a 5- or 6-quart slow cooker and mix until well combined. Cover and cook on low until the meat is tender, about 6 hours.

2 Raise the slow cooker to high. Stir in the mixed vegetables, chickpeas, and pasta. Continue to cook, covered, until the pasta is tender, about 30 minutes. Stir in the basil as desired and serve.

PER SERVING (1 generous cup): 310 calories, 11g fat (4g saturated), 560mg sodium, 19g carbohydrate, 4g fiber, 31g protein, 45% vitamin A, 10% vitamin C, 25% iron

mom's feedback

I used elbow-shaped noodles, and I was able to pull this recipe together quickly. When my husband headed back to the stove for seconds, he said, "Here's the best compliment you can get."

— Suzanne, mother of Ally, age 2 and Natalie, age 4 ▪ Winchester, CA

Mile-High Spinach Lasagna

MAKES 8 SERVINGS

It's hard to imagine lasagna cooked in the slow cooker, but we've done it, and it works like a charm. We layer no-boil noodles with pasta sauce, ricotta cheese, shredded mozzarella cheese, and frozen, chopped spinach (one of our all-time favorite convenience ingredients), so it comes together in no time. Our biggest challenge when we first created this dish was the sodium. Between the pasta and tomato sauces and the cheeses, it was too high. To keep the sodium in check, we make the switch to no-salt-added tomato sauce, and we compare labels and choose a pasta sauce with the least amount of sodium. Serve with crisp green beans or a big salad and your family will be in for an almost effortless meal.

1　10-ounce box frozen chopped spinach, thawed

1　15-ounce container part-skim ricotta cheese

⅓　cup 1% low-fat milk

¼　cup grated Parmesan cheese

1　8-ounce can no-salt-added tomato sauce

1　8- or 9-ounce box dried no-boil lasagna noodles

1　26-ounce jar pasta sauce

2　cups shredded part-skim mozzarella cheese

1　Drain the spinach in a colander. Press with the back of a large spoon to remove excess moisture. In a large bowl, stir together the spinach, ricotta, milk, and Parmesan cheese until well combined. Set aside.

2　Lightly oil or coat the bottom and sides of a 5- or 6-quart slow cooker with nonstick cooking spray. Pour the tomato sauce into the slow cooker bowl, and top with one fourth of the noodles. Cover as much of the sauce as possible by breaking some of the noodles into pieces (it's okay if they overlap a bit).

3　Spoon ½ cup pasta sauce over the noodles, then top with one third of the ricotta mixture (about 1 cup), and ½ cup mozzarella cheese. Repeat two more times with a fourth of the noodles, ½ cup sauce, 1 cup ricotta mixture, and ½ cup shredded mozzarella cheese.

4　For the final layer, cover with the remaining noodles, 1 cup sauce, and the remaining mozzarella cheese. Cover and cook on low until the noodles absorb the sauce and are tender, about 2½ hours. Turn off the slow cooker and let the noodles absorb any remaining sauce, about 15 minutes.

PER SERVING 340 calories, 11g fat (6g saturated), 580mg sodium, 37g carbohydrate, 3g fiber, 21g protein, 40% vitamin A, 10% vitamin C, 45% calcium, 15% iron

mom's feedback

Everyone actually ate this and liked it ... with no battles. We added some extra grated Parmesan cheese to the top to "disguise" the questionable ingredients from my picky eater.

— Rebecca, mother of Gwyneth, age 2, William, age 4 and Maxwell, age 6 ▪ Plover, WI

Super Veggie Pasta Sauce

MAKES 20 SERVINGS

During her four years of high school, Janice's daughter, Carolyn, played basketball and volleyball, and before big games, Janice often hosted carbo-loading dinners for the team. Ziti or penne pasta topped with our veggie-filled sauce was the girls' favorite. Instead of buying jars of prepared sauce, Janice makes this simple slow cooker sauce from scratch. She saves money — four jars of store-bought sauce can cost about $12.00 while a comparable amount of our sauce is less than $7.00 — and our sauce has half the amount of sodium. This recipe makes 10 cups, and you can easily freeze what you don't use.

2 tablespoons extra virgin olive oil, divided

2 cloves garlic, minced

1 small onion, cut into ¼-inch dice (1 cup)

1 medium red bell pepper, cut into ¼-inch dice (1½ cups)

1 medium zucchini (about 9 ounces), unpeeled and shredded (1½ cups)

Kosher salt and freshly ground black pepper

3 28-ounce cans crushed tomatoes with basil

1 6-ounce can tomato paste

3 tablespoons brown sugar

1 bay leaf

½ teaspoon dried oregano

½ teaspoon kosher salt

1 Heat 1 tablespoon of the oil in a large nonstick skillet over medium heat. Add the garlic and cook, stirring frequently, until golden, 30 seconds to 1 minute.

2 Raise the heat to medium-high, add the onion and bell pepper and cook, stirring frequently, until softened, about 5 minutes. Add the remaining oil and the zucchini and cook, stirring frequently until tender, an additional 5 minutes. Season with salt and pepper to taste.

3 Place the vegetable mixture in the bowl of a 5- or 6-quart slow cooker. Stir in the crushed tomatoes, tomato paste, brown sugar, bay leaf, oregano, and salt until well combined. Cover and cook on low until the sauce thickens slightly, 4 to 5 hours. Remove the bay leaf, and season with additional salt and pepper to taste.

PER SERVING (½ cup): 70 calories, 2g fat (0g saturated), 250 mg sodium, 13g carbohydrate, 3g fiber, 3g protein, 25% vitamin A, 40% vitamin C, 10% iron

mom's feedback

My kids are on the hook to make a meal once a week, so this was a hit because it was so easy. Zach said it tasted better than anything he's made so far.

Linda, mother of Zach, age 11 and Brenna, age 21 ▪ Lexington, MA

Polka Dot Squash Quinoa

CHAPTER 8

Meatless Meals

Fueled by concerns about health, the environment, and the economy, a growing number of people are now opting for meat-free meals. That said, the thought of going meatless may seem like a drastic idea to some families, especially if their kids are accustomed to a steady diet of chicken fingers and hot dogs. Tofu — with its reputation for being bland and boring — isn't exactly a food children clamor for, and quinoa (keen-wah) isn't even a food most people can pronounce! Read through our recipes, however, and you'll see that each of these dishes is so full of flavor, color, and texture, you may not even miss the meat.

Anna, Sarah, Emily, and Joshua team up with mom, Kim, to test and taste a healthy dish of *Polka Dot Squash Quinoa.*

See more photos of our young cooks and moms cooking their favorite meatless recipes on Flickr
http://www.flickr.com/photos/mealmakeovermoms

Beany, Cheesy, Zucchini Quesadillas

MAKES 6 SERVINGS

Kids are funny. When we first created this recipe, Liz's son, Josh, who was 14 at the time, said, "You know I don't like zucchini." But when Liz told him the zucchini was chopped up so small he wouldn't even notice it, he took a bite and declared, "Mom, this is so good … I love you!" If you think we're making this up, just ask Josh (though he'd probably deny he ever said it and disown Liz as his mom). The reason we love this recipe is because it's super easy to make and it's filled with great nutrition: fiber from the beans, calcium from the cheese, and antioxidants from the (nearly invisible) zucchini.

2 teaspoons canola oil

1 medium zucchini (about 9 ounces), unpeeled, cut into ¼-inch dice (1¾ cups)

½ small onion, cut into ¼-inch dice (½ cup)

¾ teaspoon ground cumin

½ teaspoon chili powder

1 15-ounce can cannellini beans, drained and rinsed

1½ cups shredded reduced-fat Cheddar or part-skim mozzarella cheese

6 8-inch flour tortillas

Optional sides: salsa, light sour cream, guacamole

1 Preheat the oven to 400°F. Heat the oil in a large nonstick skillet over medium-high heat. Add the zucchini, onion, cumin, and chili powder and cook, stirring frequently, until softened, 12 to 15 minutes. Gently stir in the beans and heat through.

2 To assemble the quesadillas, arrange 2 tablespoons of cheese over half of each tortilla. Top evenly with the bean mixture and then top again with the remaining cheese. Fold over, press down gently, and place on a large rimmed baking sheet.

3 Bake until the tortillas are golden and crisp on the outside, 8 to 10 minutes. Cut in half and serve with optional sides as desired.

PER SERVING (1 quesadilla): 290 calories, 10g fat (4g saturated, 0.2g omega-3), 490mg sodium, 36g carbohydrate, 5g fiber, 16g protein, 15% vitamin C, 30% calcium, 15% iron

tip For a skillet version, heat about 1 teaspoon canola oil in a large nonstick skillet over medium-high heat. Add 2 of the quesadillas and cook, pressing down occasionally with a spatula, until crisp and golden on the bottom, about 3 minutes. Flip and cook an additional 2 minutes. Repeat with the remaining oil and quesadillas.

mom's feedback I loved so many things about this dish: It was easy to prepare, inexpensive, and the zucchini was flavorful and tender. Jacob ate the whole thing.

Marissa, mother of Justin, age 1 and Jacob, age 3 ▪ League City, TX

Twice Baked Super Spuds

MAKES 4 MAIN DISH SERVINGS OR 8 SIDES

Potatoes are an excellent source of vitamin C and potassium, a mineral that's good for heart health. But top them with gobs of sour cream, bacon, and full-fat cheese, and all that great nutrition gets smothered. We take the classic recipe for twice-baked potatoes and revamp it by using low-fat milk and reduced-fat cheese. Then we up the nutrition by adding some tender baby spinach. The trick to keeping it kid-friendly is to first sauté the spinach and to then chop it into little pieces. Even if your kids are squeamish about spinach, we suspect they'll be willing to try it once it's mixed into the "creamy" potato filling.

4 large russet potatoes (about 3 pounds)

1 tablespoon extra virgin olive oil

1 clove garlic, minced

2 cups packed baby spinach (about 3 ounces)

¼ teaspoon onion powder

¾ cup 1% low-fat milk

¾ cup shredded reduced-fat Cheddar cheese, divided

¼ cup grated Parmesan cheese

2 tablespoons vegetarian-style bacon bits, divided, optional

Kosher salt and freshly ground black pepper

1 Preheat the oven to 375°F. Wash the potatoes and prick several times with a fork. Place in the oven, directly on the oven rack, and bake until the skin is crispy and the inside is softened, about 1 hour 15 minutes. Remove from the oven, slice in half lengthwise, and cool about 10 minutes.

2 While the potatoes are cooling, heat the oil in a large nonstick skillet over medium heat. Add the garlic and cook, stirring frequently, until golden, 30 seconds to 1 minute. Raise the heat to medium-high, add the spinach and onion powder and cook, stirring frequently, until the spinach wilts, about 3 minutes. Remove the spinach, place on a cutting board, and coarsely chop.

3 Scoop out the insides of the potatoes, leaving a ¼-inch rim of potato in the skins, and place in a large bowl. Add the milk, ½ cup Cheddar cheese, Parmesan cheese, and 1 tablespoon bacon bits as desired. Stir in the cooked spinach, and season with salt and pepper to taste.

4 Place the potato skins on a rimmed baking sheet and fill evenly with the potato mixture. Sprinkle with the remaining cheese and the bacon bits, as desired. Bake until the cheese melts and the potatoes are heated through, about 15 minutes.

PER SERVING (1 stuffed potato half): 200 calories, 4.5g fat (2g saturated), 140mg sodium, 34g carbohydrate, 3g fiber, 9g protein, 10% vitamin A, 20% vitamin C, 15% calcium, 10% iron

mom's feedback

We loved the flavors. Shane Walker said they were yummy!

Amanda, mother of Reagan, age 1 and Shane Walker, age 2 ▪ Louisville, KY

Spanish Tortilla Omelet

MAKES 4 SERVINGS

Janice's daughter Leah is a classic "finicky eater," but omelets are one of the foods she'll happily devour. Janice dreamed up this recipe, made with eggs, potatoes, and red bell peppers, because it reminds her of the Spanish tortillas she ate throughout Spain during her junior year in college. With a day's worth of vitamin C from the potatoes and bell peppers we say, "fantastico!"

1¼ pounds potatoes, peeled and cut into ⅓-inch dice (2½ cups)

2 tablespoons extra virgin olive oil, divided

1 medium red bell pepper, cut into ¼-inch dice (1½ cups)

½ small onion, cut into ¼-inch dice (½ cup)

1 clove garlic, minced

6 large eggs

¾ teaspoon kosher salt

1 pinch black pepper

Salsa, optional

1 Place the potatoes in a medium saucepan and add enough cold water to cover. Add a few pinches of salt, cover, and bring to a boil. Reduce the heat and cook, covered, at a low boil until very tender, about 7 minutes. Drain and set aside.

2 Heat 1 tablespoon of the oil in a large, 12-inch nonstick skillet over medium heat. Add the bell pepper, onion, and garlic, and cook, stirring frequently, until the vegetables are softened, about 8 minutes.

3 Beat the eggs in a large bowl. Gently stir in the potatoes, cooked vegetables, salt, and pepper.

4 Heat the remaining oil in the skillet over medium heat. Pour the egg mixture into the skillet, and cook until the omelet is golden brown on the bottom, about 5 minutes.

5 Heat the broiler to high. Place the skillet under the broiler (if the handle is plastic, wrap in aluminum foil) or slide the omelet onto a baking sheet. Broil until the top is golden brown, 3 to 5 minutes. Cut into wedges and serve with salsa as desired.

PER SERVING (1 slice): 320 calories, 13g fat (3g saturated, 0.3g omega-3), 310mg sodium, 34g carbohydrate, 3g fiber, 12g protein, 40% vitamin A, 140% vitamin C, 15% iron

mom's feedback

I had all the ingredients on hand, and so this was quick and easy to make. We ate it for dinner and paired it with a side of veggies and fruit. Considering the few number of ingredients, it was very flavorful. Yum!

Christina, mother of Mason, age 8, Sigilind, age 14 and Cailyn, age 15 ▪ Sultan, WA

Veggie Burger Supreme

MAKES 4 SERVINGS

Frozen veggie burgers can save the day if dinnertime rolls around and your cupboards are bare. By themselves, veggie burgers are pretty nutritious; they're low in fat and a good source of fiber and protein. To make them even healthier, we serve them on whole wheat buns and top them with baby spinach (or arugula for more adventurous eaters). As for the flavor, we boost that too with a tasty bit of feta or goat cheese and a smear of pesto.

4 frozen veggie burgers

¼ cup prepared basil pesto

4 whole wheat hamburger buns, lightly toasted

¼ cup crumbled feta or goat cheese, or 4 slices fresh mozzarella

1 cup baby spinach or arugula

1 Cook the veggie burgers according to package directions. Spread the pesto on one half of each hamburger bun.

2 Top with the veggie burgers, cheese, and spinach, place the remaining bun halves on top, and serve.

PER SERVING (1 burger): 290 calories, 12g fat (3.5g saturated), 770mg sodium, 30g carbohydrate, 8g fiber, 21g protein, 25% calcium, 20% iron

tip Prepared pesto can be a bit pricey, but it's easy — and a money saver — to make from scratch. All you need is a food processor and the following ingredients: 2 cups fresh basil leaves (ideally, from your garden), ½ cup grated Parmesan cheese, ½ cup extra virgin olive oil, ¼ to ½ cup nuts (your choice of pine nuts, walnuts, or pecans), 2 cloves garlic, and kosher salt and freshly ground black pepper to taste. Combine the ingredients in your food processor and process until smooth. Save what you don't use by placing leftover pesto in ice cube trays. Spread a layer of plastic wrap over the top (this will reduce discoloration), and freeze. Store frozen pesto cubes in zip-top bags.

 **mom's feedback** The flavors were delicious; none of us expected these to taste so good. In fact, my pickiest eater practically grabbed mine out of my hands. Emilie said it was a keeper and should become a "family recipe!"

Cindy, mother of Emilie, age 9, Anna, age 13 and Alex, age 15 ▪ DePere, WI

Quinoa with Almonds and Apricots

MAKES 5 SERVINGS

Protein-rich quinoa is an ancient grain that is gaining popularity, especially with vegetarians and people on gluten-free diets. If it's not rinsed well before cooking, quinoa can taste bitter (rinsing removes a natural, bitter coating called saponin, which protects the plant from birds, who hate the taste). There was a time when *The Meal Makeover Moms* hated the taste too (talk about "picky")! Thanks to a note we posted on our Facebook page asking for favorite quinoa recipes and preparation tips (like the importance of rinsing quinoa really well), our quinoa karma has improved considerably. Drawing from our fans' ideas, we created this delicious recipe, packed with bright colors, crunchy textures, and sweet flavors.

1 cup quinoa

All-natural vegetable broth (see tip below for amount)

½ small red bell pepper, cut into ¼-inch dice (½ cup)

⅓ cup toasted sliced almonds

⅓ cup dried apricots, coarsely chopped or golden raisins

2 tablespoons thinly sliced scallions, optional

¾ teaspoon ground cumin

½ teaspoon kosher salt

2 tablespoons lemon juice

1 tablespoon extra virgin olive oil

1 tablespoon honey

Freshly ground black pepper

1 Place the quinoa in a fine-mesh strainer and rinse several times in cold water. Drain well and set aside.

2 In a medium saucepan, bring the broth to a boil. Stir in the quinoa and cook according to package directions until the liquid is absorbed.

3 Transfer to a large bowl and fluff gently with a fork every few minutes until the grains cool.

4 Stir in the bell pepper, almonds, apricots, scallions as desired, cumin, and salt until well combined. Whisk together the lemon juice, olive oil, and honey in a small bowl until well blended. Stir into the quinoa mixture until well coated with the dressing. Season with additional salt and pepper to taste.

PER SERVING (about 1 cup): 240 calories, 8g fat (0.5g saturated), 250mg sodium, 36g carbohydrate, 4g fiber, 7g protein, 15% vitamin A, 35% vitamin C, 15% iron

tip The amount of broth needed and the cooking time will vary depending on your quinoa product. Read package directions for the suggested amount of liquid (it may range from 1¼ cups to 2 cups liquid per 1 cup quinoa). As a rule, we tend to cook the quinoa in the liquid 2 to 3 minutes longer than suggested, and then we let it stand 5 to 10 minutes until the quinoa fully absorbs all the liquid.

mom's feedback The major kid appeal of this recipe for my boys was the color. I particularly loved the honey-lemon flavor of the dressing and the combination of spices.

Lorraine, mother of Stefan, age 16 and Brian, age 20 ▪ Metuchen, NJ

Polka Dot Squash Quinoa

MAKES 5 SERVINGS

Quinoa is a complete protein — it contains all 9 essential amino acids — and it's a good source of fiber, iron, and magnesium, a mineral that, along with calcium, builds strong bones. We call for red quinoa in this recipe for no particular reason other than the fact that it's pretty, but you can certainly substitute with regular, beige-colored quinoa if that's what you find at the market. Combined with sweet, roasted butternut squash, we think your family will become quinoa converts after trying this.

12 ounces butternut squash, cut into ½-inch dice (2½ cups)

1 tablespoon extra virgin olive oil, divided

Kosher salt and freshly ground black pepper

1 cup red quinoa

¼ cup coarsely chopped shallots or red onion

2 cloves garlic, minced

All-natural vegetable broth (see tip on page 110 for amount)

½ teaspoon chopped fresh thyme

1 tablespoon lemon juice

¼ cup pine nuts, lightly toasted

1 Preheat the oven to 400°F. In a medium bowl, toss the squash with ½ tablespoon of the olive oil. Place on a large rimmed baking sheet, sprinkle with salt and pepper, and bake until tender, 20 to 25 minutes. Stir halfway through.

2 Place the quinoa in a fine-mesh strainer and rinse very well several times in cold water. Drain well and set aside.

3 Heat the remaining oil in a medium saucepan over medium-low heat. Add the shallots and garlic and cook, stirring frequently, until the shallots soften slightly, about 5 minutes. Reduce the heat if the garlic browns too quickly.

4 Add the broth and thyme, raise the heat, and bring to a boil. Stir in the quinoa, cover, reduce the heat, and simmer according to package directions until the liquid is absorbed.

5 Transfer to a large bowl. Gently stir in the cooked squash and lemon juice. Season to taste with salt and pepper, and serve with the toasted pine nuts on top.

PER SERVING (about 1 cup): 240 calories, 10g fat (0.5g saturated), 125mg sodium, 33g carbohydrate, 4g fiber, 7g protein, 150% vitamin A, 20% vitamin C, 15% iron

mom's feedback

My kids liked making this with me, and even my 11-month old loved eating it — minus the nuts, of course. This recipe was healthy and fun.

Kim, mother of Emily, age 11 months, Sarah, age 2, Anna, age 5 and Joshua, age 7 ▪ Quitman, AR

Sweet Pineapple and Red Bean Bundles

MAKES 4 TO 6 SERVINGS

The one word that best describes this recipe is, "fun." By stuffing egg roll wraps with a mixture of rice, beans, crushed pineapple, and cheese, we turn plain ol' rice and beans into adorable "bundles" your kids can (and should) pick up and eat. Older kids and adults may want to eat three bundles at mealtime while the wee ones in your house may be satisfied with just one.

1½ cups cooked white or brown rice

1 15-ounce can red beans, drained and rinsed

1 8-ounce can crushed pineapple packed in juice, drained

¾ cup shredded reduced-fat Cheddar cheese

1 teaspoon ground cumin

¾ teaspoon chili powder

1 generous pinch kosher salt

1 generous pinch black pepper

12 egg roll wraps (**not** the smaller wonton wraps)

½ teaspoon canola oil

1 Preheat the oven to 350°F. In a large bowl, stir together the rice, beans, pineapple, cheese, cumin, chili powder, salt, and pepper until well combined. Set aside.

2 To prepare the bundles, use a muffin pan with 12 medium-size cups (do not coat with nonstick cooking spray). Gently place 1 egg roll wrap into each cup, letting it extend over the sides.

3 Place about ⅓ cup of the mixture into each wrap. Bring the corners up and over the top of the filling, pressing and folding to seal the edges together. Lightly brush the oil on top of each bundle.

4 Bake until golden and crispy on top, 12 to 15 minutes. Cool slightly before eating.

PER SERVING (2 to 3 bundles): 340 calories, 3.5g fat (2g saturated), 540mg sodium, 62g carbohydrate, 6g fiber, 16g protein, 10% vitamin C, 15% calcium, 20% iron

tip If you don't have leftover cooked rice on hand, prepare ½ cup rice or ¾ cup instant rice to get the desired 1½ cups for this recipe.

mom's feedback These were extremely easy to make. My kids could assemble them themselves!
— Sarah, mother of Calvin, age 9 and Ethan, age 13 ▪ Littleton, MA

Confetti Tofu Chili (page 115)

Stuffed Spinach and Cheese Pizza (page 75)

Wild & Crazy Blueberry Cornmeal Muffins (page 161)

Coconut Chicken Fingers (page 78)

Greek Chicken and Chickpea Stew (page 94)

Pumpkin Spice Bundt Cake (page 177)

Carrot Sesame Salad (page 196)

Sweet Pineapple and Red Bean Bundles (page 112)

Scoop-It-Up-Salmon Salad (page 38)

Blueberry Cornmeal Pancakes (page 23)

Peanut Butter Power Cookies (page 183)

Brilliant Bean and Broccoli Cheese Soup (page 51)

Cowboy Chili with Sweet Potatoes and Corn (page 58)

Berry Bonanza Splash (page 149)

Quick Apple Sausage Quesadillas (page 81)

Banana Zucchini Squiggle Loaf (page 169)

Banana Brownie Waffles (page 30)

PB & Veggie Pad Thai (page 116)

Watermelon Pomegranate Pops (page 186)

Teriyaki Snow Peas and Carrots (page 143)

Smiley Face Casserole (page 122)

Turkey and Cheese Bagelwich (page 41)

Buffalo Chicken Pizza Pies (page 73)

Chili-Crusted Sweet Potato Fries (page 145)

Mile-High Spinach Lasagna (page 101)

Carrot Patch Cupcakes (page 179)

Quinoa with Almonds and Apricots (page 110)

Veggie Patch Tofu Pie

MAKES 6 SERVINGS

Liz created this recipe after a casual conversation with a neighbor (that's often where our "inspiration" comes from) who had just bought a giant bunch of spinach at the farmers' market and was about to make her favorite tofu spinach pie. The problem with her recipe, however, was that her kids hated it. The reason: too much spinach. To remove the "yuck" factor from this dish, Liz does the unthinkable — she cuts back on the amount of spinach — and switches to baby spinach, which is more tender and mild. To compensate for her culinary "crime," she adds shredded carrot for an extra kick of vitamin A.

1 16-ounce package firm tofu

1 tablespoon extra virgin olive oil

3 cloves garlic, minced

1 6-ounce bag baby spinach (4 cups)

1 medium carrot, peeled and shredded (½ cup)

2 large eggs

⅓ cup grated Parmesan cheese

½ teaspoon kosher salt

¼ teaspoon black pepper

1 cup shredded reduced-fat Cheddar cheese

1 Preheat the oven to 350°F. Drain the tofu in a colander. Place on a cutting board and cut into four 1-inch-thick slices. Pat dry with paper towels to remove excess moisture.

2 Lightly oil or coat a 9-inch pie plate with nonstick cooking spray and set aside.

3 Heat the oil in a large nonstick skillet over medium heat. Add the garlic and cook, stirring frequently, until golden, 30 seconds to 1 minute. Raise the heat to medium-high, add the spinach and carrot, and cook, stirring frequently, until the spinach wilts and the carrot is tender, about 5 minutes. Place on a cutting board and coarsely chop.

4 Meanwhile, place the tofu, eggs, Parmesan cheese, salt, and pepper in the bowl of a food processor and process until smooth and creamy. Transfer to a large bowl and stir in the Cheddar cheese and the cooked vegetables.

5 Pour the mixture evenly into the prepared pie plate and bake until golden, about 35 minutes. Let stand about 5 minutes so the pie is easier to slice.

PER SERVING (1 slice): 170 calories, 10g fat (4g saturated), 400mg sodium, 7g carbohydrate, 2g fiber, 15g protein, 60% vitamin A, 25% calcium, 15% iron

mom's **feed**back

We eat quiche a lot, and this felt like a healthier version. I used silken tofu and my immersion blender to combine the ingredients. Both of my kids liked it a lot. In fact, Alex said, "Not bad." Next time, I'll sprinkle some extra cheese on top to add even more "cheesiness."

Nicole, mother of Alex, age 10 and Nina, age 15 ▪ Havertown, PA

Crispy-on-the-Outside Coconut Tofu

MAKES 4 SERVINGS

If we told you that our kids love tofu, we'd clearly be lying. Made from the curds of soybean milk (just the word "curds" would probably freak out most kids), tofu is pretty bland, but when it's cooked with ingredients like brown sugar, shredded coconut, and peanut oil, it miraculously picks up those flavors. Tofu is rich in protein — in fact, eating soy protein has been shown to lower cholesterol levels — and it's a good source of iron, so it's ideal for people following a vegetarian diet. We hope these crispy-on-the-outside, soft-on-the-inside patties tempt your family to give tofu a try.

1 16-ounce package
    extra-firm tofu

½ cup sweetened shredded
    coconut

⅓ cup panko bread crumbs

1 tablespoon brown sugar

½ teaspoon kosher salt

1 large egg, beaten

2 tablespoons all-purpose
    flour

2 tablespoons peanut or
    canola oil, divided

1 Drain the tofu in a colander. Place on a cutting board and cut widthwise into eight ½-inch-thick slices. Pat dry with paper towels to remove excess moisture.

2 Combine the coconut, bread crumbs, brown sugar, and salt in a shallow bowl. Use a fork or your fingers to break up any clumps of coconut.

3 Place the beaten egg in another bowl and the flour on a plate. To bread the tofu, coat both sides with the flour and shake off excess. Dip in the egg and then coat evenly with the coconut mixture.

4 Heat 1 tablespoon of the oil in a large nonstick skillet over medium-high heat. Add the tofu and cook until the bottoms are golden brown, 3 to 4 minutes. Reduce the heat if the coconut browns too quickly. Carefully flip the slices, add the remaining oil, and cook until the other sides are golden brown, an additional 3 to 4 minutes. Sprinkle with additional salt before serving.

PER SERVING (2 slices): 230 calories, 12g fat (4.5g saturated), 210mg sodium, 20g carbohydrate, 3g fiber, 13g protein, 15% iron

mom's feedback Connor liked how the tofu "looked" and the crunch of the coconut. The recipe actually got all three of us to eat an entire container of tofu!

— Julia, mother of Connor, age 7 ▪ Holyoke, MA

Confetti Tofu Chili

MAKES 6 SERVINGS

Most chili recipes feature ground turkey or beef, but for this vegetarian version we make the switch to soft little cubes of tofu. We also add beans because they're packed with antioxidants, high-quality protein, and fiber. As for our choice of beans, we went with black-eyed peas; they're smaller in size than kidney beans, which are typically used in chili recipes, and they're a nice change of pace from the pinto, cannellini, and black beans that we usually grab. We like to serve this as a fast weeknight dinner or at weekend tailgating parties (if you listen to our weekly radio podcast, you'll know that Janice is the one most likely to cook for a crowd during football season), and the leftovers can be reheated and put in a thermos in your child's lunch box.

1 tablespoon canola oil

1 small onion, cut into ¼-inch dice (1 cup)

1 large carrot, cut into ¼-inch dice (1 cup)

3 cloves garlic, minced

1 tablespoon ground cumin

1 tablespoon chili powder

1 28-ounce can crushed tomatoes

1 15-ounce can black-eyed peas, drained and rinsed

1 cup all-natural vegetable broth

1 8-ounce package cubed super firm tofu, drained

1 cup frozen corn, thawed

Kosher salt and freshly ground black pepper

1 cup shredded reduced-fat Cheddar cheese

⅓ cup light sour cream, optional

1 Heat the oil in a large Dutch oven or saucepan over medium-high heat. Add the onion and the carrot and cook, stirring frequently, until softened, about 7 minutes.

2 Stir in the garlic, cumin, and chili powder and cook an additional 2 minutes.

3 Stir in the crushed tomatoes, beans, broth, tofu, and corn. Cover, raise the heat, and bring to a boil. Reduce the heat and simmer, covered, stirring occasionally, until the carrots are tender, about 30 minutes. Season with salt and pepper to taste.

4 Top each serving with cheese and the sour cream as desired.

PER SERVING (1 generous cup): 280 calories, 8g fat (2.5g saturated, 0.2g omega-3), 490mg sodium, 38g carbohydrate, 10g fiber, 19g protein, 100% vitamin A, 20% vitamin C, 20% calcium, 20% iron

tip If you can't find pre-cubed tofu in the produce section of your supermarket, use half a 16-ounce package, drained (see tip on page 117), and cut into ½-inch cubes.

mom's feedback

This was the first time I ever used tofu in a recipe, so everyone was a little apprehensive about it. Daniel isn't very adventurous food-wise, but after his first taste, he started searching through his bowl for pieces of tofu and he actually said, "It was an extraordinary journey for my taste buds."

Susan, mother of Daniel, age 11 and Matt, age 19 • Vienna, VA

PB & Veggie Pad Thai

MAKES 5 SERVINGS

When Janice is too tired to cook (imagine that!), she's been known to order Pad Thai from her local Thai restaurant. So it was no surprise when daughter Carolyn asked if she could whip up a made-from-home version for our next cookbook. Since neither of us had ever made Pad Thai before, it took some experimentation in the kitchen and a few trips to the Asian market before we nailed it. This is probably one of the "fussiest" recipes in the book and may call for a few unfamiliar ingredients. Traditional Pad Thai uses fish sauce, but because this is a "vegetarian" recipe, we use soy sauce. For a seafood version, feel free to switch back to the fish sauce and replace the tofu with a pound of shrimp.

8 ounces dry rice noodles (rice stick or bahn pho)	1 tablespoon canola or peanut oil
1 16-ounce package extra firm tofu	3 scallions, thinly sliced
½ cup all-natural vegetable broth or water	2 medium carrots, peeled and cut into 2-inch-long matchsticks (1⅓ cups)
¼ cup reduced-sodium soy sauce	1 cup snow pea pods, trimmed and cut in half crosswise
¼ cup rice vinegar	1 large egg, beaten
3 tablespoons brown sugar	¼ cup roasted peanuts, chopped, optional
2 tablespoons peanut butter	1 lime, cut into wedges, optional

1 Place the noodles in a large bowl and cover with warm water. Soak about 40 minutes, or until softened but not mushy. They should be pliable and almost edible, the texture of al dente pasta. Drain well.

2 Drain the tofu (see tip on page 117) and cut into ½-inch cubes. Set aside in a large bowl.

3 Whisk together the broth, soy sauce, vinegar, brown sugar, and peanut butter in a medium bowl until well blended. Pour 2 tablespoons of the mixture over the tofu and gently stir to combine. Marinate about 15 minutes.

4 Heat the oil in a large wok or Dutch oven over medium-high heat. Add the scallions, carrots, and snow peas and stir-fry until crisp-tender, 3 minutes. Add the tofu and stir-fry until warmed through, 2 minutes.

5 Move the tofu and vegetables to the sides, creating a well in the center of the wok. Add the egg and scramble until set, about 1 minute. Stir in the noodles and the sauce and toss until most of the liquid is absorbed, about 3 minutes. Serve with the chopped peanuts and lime wedges as desired.

PER SERVING 380 calories, 12g fat (1g saturated, 0.3g omega-3), 610mg sodium, 57g carbohydrate, 3g fiber, 12g protein, 120% vitamin A, 25% vitamin C, 20% calcium, 20% iron

tip To drain tofu, follow these steps:

- Place two layers of paper towels or a clean dish towel on a cutting board.
- Place the block of tofu on the towels, and top with another layer of paper towels.
- Gently press down on the towels to remove any water.
- Remove the wet towels and place two new layers on the top and bottom.
- Place a saucepan or other weight on top of the towels and let sit about 15 minutes to remove even more liquid from the tofu.

mom's feedback

My daughter is a tomato sauce-type of girl, so I was surprised by how much she liked the peanut sauce. Making this with Olivia really motivated her to try a new sauce on her noodles.

Amy, mother of Olivia, age 3 ▪ Westford, MA

Cutie Quiche Cakes

MAKES 6 SERVINGS

If your children's repertoire of vegetables includes mostly carrots, corn, and peas, here's an easy way to expand it at dinner or brunch. The taste may be subtle, but frozen pureed winter squash — rich in vitamin A and available year-round — gives these pint-size quiche cakes the golden color and hint of sweetness most kids can't resist. You can make our mild mini quiche cakes more savory by dipping in ketchup, or enhance their sweetness with some maple syrup on the side.

3 slices 100% whole wheat bread, cut into ½-inch pieces

6 large eggs, beaten

1 12-ounce box frozen cooked pureed winter squash, thawed and drained

1 cup shredded reduced-fat Cheddar cheese

⅓ cup grated Parmesan cheese

2 tablespoons vegetarian-style bacon bits

Pure maple syrup or ketchup, optional

1 Preheat the oven to 375°F. Generously oil or coat a 12-cup muffin pan with nonstick cooking spray and set aside. Divide the bread evenly and place into the muffin cups.

2 Whisk together the eggs, squash, Cheddar cheese, Parmesan cheese, and vegetarian bacon bits in a large bowl until well blended. Using a ¼-cup measuring cup, pour the egg mixture into each of the bread-filled muffin cups.

3 Bake until golden brown, about 22 minutes. Cool slightly, remove from muffin tins, and serve with maple syrup or ketchup as desired.

PER SERVING (2 mini quiches): 200 calories, 9g fat (4g saturated, 0.3g omega-3), 350mg sodium, 12g carbohydrate, 3g fiber, 16g protein, 40% vitamin A, 25% calcium, 10% iron

tip For a sweet alternative, replace the 100% whole wheat bread with 100% whole wheat cinnamon with raisins swirl bread and replace the bacon bits with 2 tablespoons brown sugar.

mom's **feed**back When my daughter asked if she could dip the quiche in maple syrup, she devoured every bite. I'd like to try these with a diced bell pepper.

Kristin, mother of Kaeden, age 4 and Wynne, age 7 ▪ O Fallon, IL

Simply Delicious Shepherd's Pie

CHAPTER 9

Crazy About Casseroles

"Gooey" and "gloppy" are just two of the words that come to mind when we think about the classic casseroles our moms used to make. Typically made with creamed soups, lots of butter, and full-fat cheese, casseroles got a bad nutrition rap because of their tendency to stick to the ribs ... and to the waistline. We give a contemporary twist to dishes like tuna-noodle and Tater Tots® casseroles by skimming some of the fat and excess calories and weaving in lots of veggies and other better-for-you ingredients. Kids and parents will be happy to know that we do it all without sacrificing those old-fashioned flavors.

Sisters, Alex and Danica, team up to make our *Simply Delicious Shepherd's Pie*. They show off their "delicious" results with their mom, Beth.

See more photos of our young cooks and moms cooking their favorite casserole recipes on Flickr http://www.flickr.com/photos/mealmakeovermoms

Smiley Face Casserole

MAKES 10 SERVINGS

Tater Tots® Casserole. The name alone sounds like every bite is drenched in fat and calories. The original recipe, sent to us by a blog reader, called for Tater Tots®, a pound of ground meat, lots of cheese, a can of cream-of-something soup, and a stick of butter. The nutritional damage: 15 grams of saturated fat (nearly a day's worth) and over 1,000 milligrams of sodium in each serving. For our easy makeover, we switch to 90% (or higher) lean ground meat, a lower-sodium soup, add a few nutritious veggies, and top it off with playful smiley-face baked fries. We figure that even the most fickle kids out there will smile right back.

1 26-ounce bag frozen smiley-face potato fries

1 tablespoon canola oil

8 ounces mushrooms, coarsely chopped

1 pound lean ground beef or turkey (90% or higher)

1 large carrot, peeled and shredded (1 cup)

½ teaspoon garlic powder

½ teaspoon black pepper

Kosher salt

1 10¾-ounce can condensed lower-fat, lower-sodium cream of mushroom soup

1 10¾-ounce can filled with 1% low-fat milk

2 cups shredded reduced-fat Cheddar cheese, divided

1 Preheat the oven and bake the fries according to package directions. Remove from the oven and set aside.

2 While the fries are cooking, heat the oil in a large Dutch oven or saucepan over medium-high heat. Add the mushrooms and cook, stirring frequently, until softened, about 5 minutes.

3 Add the meat, carrot, garlic powder, and pepper and cook, breaking up the large pieces, until the meat is no longer pink and the carrot is tender, about 5 minutes. Drain excess fat and season with salt and additional pepper to taste.

4 Stir in the soup, milk, and 1½ cups of the cheese (the mixture will seem very thin at this point, but don't worry). Heat, stirring frequently, until the mixture comes to a simmer. Remove from the heat.

5 Set the oven to 425°F. Arrange half the cooked fries in a 9 x 13-inch baking pan or dish. Top with the meat mixture, the remaining ½ cup of cheese, and the remaining potato smiles. Cover loosely with aluminum foil and bake until the mixture is bubbly, about 10 minutes.

PER SERVING 310 calories, 14g fat (5g saturated), 620mg sodium, 26g carbohydrate, 2g fiber, 20g protein, 40% vitamin A, 25% calcium

 tip If you can't find smiley-face potato fries, use waffle, alphabet or another fun-shaped fry.

 **mom's feedback** My middle child loved the potatoes the most, but he ate the whole thing ... and there were no complaints about the added veggies.

Karen, mother of Steven, age 7, Michael, age 11 and Rebecca, age 15 ▪ Dublin, CA

Whole Enchilada Bake

MAKES 8 SERVINGS

The star ingredient in this dish, from our dietitians' point of view, is the squash. It provides nutrients like vitamin A, and it blends right into the filling when mixed with eggs and creamy cottage cheese. This casserole comes together quickly, and if you have leftover rotisserie chicken in your fridge, the dish is that much easier to assemble. For families whose taste buds crave spicy, mouth-on-fire foods, use a medium or hot enchilada sauce or double the seasoning.

- 1 16-ounce container low-fat cottage cheese
- 1 12-ounce box frozen cooked pureed winter squash, thawed and drained
- 2 large eggs, beaten
- 1½ teaspoons ground cumin
- 1 teaspoon chili powder
- 1 15-ounce can enchilada sauce
- 12 6-inch corn tortillas, halved
- 2 cups diced cooked chicken (12 ounces)
- 1½ cups frozen corn, thawed
- 1½ cups shredded reduced-fat Cheddar cheese

1 Preheat the oven to 375°F. Lightly oil or coat a 9 x 13-inch baking pan or dish with nonstick cooking spray and set aside.

2 In a large bowl, mix together the cottage cheese, squash, eggs, cumin, and chili powder until well combined.

3 Spread ¼ cup enchilada sauce in the prepared pan. Arrange 8 tortilla halves over the sauce, allowing them to overlap slightly. Top evenly with 1 cup squash mixture, 1 cup chicken, half the corn, ½ cup cheese, and ½ cup enchilada sauce.

4 Repeat the next layer with 8 tortilla halves, 1 cup squash mixture, 1 cup chicken, the remaining corn, ½ cup cheese, and ½ cup enchilada sauce. Top with the remaining tortillas, squash mixture, enchilada sauce, and ½ cup cheese.

5 Bake, uncovered, until the casserole is heated through and bubbly, about 35 minutes.

PER SERVING 290 calories, 9g fat (3.5g saturated), 710mg sodium, 28g carbohydrate, 3g fiber, 28g protein, 35% vitamin A, 20% calcium

mom's feedback Half of my family members are on gluten-free diets, so this was a perfect recipe for us. We were pleasantly surprised that it included squash.

Tanya, mother of Maxwell, age 3 and Alexander, age 4 ▪ Stillwater, MN

Chicken Broccoli Crunch

MAKES 5 TO 6 SERVINGS

Over the years, we've been asked to give everything from luscious chocolate chip cookies to creamy clam chowder a healthy makeover. But perhaps the most popular recipe rehab request of all time was for the classic chicken casserole — made with chicken, a veggie, and a can of cream soup. For this recipe, we pair cubes of cooked chicken with cute little broccoli florets, add an all-natural cream of mushroom soup, and create a crunchy topping with heart-healthy almonds, ground flaxseed, and panko (Japanese bread crumbs). Serve over rice or noodles and we bet you'll have a new family classic on your hands.

3 cups fresh or frozen small broccoli florets

1 14½-ounce can ready-to-serve all-natural cream of mushroom or chicken soup

¼ cup light mayonnaise

1 pound cooked chicken, cut into ½-inch dice (2½ cups)

¼ cup almonds, very finely chopped

¼ cup panko bread crumbs

2 tablespoons ground flaxseed

2 tablespoons grated Parmesan cheese

1 Preheat the oven to 350°F. Lightly oil or coat a 2-quart casserole dish or an 8 x 8-inch baking pan or dish with nonstick cooking spray and set aside.

2 Thaw the broccoli if frozen. Steam until crisp-tender, about 3 minutes. Uncover and set aside.

3 Whisk together the soup and mayonnaise in a large bowl until well blended. Add the chicken and broccoli and stir gently to combine. Spread the mixture evenly in the prepared pan and set aside.

4 To make the topping, place the almonds, bread crumbs, flaxseed, and Parmesan cheese in a small bowl and stir to combine. Spread evenly over the chicken mixture.

5 Bake until the mixture bubbles and the topping turns golden brown, about 20 minutes.

PER SERVING 240 calories, 11g fat (2g saturated, 0.9g omega-3), 390mg sodium, 12g carbohydrate, 3g fiber, 21g protein, 25% vitamin A, 60% vitamin C

tip If you can't find the 14½-ounce can of all-natural soup at your market, use one 10 ¾-ounce can condensed lower-fat, lower-sodium cream of mushroom or chicken soup plus ⅓ cup 1% low-fat milk.

mom's feedback My daughter said, "Yum, yum, yum," and she ate broccoli for the very first time!
Jackie, mother of Matthias, age 2 and Danika, age 3 ▪ Roseville, MN

Crushed Tortilla Chip Casserole

MAKES 8 SERVINGS

Kids love chips, so imagine their delight when you serve this casserole covered with a layer of crushed tortilla chips. The chips in this dish provide crunch, and they're a nice contrast to the almost-creamy consistency of the refried bean filling. When shopping for canned refried beans — a fiber-rich favorite of ours — look for fat-free or vegetarian versions made without lard. Serve with a few extra chips and the kids will scoop up every last bite.

1 tablespoon canola oil

1 small onion, cut into ¼-inch dice (1 cup)

2 cloves garlic, minced

1 pound lean ground turkey or chicken

1½ cups frozen corn, thawed

1 15-ounce can refried beans

1 15-ounce can enchilada sauce

1 8-ounce can no-salt-added tomato sauce

3 cups coarsely crushed corn tortilla chips, divided (8 ounces)

1 cup shredded reduced-fat Cheddar cheese

1 Preheat the oven to 350°F. Heat the oil in a large Dutch oven or nonstick skillet over medium heat. Add the onion and cook, stirring frequently, until softened, about 7 minutes. Add the garlic and cook an additional 1 minute.

2 Add the turkey and cook, breaking up the large pieces, until no longer pink, about 5 minutes. Drain excess fat.

3 Stir in the corn, refried beans, enchilada sauce, and tomato sauce until well combined (use a whisk or spoon to get all the ingredients well blended).

4 Spread 1 cup of the crushed tortilla chips in a 9 x 13-inch baking pan or dish. Arrange the meat mixture over the chips. Top evenly with the grated cheese and the remaining chips.

5 Bake, uncovered, until the cheese melts and the casserole is heated through, about 15 minutes.

PER SERVING 370 calories, 13g fat (3g saturated, 0.2g omega-3), 540mg sodium, 42g carbohydrate, 9g fiber, 23g protein, 15% calcium, 10% iron

mom's feedback

My husband said the dish "was amazing," and my daughter declared it "the best meal ever." Even the cat tried to steal a bite!

Tamara, mother of Hannah, age 5 ▪ Cumberland, RI

Simply Delicious Shepherd's Pie

Liz's husband grew up in England, which means he grew up eating lots of classic British dishes such as Shepherd's Pie. The best part about Shepherd's Pie — at least according to Tim — is that each forkful provides a little taste of everything: meat 'n potatoes and vegetables. To add a modern twist to this hearty dinner, we use lean ground beef, fiber-rich beans (which also extend the meat and cost pennies), and a light tomato soup as the base. For the mashed potatoes, you can use leftovers, frozen, instant, or make them from scratch (check out our microwave mashed potato tip on page 140).

1½ pounds lean ground beef (90% or higher)

2 large carrots, peeled and shredded (2 cups)

1 teaspoon garlic powder

1 teaspoon onion powder

1 15-ounce can pinto beans, drained and rinsed

1 14½-ounce can ready-to-serve all-natural tomato soup

1½ cups shredded reduced-fat Cheddar cheese

1 cup frozen corn, thawed

Kosher salt and freshly ground black pepper

4 cups mashed potatoes

2 tablespoons grated Parmesan cheese

1 Preheat the oven to 375°F. Lightly oil or coat a 9 x 13-inch baking pan or dish with nonstick cooking spray and set aside.

2 Place a large Dutch oven or nonstick skillet over medium-high heat. Add the meat, carrots, garlic powder, and onion powder and cook, breaking up the large pieces, until the meat is no longer pink and the carrots are tender, about 5 minutes. Drain excess fat.

3 Stir in the beans, tomato soup, cheese, and corn. Simmer until heated through, 2 to 3 minutes. Season with salt and pepper to taste.

4 Arrange the meat mixture evenly in the prepared pan. Spread the mashed potatoes evenly on top, and sprinkle with the Parmesan cheese.

5 Bake until the meat mixture starts to bubble and the potatoes are heated through, about 15 minutes. Turn the oven to broil and broil until the top turns golden brown, 2 to 4 minutes.

PER SERVING 370 calories, 10g fat (5g saturated), 520mg sodium, 41g carbohydrate, 7g fiber, 30g protein, 90% vitamin A, 45% vitamin C, 25% calcium, 15% iron

mom's feedback

I would typically add chopped onion and garlic to a dish like this, but the onion and garlic powder made it so much faster. I liked the cheesy tomato flavor; my husband said it was a great meal to come home to. Everyone gave it two-thumbs up.

Beth, mother of Danica, age 2 and Alex, age 4 ▪ Garner, NC

Silly Salmon Noodle Bake

Tuna noodle casserole is a classic, but we've met a lot of kids, ours included, who are not big fans. To add more appeal as well as nutrition, we use salmon instead of tuna because it's higher in brain-boosting omega-3s, and we use whole wheat blend pasta instead of white for more fiber. Cream of mushroom soup gets nixed for a lighter, from-scratch mushroom sauce, and we replace the usual crushed potato chip topping with a crispy mixture of Japanese-style bread crumbs (AKA panko) and Parmesan cheese.

½ cup panko bread crumbs

½ cup grated Parmesan cheese

1 12-ounce package whole wheat blend egg noodles

2 5-ounce cans boneless, skinless pink salmon, drained and flaked

1 cup frozen petite peas, thawed

1 tablespoon unsalted butter

8 ounces mushrooms, coarsely chopped

½ teaspoon dried dill

½ teaspoon onion powder

¼ teaspoon kosher salt

¼ teaspoon black pepper

3 tablespoons canola oil

¼ cup all-purpose flour

3½ cups 1% low-fat milk

2 tablespoons reduced-sodium soy sauce

½ cup light sour cream

1 Preheat the oven to 400°F. Lightly oil or coat a 9 x 13-inch baking pan or dish with nonstick cooking spray and set aside. Combine the bread crumbs and Parmesan cheese in a bowl and set aside.

2 Cook the noodles according to package directions. Drain and return to the saucepan. Stir in the salmon and peas and set aside.

3 While the pasta is cooking, melt the butter in a medium saucepan over medium heat. Add the mushrooms, dill, onion powder, salt, and pepper and cook, stirring occasionally, until the mushrooms are tender, about 7 minutes.

4 Stir the oil and flour into the mushroom mixture and whisk constantly until smooth, about 2 minutes. Whisk the milk and soy sauce slowly into the flour mixture. Raise the heat and bring to a low boil, stirring constantly. Reduce the heat and continue to simmer and stir gently until the mixture thickens, about 3 minutes.

5 Remove from the heat and stir in the sour cream. Pour the sauce over the pasta mixture and stir to combine. Spread the mixture evenly in the prepared pan. Top with the bread crumb mixture.

6 Bake until the casserole is bubbly and the topping turns golden brown, 15 to 17 minutes.

PER SERVING 390 calories, 13g fat (5g saturated, 0.8g omega-3), 660mg sodium, 50g carbohydrate, 6g fiber, 22g protein, 25% calcium, 10% iron

mom's feedback

I always struggle to find fish recipes my family will eat, so I'll keep this one in the rotation. The salmon flavor was not too strong, which helped get it past the pickier palates in my house.

Kirsten, mother of Luke, age 10 months and Jackson, age 3 ▪ Danville, CA

Ham and Broccoli Hash Brown Casserole

MAKES 8 SERVINGS

There are so many words to describe this dish: Crowd pleaser, stick to your ribs, hearty, perfect for brunch, comforting — we could go on and on. But we realize that when it comes to casseroles, kids either love them and gobble them up, or run for the nearest PB&J sandwich. We certainly hope this great-tasting casserole convinces reluctant kids to take a bite … or two. Made with frozen hash brown potatoes, reduced-fat cheese, vitamin C-rich broccoli, and savory bites of ham, this dish comes together quickly, and in the case of our kids, disappears just as quickly.

1 10¾-ounce can condensed lower-fat, lower-sodium cream of celery soup

1 cup light sour cream

½ cup 1% low-fat milk

½ teaspoon onion powder

½ teaspoon garlic powder

½ teaspoon kosher salt

½ teaspoon black pepper

1 30-ounce bag frozen shredded potatoes, thawed

2 cups shredded reduced-fat Cheddar cheese, divided

1 10-ounce box frozen chopped broccoli, thawed and drained

8 ounces lower-sodium deli ham, cut into ½-inch pieces (2 cups)

1 Preheat the oven to 350°F. Lightly oil or coat a 9 x 13-inch baking pan or dish with nonstick cooking spray and set aside.

2 In a very large bowl, whisk together the soup, sour cream, milk, onion powder, garlic powder, salt, and pepper until well combined.

3 Mix in the shredded potatoes, 1½ cups of the cheese, broccoli, and ham.

4 Spread the mixture evenly in the prepared pan, top with the remaining ½ cup cheese, and bake, uncovered, until the cheese melts and the casserole is heated through, about 45 minutes. Cool about 10 minutes before serving.

PER SERVING 240 calories, 8g fat (4.5g saturated), 460mg sodium, 29g carbohydrate, 4g fiber, 17g protein, 20% vitamin A, 45% vitamin C, 30% calcium

tip The fastest way to thaw frozen vegetables is to defrost them using the microwave. You can also measure out what you need and defrost it overnight in the fridge.

mom's **feed**back We liked the flavor and texture combination of the ham and the broccoli and the bits of color they added to the dish.

— Elisia, mother of Brandt, age 3 and Cade, age 5 ▪ Sharpsburg, GA

Hot Diggity Dog Cornbread Casserole

MAKES 10 SERVINGS

Recently, a recipe for hot dog casserole caught our eye. Knowing how much kids love hot dogs and corn dogs, it seemed like a fun thing to make. Between the full-fat cheese, cornbread mix, and hot dogs, however, the saturated fat and sodium were off the charts. In *Meal Makeover Moms* fashion, we came up with a slimmed-down version. We make our cornbread from scratch, use low-fat veggie dogs, and add yellow bell pepper and corn, which blend in. For a kick, add a small can of diced green chile peppers.

1 12-ounce package vegetarian hot dogs

1 teaspoon canola oil

1 medium yellow bell pepper, cut into ¼-inch dice (1½ cups)

1¼ cups all-purpose flour

1 cup cornmeal

¼ cup granulated sugar

1 tablespoon baking powder

1 teaspoon chili powder

1 teaspoon kosher salt

½ teaspoon black pepper

1½ cups 1% low-fat milk

3 large eggs, beaten

⅓ cup canola oil

2 tablespoons honey mustard

1 cup frozen corn, thawed

1 cup shredded reduced-fat Cheddar cheese

1 Preheat the oven to 400°F. Lightly oil or coat a 9 x 13-inch baking pan or dish with nonstick cooking spray and set aside.

2 Slice the hot dogs in half lengthwise and then cut into ½-inch pieces. Set aside.

3 Heat 1 teaspoon oil in a large nonstick skillet over medium-high heat. Add the bell pepper and cook, stirring frequently, until softened, about 7 minutes. Add the hot dogs and cook until lightly browned, about 5 minutes. Set aside.

4 Meanwhile, whisk together the flour, cornmeal, sugar, baking powder, chili powder, salt, and pepper in a large bowl until well combined.

5 In a separate bowl, whisk the milk, eggs, ⅓ cup canola oil, and honey mustard until well blended. Stir into the flour mixture until just combined. Stir in the corn, cheese, and cooked hot dog mixture.

6 Spread the mixture evenly in the prepared pan and bake until a toothpick inserted in the center comes out clean and the casserole is golden brown on top, 25 to 30 minutes.

PER SERVING 310 calories, 12g fat (2.5g saturated, 0.8 omega-3), 540mg sodium, 32g carbohydrate, 2g fiber, 16g protein, 70% vitamin C, 20% calcium, 20% iron

mom's feedback

I have two, always-hungry teenage boys, so I would add a large can of chili to the baking dish before pouring in the cornbread mixture and baking.
— Rosey, mother of Teddy, age 13 and Joey, age 15 ▪ Camano Island, WA

Oodles of Orzo Zucchini Bake

MAKES 4 TO 5 SERVINGS

Well before their girls were born, Janice and Don planted their first backyard vegetable garden. If you ask Don (who's the chief farmer in the family) what he likes best, chances are he'll say zucchini. Ask Janice about zucchini, and she'll laugh about the bounty Don harvests each summer. It's just one of those vegetables that keeps growing and growing and growing. Try as she might to give it away to every neighbor on the street, Janice always has a lot left over. Of course, that's a good thing. Zucchini is rich in manganese — a nutrient needed for strong bones — and Carolyn and Leah are happy to eat it in everything from our *Tuscan Minestrone Soup* (page 54) and *Banana Zucchini Squiggle Loaf* (page 169) to this fresh and flavorful casserole.

1 cup dried orzo pasta (6 ounces)

1 tablespoon extra virgin olive oil, divided

½ small onion, cut into ¼-inch dice (½ cup)

1 medium zucchini (about 9 ounces), unpeeled and shredded (1½ cups)

2 large eggs, beaten

1 cup coarsely chopped cooked chicken (6 ounces)

1 cup shredded reduced-fat Italian blend cheese, divided

¼ cup grated Parmesan cheese

¼ teaspoon kosher salt

¼ teaspoon black pepper

1 pinch ground nutmeg

1 Preheat the oven to 350°F. Lightly oil or coat an 8 x 8-inch baking pan or dish with nonstick cooking spray and set aside.

2 Cook the orzo according to package directions. Drain and transfer to a large bowl.

3 Meanwhile, heat ½ tablespoon of the oil in a large nonstick skillet over medium heat. Add the onion and cook, stirring frequently, until softened, about 7 minutes. Raise the heat to medium-high, add the remaining ½ tablespoon oil and the zucchini, and cook, stirring frequently, until tender, about 5 minutes.

4 Stir the cooked vegetables, eggs, chicken, ½ cup cheese, Parmesan cheese, salt, pepper, and nutmeg into the orzo. Spread the mixture evenly in the prepared pan, top with the remaining ½ cup cheese and bake until the cheese melts and the casserole is cooked through, about 15 minutes.

PER SERVING 360 calories, 13g fat (5g saturated, 0.2g omega-3), 380mg sodium, 33g carbohydrate, 2g fiber, 29g protein, 10% vitamin A, 35% vitamin C, 25% calcium, 15% iron

mom's feedback

My 1-year old gobbled up the "cheesy chicken," and Eli said he loved the chicken and didn't mind the green stuff.

Jennifer, mother of Owen, age 1 and Eli, age 4 ▪ Laurinburg, NC

Cheesy Spinach Bake

CHAPTER 10

Vegetables You Don't Have to Hide

There's an assumption out there that kids hate the taste of vegetables, and the only way to get them down is to cook, puree, and conceal them in everything from chocolate pudding to macaroni and cheese. We disagree with this sneaky strategy and prefer to serve our veggies out in the open. Admittedly, some vegetables can be a tough sell with kids, but with such flavorful recipes as *Perfect Parsnip Fries, Mommy's Edamame,* and *Golden Mashed Potatoes,* even the pickiest eaters at your table will be tempted to try them. Buying fresh vegetables in season is ideal, but frozen and canned can also provide your family with a big burst of great nutrition, so use them too!

Stella and Vera stir up our *Cheesy Spinach Bake*, and proud mom, Jane shows off their work.

See more photos of our young cooks and moms cooking their favorite vegetable recipes on Flickr http://www.flickr.com/photos/mealmakeovermoms

Cheesy Spinach Bake

MAKES 8 SERVINGS

Frozen spinach rocks: it's inexpensive, nutritious, and a convenience ingredient you can feel good about. On its own, it's far from appetizing — and one could argue that from a child's perspective, it's kind of gross. But combined with seasoned bread crumbs, Cheddar cheese, and grated Parmesan, this simple side dish takes on a flavor and texture that appeal to kids. With 20 percent bone-building calcium in each serving, plus a boatload of vitamin A, we hope you'll add these gooey, cheesy spinach bites to your lineup of favorite family sides.

1 10-ounce box frozen chopped spinach, thawed

2 large eggs

½ cup 1% low-fat milk

1 tablespoon extra virgin olive oil or melted butter

½ cup seasoned dried bread crumbs

½ teaspoon baking powder

1 cup shredded reduced-fat Cheddar cheese

¼ cup grated Parmesan cheese

   Kosher salt

1 Preheat the oven to 350°F. Lightly oil or coat an 8 x 8-inch baking pan or dish with nonstick cooking spray and set aside.

2 Drain the spinach in a colander. Press with the back of a large spoon to remove excess moisture. Set aside.

3 Whisk together the eggs, milk, and olive oil in a large bowl. Whisk in the bread crumbs and baking powder. Stir in the spinach, Cheddar cheese, and Parmesan cheese until well combined.

4 Spread the mixture evenly in the prepared pan. Bake until the mixture is set and the top is golden brown, 25 to 30 minutes. Slice into 2 x 4-inch rectangles and serve. Sprinkle the tops with a few pinches of salt to taste.

PER SERVING (1 slice): 120 calories, 7g fat (3g saturated), 340mg sodium, 8g carbohydrate, 1g fiber, 9g protein, 90% vitamin A, 20% calcium

mom's **feed**back

My 3-year old thought it was quiche and my younger daughter asked for more. They like spinach, eggs, and cheese, so this was a winning combination.

Jane, mother of Stella, age 1 and Vera, age 3 ▪ Aalen, Germany

Roasted Cauliflower with Crispy Leek Rings

MAKES 4 TO 5 SERVINGS

Vegetables don't have to be brightly colored to be nutritious. Consider cauliflower. The reason it's so pale is because the leaves of the plant shield the florets from the sun's rays as it grows. Cauliflower, along with broccoli and cabbage, is a cruciferous vegetable, and research shows it may protect against certain cancers. It's also a veggie lots of kids like. For this recipe, we bring out the natural sweetness of cauliflower by roasting it, and we add sliced leeks, which end up resembling mini onion rings.

1 large leek, white part only

1 head cauliflower (about 2¼ pounds), trimmed and cut into 1-inch florets

2 tablespoons extra virgin olive oil

½ teaspoon kosher salt

Freshly ground black pepper

1 Preheat the oven to 425°F. Wash the leek well to remove any dirt trapped between the layers. Slice into ½-inch-thick rounds and break them apart into little "rings."

2 Place the leeks, cauliflower, oil, salt, and a few cranks of pepper in a large bowl and toss to coat with the oil. Transfer to a 9 x 13-inch glass baking dish.

3 Bake until the cauliflower turns golden and the leek "rings" become crispy, 20 to 25 minutes. Stir well every 10 minutes so the leeks don't burn. Season with additional salt and pepper to taste.

PER SERVING 100 calories, 7g fat (1g saturated), 170mg sodium, 10g carbohydrate, 3g fiber, 3g protein, 120% vitamin C

tip If you use a metal baking sheet or pan, cook the cauliflower on its own for 10 minutes, then stir in the leeks for the remainder of the cooking time.

mom's feedback

We live in Wisconsin, and when I saw this simple recipe, I thought, "What, no cheese?" We were all pleasantly surprised at how much flavor the leek, salt, and pepper added to the cauliflower.

Christa, mother of Grant, age 8 months and Ryan, age 4 ▪ Plymouth, WI

Sweeeeet Brussels Sprouts

MAKES 4 SERVINGS

Ask 100 kids to name their favorite vegetable and chances are the words "Brussels sprouts" will never cross their lips. To turn these mini cabbage look-alikes into a vegetable kids will clamor for, we toss them with sautéed bits of bacon and onion and a drizzle of maple syrup. The slightly sweet and salty combo is just what the Brussels sprouts need to turn them from "yuck" to "yum." As for their nutritional merits, they're packed with vitamin C, as well as vitamin K, a nutrient needed for strong bones.

1 pound Brussels sprouts

2 slices nitrite-free bacon, cut crosswise into ¼-inch-wide pieces

½ small onion, cut into ¼-inch dice (½ cup)

1 tablespoon pure maple syrup

¼ teaspoon kosher salt

1 generous pinch freshly ground black pepper

1 Trim the stem ends of the Brussels sprouts using a sharp knife. Peel off the loose leaves around the stems and slice each sprout in half lengthwise.

2 Bring a pot of water to a boil. Add the Brussels sprouts, bring the water back to a low boil, and cook, uncovered, until tender, 8 to 10 minutes. Drain and set aside.

3 While the sprouts are cooking, heat a large nonstick skillet over medium heat. Add the bacon and onion and cook, stirring frequently, until the bacon is crisp and the onion is softened, about 7 minutes.

4 Add the cooked Brussels sprouts, maple syrup, salt, and pepper and toss until the vegetables are coated.

PER SERVING (about 15 halves): 80 calories, 2g fat (0.5g saturated), 190mg sodium, 14g carbohydrate, 4g fiber, 5g protein, 15% vitamin A, 150% vitamin C

tip You may be surprised to find bacon in a few of our recipes, including this one. The truth is, adding just 2 small slices of bacon (we use the uncured, nitrite-free kind) doesn't really contribute much fat to the dish. What it does add, however, is a huge burst of flavor that kids really like.

mom's feedback These weren't bitter like most Brussels sprouts I've tried. They had a touch of sweetness from the maple syrup and everyone loved the bacon.

Heather, mother of Brandon, age 6, Caroline, age 10 and TJ, age 14 ▪ Laytonsville, MD

Mommy's Edamame

MAKES 6 SERVINGS

Vegetables aren't often called "fun" by kids, but that's exactly how Janice's daughter, Leah, describes this recipe. She gets a big kick out of "popping" the beans from their pods and asks for edamame a lot. (To see Leah in action, check out the Cooking Videos section of our website and watch her devour them.) Edamame, AKA soybeans, are the most widely grown legume in the world. Soy is high in protein, low in fat, and eating it has been shown to lower cholesterol levels and boost heart health. Not bad for a side dish that takes just 10 minutes to prepare!

1 16-ounce bag frozen edamame (soybeans in pods)

2 teaspoons extra virgin olive oil

½ teaspoon kosher salt

1 Bring a large saucepan of salted water to a boil. Add the frozen edamame and cook according to package directions.

2 Drain and return to the pan. Toss with the olive oil and salt.

3 When cool enough to pick up, pop the beans out of the pod directly into your mouth.

PER SERVING (about ¾ cup): 100 calories, 5g fat (0g saturated), 100mg sodium, 6g carbohydrate, 4g fiber, 8g protein, 10% vitamin C

tip The pods are not edible, so don't eat them! For younger children, you may want to buy edamame already shelled.

mom's feedback

I served these for a snack while I was making dinner. I liked that it was healthy, and my son thought it was fun to open up the pods to find the edamame. Madeleine had trouble getting the pods open, so next time I'll make the shelled ones for her instead. For an Asian touch, I'm going to try using a little bit of sesame oil.

Danielle, mother of Madeleine, age 2 and Spencer, age 5 ▪ Chelmsford, MA

Creamy Caesar Salad with Feta and Dill

MAKES 4 SERVINGS

Sometimes the easiest way to get kids to try a new vegetable is to start with something familiar. If your family eats iceberg lettuce without complaint, consider a switch to its more nutritious relative: romaine. Like iceberg, romaine lettuce is mild in flavor and packed with crunch, but when it comes to nutrition, it blows the roof off iceberg. Surprisingly (because it's mostly water), romaine is loaded with three heart-healthy vitamins: A, C, and folate. Don't be afraid of the full-fat dressing in this salad. We use it because it adds a huge kick of flavor and because the fat boosts our bodies' ability to absorb certain nutrients. If you're concerned about the fat, by all means, substitute with a light dressing.

1 head romaine lettuce (about 8 ounces), coarsely chopped (5 cups)

¼ cup crumbled feta cheese

2 tablespoons creamy Caesar salad dressing

1 tablespoon chopped fresh dill

Freshly ground black pepper

¾ cup seasoned croutons, preferably whole wheat

 Combine the lettuce, feta cheese, dressing, and dill in a large bowl and toss to coat evenly with the dressing. Season with pepper to taste, and top with the croutons.

PER SERVING (1 side salad): 90 calories, 7g fat (2g saturated), 230mg sodium, 5g carbohydrate, 1g fiber, 2g protein, 100% vitamin A, 25% vitamin C

tip If you're left with a bunch of fresh dill, you can freeze what you don't use. Herbs like dill freeze well and are best frozen while still on the stalk. Clean the leaves, dry them, and place in zip-top bags. Once frozen, just snip off what you need.

 **mom's feedback** My 3-year old's favorite cheese is feta, so her response, "Yummy, yummy, yummy," wasn't a surprise.

Elaine, mother of Allison, age 2 months and Emily, age 3 ▪ Vienna, VA

Buttery Brown Sugar Carrots

MAKES 6 SERVINGS

It's hard to say what makes kids hit the "reject" button when vegetables are served, but mushy and bland are probably two of the main reasons. For this simple side dish, we steam the carrots so they're tender but still a bit crunchy (research shows kids prefer crunchy textures), and we stir in a small amount of brown sugar and butter. As dietitians, we don't worry too much about that. After all, a tablespoon each of sugar and butter split between six servings is no big deal — especially if every single carrot gets gobbled up.

1 16-ounce bag baby carrots

1 tablespoon unsalted butter

1 tablespoon brown sugar

¼ teaspoon kosher salt

1 generous pinch ground cinnamon

1 generous pinch ground cloves

1 Steam the carrots until crisp-tender, 12 to 15 minutes.

2 Melt the butter in a large nonstick skillet over low heat. Whisk or stir in the brown sugar, salt, cinnamon, and cloves until the sugar dissolves.

3 Remove from the heat, stir in the carrots until well coated, and season with additional cinnamon and cloves to taste.

PER SERVING (about ½ cup): 60 calories, 2g fat (1g saturated), 100mg sodium, 10g carbohydrate, 2g fiber, 1g protein, 220% vitamin A

mom's feedback

Rosie said these were the best carrots in the world. The best parts about this recipe were the butter — which I don't usually use with vegetables — and the cinnamon and cloves.

— Laura, mother of Rosie, age 5 and Jonah, age 7 ▪ La Crosse, WI

Golden Mashed Potatoes

MAKES 8 SERVINGS

Mashed potatoes are the ultimate comfort food. But when they're made with gobs of butter and cream, the nutritional benefits of potatoes — vitamin C, heart-healthy potassium, and fiber — get overshadowed. Our makeover is a lot lower in the bad fat because we use low-fat milk, light cream cheese, and just a bit of butter, plus we add sweet potato for a splash of color and to boost the nutrition even more. Sweet potatoes take a bit longer to cook which is why we cut them into smaller pieces.

2 pounds Yukon Gold or russet potatoes, peeled and cut into ¾-inch dice (4 cups)

1 pound sweet potatoes, peeled and cut into ½-inch dice (2½ cups)

½ cup 1% low-fat milk

2 ounces light cream cheese

2 tablespoons unsalted butter

1½ teaspoons kosher salt

Freshly ground black pepper

1 Place the potatoes and sweet potato in a large saucepan and add enough cold water to cover. Add a few pinches of salt, cover, and bring to a boil. Reduce the heat and cook, covered, at a low boil until very tender, about 12 minutes.

2 When done, drain well and return to the saucepan. Place over low heat and add the milk, cream cheese, butter, and salt. Use a potato masher, and mash until smooth. Season with pepper to taste.

PER SERVING (about ⅔ cup): 180 calories, 4.5g fat (2.5g saturated), 270mg sodium, 32g carbohydrate, 3g fiber, 4g protein, 140% vitamin A, 25% vitamin C

tip You can also make mashed potatoes in the microwave. Wash the potatoes and place them in a microwave-safe dish. Avoid piercing the skin in order to retain steam and speed up the cooking time. Cover the dish (if covering with plastic wrap, poke a small hole in the plastic) and microwave on high, about 10 minutes. Use oven mitts to remove the dish, uncover, and mash well. Add your favorite mashed potato ingredients.

mom's feedback
Paige liked these even more the next day when we reheated them for leftovers!
Beth, mother of Kate, age 9 and Paige, age 12 ▪ Wilmington, NC

Broccoli Trees with Cheesy Dipping Sauce

MAKES 6 SERVINGS

Broccoli usually goes over pretty well with kids, but when it's steamed until mushy and served with nothing on it, broccoli can be pretty bland and boring. To jazz things up, we suggest you top crisp florets with our tangy cheese sauce. Your kids can drizzle it all over their bright-green florets or use it as a dip. It bolsters the flavor and adds a hefty helping of calcium.

1 head broccoli (about 1½ pounds), cut into florets

1 tablespoon olive oil or unsalted butter

1 tablespoon all-purpose flour

1 cup 1% low-fat milk

½ teaspoon Dijon mustard

⅛ teaspoon garlic powder

1 cup shredded reduced-fat Cheddar cheese

Kosher salt and freshly ground black pepper

1 Steam the broccoli until crisp-tender, about 5 minutes. Remove from the heat and set aside, uncovered.

2 While the broccoli is steaming, heat the oil in a small saucepan over medium heat. Add the flour and whisk constantly until smooth, about 2 minutes. Whisk the milk, mustard, and garlic powder slowly into the flour mixture. Raise the heat and bring to a low boil, stirring constantly. Reduce the heat and continue to simmer and stir gently until the mixture thickens, about 3 minutes.

3 Remove from the heat and stir in the cheese until it melts. Season with salt and pepper to taste, and serve with the broccoli.

PER SERVING (1 cup broccoli & 3 tablespoons sauce): 110 calories, 6g fat (2.5g saturated), 160mg sodium, 8g carbohydrate, 2g fiber, 9g protein, 50% vitamin A, 110% vitamin C, 20% calcium

mom's feedback

My son, Alex, loves Dijon mustard, and I'm always looking for ways to get more calcium and protein into my "vegetarian" 13-year old, so this recipe gets a "wow" from all of us.

Cindy, mother of Emilie, age 9, Anna, age 13 and Alex, age 15 ▪ De Pere, WI

Over-the-Rainbow Brown Rice

MAKES 6 SERVINGS

Brown rice takes about 40 minutes to cook, but we think it's worth the time. Brown rice is nutritionally superior to white — it's higher in B vitamins, iron, and fiber — plus, it's a whole grain which kids and adults don't get enough of. The rainbow of colors from the carrots, corn, and peas makes this savory side dish hard to resist. And despite all the veggies, the hands-on prep time is really quick.

1 tablespoon extra virgin olive oil

½ small onion, cut into ¼-inch dice (½ cup)

1 medium carrot, peeled and cut into ¼-inch dice (½ cup)

1 clove garlic, minced

1 cup long grain brown rice

½ teaspoon chopped fresh thyme, optional

2 cups all-natural vegetable or chicken broth

¼ cup frozen corn, thawed

¼ cup frozen petite peas, thawed

Kosher salt and freshly ground black pepper

1 Heat the oil in a medium saucepan over medium heat. Add the onion, carrot, and garlic and cook, stirring frequently, until the vegetables are softened, about 7 minutes.

2 Stir in the rice and thyme as desired, and cook, stirring a few times, for 1 minute. Stir in the broth, raise the heat, cover, and bring to a boil. Reduce the heat and simmer, covered, until all the liquid is absorbed, 40 to 45 minutes.

3 Remove from the heat and fluff the rice with a fork. Stir in the corn and peas, replace the cover, and let stand an additional 5 to 10 minutes.

PER SERVING (generous ½ cup): 160 calories, 3.5g fat (0.5g saturated), 160mg sodium, 30g carbohydrate, 2g fiber, 4g protein, 45% vitamin A

mom's feedback

I love using brown rice. Sometimes the kids like it and sometimes they don't. This recipe was a huge hit — I think it was because of the chicken broth. The kids kept asking, "Mom, are you sure this is brown rice?" Next time I'm going to add one or two more garlic cloves.

Susan, mother of Emily, age 11 and Anna and Naomi, age 15 ▪ Du Quoin, IL

Teriyaki Snow Peas and Carrots

MAKES 4 SERVINGS

If getting a vegetable on the dinner table is a challenge in your house, you'll welcome this quick, weeknight stir fry. We pair crunchy snow peas (a variety of pea eaten whole in its flat-shaped pod) with kid-friendly carrots and stir in a smidgen of teriyaki sauce. Most people know carrots are high in vitamin A, but snow peas have some too — plus they're a good source of vitamin C.

1 teaspoon canola oil

1 9-ounce bag snow peas, strings removed (3 cups)

1 medium carrot, peeled and cut into 1/16-inch rounds (2/3 cup)

2 teaspoons reduced-sodium teriyaki sauce

1 teaspoon toasted sesame seeds, optional

1 Heat the oil in a large nonstick skillet over medium-high heat. Add the snow peas and carrot and cook, stirring frequently, until the vegetables are crisp-tender, about 5 minutes.

2 Transfer to a bowl and stir in the teriyaki sauce until the vegetables are well coated. Top with the sesame seeds as desired.

PER SERVING (¾ cup): 50 calories, 1.5g fat (0g saturated), 95mg sodium, 8g carbohydrate, 2g fiber, 2g protein, 100% vitamin A, 50% vitamin C

tip To remove the tough, stringlike fiber that runs along both sides of the pod, snap off one end with your fingers (or a paring knife), and pull the string along the length of the pod. Do the same thing on the other side.

mom's feedback

The night we prepared this recipe, Brianna peeled a carrot while Kyle watched. I did all the slicing, and then at dinner, Kyle — who's normally my "picky" eater — ate all the vegetables on his plate. It just goes to show that the more you get your kids involved in the planning, prepping, and cooking process, the more they will try new foods!

Leah, mother of Kyle, age 2 and Brianna, age 5 ▪ Leander, TX

Perfect Parsnip Fries

MAKES 4 SERVINGS

Parsnips are cousins to carrots but they're even higher in fiber and vitamin C (and they're cream colored versus orange). Popular in Europe — Liz's British husband remembers eating parsnips at many Sunday dinners — their flavor becomes surprisingly sweet when you roast them. Shaped into "fries," our own kids could eat them every day, which wouldn't be a problem since they're so low in calories. Don't be surprised if you end up doubling this recipe!

1 16-ounce bag parsnips

1 tablespoon extra virgin olive oil

¼ teaspoon kosher salt

⅛ teaspoon garlic powder

Freshly ground black pepper

1 Preheat the oven to 400°F. Peel the parsnips and trim the tops and bottoms. Slice each in half crosswise to separate the thick end and the narrow end. Cut the narrow piece in half lengthwise and the thick piece in quarters lengthwise. Each "fry" will be about 2½ to 3 inches long and about ½-inch wide.

2 Place the fries in a bowl and toss with the oil, salt, and garlic powder. Spread in a single layer on a large rimmed baking sheet, and bake for 15 minutes.

3 Remove from the oven, turn each parsnip with a spatula or tongs (this will allow even baking), place back in the oven, and bake until golden brown and tender, about 10 minutes. Season with additional salt and pepper to taste.

PER SERVING (about 9 fries): 110 calories, 4g fat (0.5g saturated), 80mg sodium, 18g carbohydrate, 5g fiber, 1g protein, 30% vitamin C

mom's feedback We wouldn't change a thing about this recipe; the parsnips were "perfect." Liliana said it was fun to make them together.

Lara, mother of Liliana, age 9 and Jens, age 12 ▪ Arlington, VA

Chili-Crusted Sweet Potato Fries

MAKES 4 SERVINGS

French fries are the most popular "vegetable" among the under-five crowd. But many are deep-fat fried or made with partially hydrogenated vegetable oils. If your kids are hooked on fries, cook up your own with white potatoes, parsnips (see page 144), or sweet potatoes. For this recipe, the chili powder and cumin add a nice little kick of flavor (cut back if you think it's too strong for your kids), and the cornmeal gives a crispy coating. Janice's daughter, Carolyn, never liked sweet potato fries because she thought they were "soggy." After trying ours, she "loves" them.

2 medium sweet potatoes (about 1¼ pounds), peeled

3 tablespoons cornmeal

1 tablespoon granulated sugar

¾ teaspoon chili powder

½ teaspoon ground cumin

½ teaspoon kosher salt

1 pinch onion powder

1 pinch garlic powder

2 egg whites

1 Preheat the oven to 425°F. Generously oil or coat a large rimmed baking sheet with nonstick cooking spray and set aside.

2 Cut the sweet potatoes in half lengthwise. Cut each half into 6 wedges and then cut each of the wedges in half, lengthwise, so you end up with a total of about 48 thin "fries."

3 Whisk together the cornmeal, sugar, chili powder, cumin, salt, onion powder, and garlic powder in a large bowl.

4 In a separate bowl, whisk the egg whites until frothy. Add the sweet potatoes and toss to coat evenly with the egg whites.

5 Add the sweet potatoes to the cornmeal mixture and toss until lightly coated. Place on the prepared baking sheet and mist with nonstick cooking spray. Bake until golden brown on the bottoms, about 12 minutes. Remove from the oven, turn each fry with a spatula or tongs, and bake until slightly crisp on the outside and soft on the inside, 10 to 12 minutes.

PER SERVING (about 12 fries): 150 calories, 1g fat (0g saturated), 230mg sodium, 31g carbohydrate, 4g fiber, 4g protein, 290% vitamin A

tip Be sure to coat the baking sheet generously with cooking spray. Keep a watchful eye on the wedges as they cook so they don't burn.

mom's feedback This recipe was great for letting my girls practice using measuring spoons and to reinforce counting. My oldest daughter said, "These were so fun to make! I'm going to be a famous chef on TV some day!"
— Rachel, mother of Lilly, age 1, Maggie, age 3 and Giselle, age 5 ▪ Columbus, OH

Mom's Mango Smoothie

CHAPTER 11

Sips & Smoothies

It's a rare kid (or adult) who will resist a colorful, sweet, and refreshing drink. That's why sips and smoothies are ideal for filling the nutritional gaps in your family's diet. They're one of the easiest ways to help meet kids' daily recommended servings of fruit. Made with low-fat milk, yogurt, or soy milk, they also provide boosts of protein and bone-building calcium. Our recipes are incredibly versatile, so you can tailor them to your kids' individual tastes. For more sweetness in our *Muddy Berry Smoothie*, add more banana. To make our *Peanut Butter Banana Split Shake* even thicker, toss in extra ice cubes. Even swap the blueberries for strawberries in our *Blueberry Frosty*. Serve these with breakfast, as an after-school snack, before a soccer game, or as an anytime treat. Cheers!

Little chefs, Evan and McKenzie, make our *Mom's Mango Smoothie* by filling the blender with nutritious yogurt, juice, and chunks of mango.

See more photos of our young cooks and moms making their favorite smoothies on Flickr
http://www.flickr.com/photos/mealmakeovermoms

Strawberry Banana Smoothie

MAKES 3 SERVINGS

This is Liz's go-to smoothie. She serves it with breakfast before her boys head off for school, or whips it up for an after-school pick-me-up when the kids are famished and thirsty. Made with the simplest of ingredients — juice, frozen fruit, yogurt, and banana — it goes down quickly with just a few slurps. Josh and Simon can easily make it themselves, and there's always plenty left over for Liz.

1½ cups 100% tropical juice blend or apple juice

1 cup frozen strawberries

½ cup low-fat strawberry or vanilla yogurt

½ large ripe banana

1 Place the juice, strawberries, yogurt, and banana in a blender, and blend until well combined.

2 Pour into individual glasses and serve with a straw.

PER SERVING (1 cup): 150 calories, 0.5g fat (0g saturated), 40mg sodium, 35g carbohydrate, 2g fiber, 2g protein, 90% vitamin C

tip Over-ripe bananas are perfect for smoothies. Peel, cut in half, and stash in your freezer in zip-top bags. Whenever you're craving a smoothie, toss one into the blender for some added slush and sweetness.

mom's feedback This is the perfect healthy snack to fill in those nutritional gaps during the day. Jasmine said it tastes like dessert ... but it's healthy!

Jen, mother of Jade, age 5 and Jasmine, age 6 ▪ Ft. Thomas, KY

Muddy Berry Smoothie

MAKES 3 SERVINGS

The thought of drinking mud is enough to ruin anyone's appetite, but it's the perfect name for this thick, brownish-blue smoothie made with blueberries and chocolate milk. Blueberries are one of nature's most antioxidant-rich fruits. Pair them with calcium-rich low-fat chocolate milk, and you've got a nutritional power drink on your hands — no matter what you call it.

2 cups low-fat chocolate milk or light chocolate soy milk

4 ice cubes

1½ cups frozen blueberries

½ large ripe banana

1 Place the milk, ice cubes, blueberries, and banana in a blender, and blend until well combined.

2 Pour into individual glasses and serve with a straw.

PER SERVING (1 cup): 150 calories, 1.5g fat (0g saturated), 80mg sodium, 31g carbohydrate, 3g fiber, 6g protein, 20% calcium

mom's feedback We all loved the sweetness of this smoothie. In fact, my husband said it tasted like maraschino cherries!

Courtney, mother of Rylea, age 5 ▪ Calgary, Alberta, Canada

Berry Bonanza Splash

MAKES 3 SERVINGS

When Janice's daughter, Leah, first tried this smoothie, she declared (between sips), "This is the best smoothie I've had in ten years." Leah is ten, so we took it as a compliment. The frozen mixed berries called for in this recipe — a medley of blueberries, strawberries, raspberries, and blackberries — have seeds. If you anticipate "yucks," pour the mixture through a fine-mesh strainer to remove them.

1½ cups 100% apple juice

1½ cups frozen mixed berries

¾ cup low-fat strawberry yogurt

1 Place the juice, berries, and yogurt in a blender, and blend until well combined.

2 Pour into individual glasses and serve with a straw.

PER SERVING (1 cup): 140 calories, 1g fat (0g saturated), 40mg sodium, 34g carbohydrate, 2g fiber, 2g protein, 15% vitamin C

mom's feedback Blake said it was the best smoothie ever, and Riley said it was awesome! I may add ice cubes to the blender the next time.

Kathi, mother of Blake, age 7 and Riley, age 11 ▪ Grand Blanc, MI

Tropical Soy Milk Smoothie

MAKES 3 SERVINGS

A dairy allergy or intolerance shouldn't prevent you and your kids from enjoying creamy, rich smoothies. The vanilla soy milk that we use for this island-inspired concoction enhances the natural sweetness of the frozen fruit, banana, and honey. And with the same amount of calcium and vitamin D as a regular glass of milk, it's an ideal alternative to dairy.

1½ cups light vanilla soy milk

1 medium ripe banana

⅔ cup frozen mango

⅔ cup frozen strawberries

1 tablespoon honey

1 Place the soy milk, banana, mango, strawberries, and honey in a blender, and blend until well combined.

2 Pour into individual glasses and serve with a straw.

PER SERVING (1 cup): 150 calories, 1g fat (0g saturated), 35mg sodium, 34g carbohydrate, 3g fiber, 3g protein, 10% vitamin A, 40% vitamin C, 15% calcium

mom's feedback The soy milk worked for us because we have a dairy allergy in the family, but I think low-fat milk could also be used. My 6-year old asked me to make it again.

— Amy, mother of Lindsey, age 3, Abigail, age 5 and Caleb, age 6 ▪ Kewaunee, WI

Pint-Size Pina Colada

MAKES 3 SERVINGS

When we think of pina coladas, we envision sipping icy drinks while lolling on a beautiful beach in the tropics. In reality, the only pina coladas we drink nowadays are these pint-size, vitamin C-packed versions that we share with our kids in our Massachusetts kitchens! For this tropical treat, we blend together naturally sweet, frozen pineapple chunks with pineapple juice and light coconut milk. We use the light kind because 1 cup has just 150 calories compared to 450 in the regular, full-fat version. In the unlikely event you have leftovers, pour the smoothie into ice pop molds and freeze.

2 cups frozen pineapple chunks

1½ cups 100% pineapple juice (we use two 6-ounce cans)

⅓ cup light coconut milk or ½ cup low-fat vanilla yogurt

1 Place the pineapple, juice, and coconut milk in a blender, and blend until well combined.

2 Pour into individual glasses and serve with a straw.

PER SERVING (1 cup): 120 calories, 1.5g fat (1.5g saturated), 15mg sodium, 27g carbohydrate, 1g fiber, 0g protein, 130% vitamin C

tip Our recipe only calls for a third cup coconut milk, but you can freeze what you don't use. Measure out ⅓ cup portions, pour into zip-top bags, and place in your freezer. Thaw slightly before adding to your next pina colada.

mom's feedback

We love coconut milk, and my kids asked me to make these again. They were easy and fun to make, and tasted so good with just a handful of ingredients.

Kate, mother of Mairead, age 3, Nuala, age 7, Dori, age 9 and Phoebe, age 11 ▪ Cheshire, CT

Peanut Butter Banana Split Shake

MAKES 3 SERVINGS

This super cool drink is reminiscent of an old-fashioned milkshake (with a hint of Reese's® Peanut Butter Cups). But it's a whole lot healthier, and surprisingly, doesn't contain any ice cream at all. Made with calcium-rich low-fat milk, lots of ice cubes, peanut butter, banana, and a bit of chocolate syrup, your kids will feel like they're drinking an ice cream sundae through a straw.

1½ cups 1% low-fat milk

6 ice cubes

1 small ripe banana

2 tablespoons peanut butter

2 tablespoons chocolate syrup

1 Place the milk, ice cubes, banana, peanut butter, and chocolate syrup in a blender, and blend until well combined.

2 Pour into individual glasses over additional ice as desired and serve with a straw.

PER SERVING (1 cup): 180 calories, 7g fat (2g saturated), 125mg sodium, 24g carbohydrate, 2g fiber, 8g protein, 15% calcium

tip Since we don't add ice cream or frozen yogurt to this drink, we use a generous helping of ice cubes to make it thick and frosty.

mom's feedback

My daughter said it tasted like a "Reese's banana split!"

Karen, mother of Niki, age 13, Sean, age 16, Erin, age 19 and Marc, age 21 ■ Steilacoom, WA

Blueberry Frosty

MAKES 4 SERVINGS

This frozen treat is the perfect antidote to a hot summer's day. Our make-in-minutes frosty hits the nutritional spot with three good-for-you ingredients: calcium-rich frozen yogurt, blueberries (an antioxidant superstar), and 100% fruit juice. This recipe is as versatile as it is easy: You can substitute the blueberries with frozen mango, strawberries, or peaches.

2 cups low-fat vanilla
frozen yogurt

2 cups frozen or fresh
blueberries

½ cup 100% cranberry
blueberry juice

1 Place the frozen yogurt, blueberries, and juice in a blender, and blend until well combined. To keep things moving, you may need to stop the blender a few times and stir the ingredients around with a spoon.

2 Pour into individual glasses or bowls and serve with a spoon.

PER SERVING (¾ cup): 180 calories, 2g fat (1g saturated), 70mg sodium, 36g carbohydrate, 2g fiber, 6g protein, 25% vitamin C, 20% calcium

mom's feedback This tasted so good and had two of my favorite things in it: protein and fiber. My daughter couldn't believe something so tasty could be healthy.

— Jennifer, mother of Sean, age 9 and Laurie, age 11 ▪ Jackson, MI

Immunity Booster Blast

MAKES 4 SERVINGS

Keeping kids healthy and strong, especially during cold and flu season, is the reason we originally whipped up this smoothie. It's made with strawberries and pomegranate juice — both rich in immune-bolstering vitamin C — and kefir, a beverage teaming with probiotics, so-called good bacteria that some research shows may reduce upper respiratory infections. We also whirl in some Greek yogurt (it has more protein than regular yogurt) and ground flaxseed for its omega-3 prowess. This smoothie has it all!

1 cup 100% pomegranate blueberry juice

1 cup frozen strawberries

1 small ripe banana

1 6-ounce container 0%-fat strawberry Greek yogurt

½ cup strawberry kefir

4 ice cubes

2 tablespoons honey

1 teaspoon ground flaxseed

1 Place the juice, strawberries, banana, yogurt, kefir, ice cubes, honey, and flaxseed in a blender, and blend until well combined.

2 Pour into individual glasses and serve with a straw.

PER SERVING (1 cup): 150 calories, 1g fat (0g saturated, 0.2g omega-3), 35mg sodium, 32g carbohydrate, 2g fiber, 5g protein, 60% vitamin C

tip In our Pantry Picks sidebar (page 16), we recommend a variety of products including the 100% juices we like to use. The one we suggest for this recipe is Minute Maid Enhanced because it has a sweet, mild flavor and has added omega-3 fat.

mom's feedback We turned the extra smoothie into frozen pops. If you used a frozen banana in this smoothie, you could leave out the ice.

Alyssa, mother of Evan, age 6 and Ryan, age 7 ▪ Arlington, MA

Make-It-Yourself Sports Drink

MAKES 4 SERVINGS

There is a time and a place for sports drinks. For instance, on hot summer days when our kids are playing sports for long stretches, we pack them along without a second thought. However, sports drinks can be pricey and we're not thrilled with the artificial colors found in most of them. For this recipe, we turn to sports nutritionist and author, Nancy Clark, for her do-it-yourself sports drink. Having shared this easy-to-make thirst quencher with some of the world's most elite athletes, Nancy is happy to pass it on to your favorite athletes.

¼ cup granulated sugar

¼ cup hot water

¼ teaspoon salt

¼ cup orange juice or any 100% juice your kids love (not concentrate)

2 tablespoons lemon juice

3½ cups cold water

1 Place the sugar, hot water, and salt in a large pitcher and stir until the sugar dissolves.

2 Mix in the orange juice, lemon juice, and the remaining water. Chill before serving.

PER SERVING (1 cup): 60 calories, 0g fat (0g saturated), 150mg sodium, 15g carbohydrate, 0g fiber, 0g protein, 15% vitamin C

mom's feedback The kids loved the taste and thought it tasted like their usual sports drink. I put all the ingredients out and the kids made it themselves.

Robin, mother of Naomi, age 8 and Maya, age 11 ▪ Arlington, MA

Juicy Sherbet Party Punch

MAKES 12 SERVINGS

Janice entertains a lot, and this punch has served her well over the years. In the summer, limes and lime sherbet add a cool, refreshing zing to the mix; around the holidays, she floats cranberries on top; and at Halloween, orange sherbet and thin slices of fresh oranges add a festive touch. With a punch like this one, no one will complain if you don't serve soft drinks at your next party.

1　64-ounce bottle 100% cranberry raspberry juice

1　1-liter bottle lime or lemon seltzer

4　scoops lime sherbet (about 1 cup)

1　lime, sliced into thin rounds

1　Pour the juice and seltzer into a large punch bowl. Add about a dozen ice cubes or an ice ring (see tip below), sherbet, and lime slices.

2　Ladle into individual glasses and serve.

PER SERVING (1 cup): 100 calories, 0g fat (0g saturated), 50mg sodium, 24g carbohydrate, 0g fiber, 0g protein, 70% vitamin C

tip　If you have an ice-ring mold, add lime slices and water to it the day before and freeze. You can also create your own "ice ring" by freezing water and several lime slices in a square, rectangular, or round plastic container.

mom's feedback

My 2-year old said, "Yum," over and over as she slurped down three kid-size glasses. She's my very picky eater so that's a great endorsement. I love how it is made with 100% juice and no added sugar; I could see experimenting using different juices such as fresh orange juice.

Molly, mother of Chloe, age 2 and Lydia, age 4 ▪ Melrose, MA

Mom's Mango Smoothie

MAKES 4 SERVINGS

This smoothie is a *Meal Makeover Moms* favorite because it uses mango, a good source of vitamins A and C, and fiber. We first created it for a series of cooking videos we put on our website to showcase some family-friendly recipes. In the video, Janice and Leah prepare the smoothie together, demonstrating that kids of all ages can easily whip one up with little help — just be sure to place the blender lid on tightly!

2 cups frozen mango chunks (one 10-ounce package)

1½ cups 100% mango juice, tropical juice, or orange juice

1 cup low-fat vanilla yogurt

1 Place the mango, juice, and yogurt in a blender, and blend until well combined.

2 Pour into individual glasses and serve with a straw.

PER SERVING (1 cup): 150 calories, 1g fat (0g saturated), 65mg sodium, 33g carbohydrate, 2g fiber, 4g protein, 10% vitamin A, 30% vitamin C, 10% calcium

 mom's **feed**back

My 1-year old sipped her drink to the bottom and signed for more, adding her little "mooore" word.

— Rebecca, mother of McKenzie, age 1 and Evan, age 4 ▪ Wichita, KS

Grab-and-Go Granola Bars

CHAPTER 12

Snack Attack

"Mooooom, can I have a snack?" Kids gobble up an average of 850 between-meal nibbles every year. The quality of all those snacks — from carrots to cookies — can make or break a child's diet. We consider snack time the perfect opportunity to improve kids' overall nutritional GPA.

Between meals, when kids are hungry, they're more likely to try new foods, especially if you keep them finger-friendly, bite size, or add a suggestion of sweetness. These kid-approved snacks are designed to add a tasty variety of fruits, vegetables, nuts, beans, whole grains, and calcium-rich foods to the diet ... things kids often don't get enough of and may think they don't like.

Zach, Emi, and Izzi take turns making our *Grab-and-Go Granola Bars*. Even mom, Heidi, eats them on the run.

See more photos of our young cooks and moms cooking their favorite snack recipes on Flickr
http://www.flickr.com/photos/mealmakeovermoms

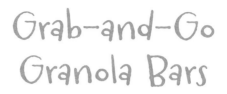

Grab-and-Go Granola Bars

MAKES 12 BARS

When it comes to breakfast-on-the-go, lunch box treats, and quick snacks between school and soccer practice, granola bars can be a busy mom's best friend. How healthy those bars are is tough to say. There are literally dozens on the market, so their nutritional merits (or demerits) vary considerably. Some store-bought bars are indeed healthy — made with big chunks of dried fruit and nuts — but they're more adult-friendly than kid-friendly. It took a lot of trial and error before we got our bar recipe just right. By using fiber-rich whole grain cereal and oats, chopped bits of walnuts and dried fruit, and just a handful of chocolate chips, they get rave reviews from kids big and small.

1 cup quick-cooking or old-fashioned oats

1 cup spoon-size shredded wheat cereal

1 cup walnuts

1½ cups dried fruit (choose one or more of the following: raisins, cherries, apricots, cranberries, prunes)

½ teaspoon ground cinnamon

½ teaspoon salt

2 large eggs

¼ cup honey

1 teaspoon vanilla extract

¼ cup mini semi-sweet chocolate chips

1 Preheat the oven to 350°F. Lightly oil or coat an 8 x 8-inch baking pan or dish with nonstick cooking spray and set aside.

2 Place the oats, shredded wheat, walnuts, dried fruit, cinnamon, and salt in the bowl of a food processor and pulse until the mixture is finely chopped (the fruit should be the size of a dried pea or lentil).

3 Whisk together the eggs, honey, and vanilla in a large bowl until well blended. Add the oat mixture and chocolate chips and stir to combine.

4 Spread the mixture evenly in the prepared pan, and flatten gently with the back of a spoon or rubber spatula.

5 Bake about 18 minutes, or until the edges turn golden brown. Let cool completely in the pan before slicing into twelve 2 x 2½-inch bars.

PER SERVING (1 bar): 200 calories, 9g fat (1.5g saturated, 0.9g omega-3), 115mg sodium, 30g carbohydrate, 3g fiber, 4g protein

tip Our kids are especially fond of raisins in this recipe, and we're fond of the fact that ¼ cup counts as a full serving of fruit. California raisins are low in sodium, fat- and cholesterol-free, and loaded with antioxidants ... and they're portable too.

mom's feedback

This is the first granola bar recipe that I've been able to bake with success (others would crumble or bake solid). The ratio of the fruit and the nuts was just right, and all of my kids wanted seconds.

— Heidi, mother of Jeremiah, age 1, Isabelle, age 3, Emily, age 5 and Zachariah, age 6 ▪ Rothschild, WI

Wild & Crazy Blueberry Cornmeal Muffins

MAKES 24 MINI MUFFINS

At first glance, muffins seem pretty healthy. But when they're made with white sugar, white flour, and egg whites (many so-called healthy recipes eliminate the nutritious yolks), there's not a whole lot to 'em. These muffins are bursting with great nutrition thanks to the whole wheat flour, canola oil, and the wild blueberries — one of nature's most antioxidant-rich foods. We also use cornmeal, a whole grain that adds a little bit of crunch to the muffins. Baking them in mini cups makes two of them seem just right for a satisfying, but not ruin-your-dinner, snack.

1 cup all-purpose flour

⅓ cup whole wheat flour

⅓ cup cornmeal

2 teaspoons baking powder

½ teaspoon baking soda

½ teaspoon salt

½ teaspoon ground cinnamon

2 large eggs, beaten

½ cup brown sugar

⅓ cup canola oil

½ cup 1% low-fat milk

2 tablespoons lemon juice (juice of half a lemon)

1 teaspoon lemon zest (zest of half a lemon)

1 teaspoon vanilla extract

1 cup frozen or fresh wild blueberries

1 Preheat the oven to 350°F. Lightly oil or coat 24 mini muffin cups with nonstick cooking spray and set aside.

2 Whisk together the all-purpose flour, whole wheat flour, cornmeal, baking powder, baking soda, salt, and cinnamon in a large bowl.

3 In a separate bowl, whisk the eggs, brown sugar, and oil until well blended. Whisk in the milk, lemon juice, lemon zest, and vanilla. Pour the liquid ingredients over the dry ingredients and stir until just combined. Gently stir in the blueberries.

4 Spoon the batter into the prepared muffin cups. Bake 15 to 17 minutes, or until the muffins are golden and a toothpick inserted in the center comes out clean. Transfer the pan to a wire rack and cool for 5 minutes. Remove the muffins and cool an additional 5 minutes before serving. When making 12 full-size muffins, bake for 20 to 23 minutes.

PER SERVING (2 mini muffins): 170 calories, 7g fat (0.5g saturated, 0.6g omega-3), 190mg sodium, 24g carbohydrate, 1g fiber, 3g protein

mom's feedback

When I tested this recipe, I had all the ingredients already in the house, so it was a fast and easy treat. I made 12 full-size muffins instead of 24 mini ones since I don't own a mini muffin tin. Next time, I'd even consider putting the batter into a small bread loaf pan, because I think it would be an amazing quick bread too.

— Lara, mother of Amanda, age 11 ▪ Los Gatos, CA

No-Nut Pumpkin Chocolate Chip Muffins

MAKES 24 MINI MUFFINS

Even though these muffins are similar to our *Chocolaty Pumpkin Bars* on page 163, we couldn't resist including them in the book. Both recipes feature nutrient-rich canned pumpkin — one of our favorite convenience foods. The main difference is that the muffins are nut free. Don't get us wrong … we love nuts. But if they're off-limits for your family, you can still get the taste and nutritional benefit of the pumpkin. We hope you and your kids like these as much as we do.

1 cup all-purpose flour

½ cup whole wheat flour

¼ cup ground flaxseed or wheat germ

2 teaspoons baking powder

½ teaspoon ground cinnamon

¼ teaspoon salt

1 cup canned 100% pure pumpkin

2 large eggs, beaten

½ cup brown sugar

½ cup 1% low-fat milk

⅓ cup canola oil

1 teaspoon vanilla extract

½ cup mini semi-sweet chocolate chips

1 Preheat the oven to 350°F. Lightly oil or coat 24 mini muffin cups with nonstick cooking spray and set aside.

2 Whisk together the all-purpose flour, whole wheat flour, ground flaxseed, baking powder, cinnamon, and salt in a large bowl.

3 In a separate bowl, whisk the pumpkin, eggs, brown sugar, milk, oil, and vanilla until well blended. Pour the liquid ingredients over the dry ingredients and stir until just combined. Stir in the chocolate chips.

4 Spoon the batter into the prepared muffin cups. Bake 15 to 18 minutes, or until a toothpick inserted in the center comes out clean. Transfer the pan to a wire rack and cool for 5 minutes. Remove the muffins and cool an additional 5 minutes before serving. When making 12 full-size muffins, bake for 20 to 23 minutes.

PER SERVING (2 mini muffins): 220 calories, 10g fat (2g saturated, 1.1g omega-3), 135mg sodium, 28g carbohydrate, 3g fiber, 4g protein, 60% vitamin A

mom's feedback

I've been making your Chocolaty Pumpkin Bars for years and they're always a crowd pleaser. My son doesn't like nuts, so this was better for him than the other recipe. When we got down to the last muffin, Grant asked if we could all share it.

Jill, mother of Grant, age 6 and Anna, age 8 ▪ Austin, TX

Chocolaty Pumpkin Bars

MAKES 30 BARS

When we launched *MealMakeoverMoms.com* in 2004, this was one of the first recipes we created for the site. Since then, we have sampled it at book signings, delivered it to new neighbors, and served it to kids at more play dates than we can count. Bottom line: this recipe is always a winner! And thanks to the canned pumpkin, each serving has almost half a day's worth of vitamin A. Note: If your family is nut-free, try our *No-Nut Pumpkin Chocolate Chip Muffins* (page 162) for a similar taste.

- 1 cup all-purpose flour
- 1 cup whole wheat flour
- 1 cup pecans, very finely chopped
- ¾ cup granulated sugar
- 2 teaspoons baking powder
- 1 teaspoon ground cinnamon
- ½ teaspoon baking soda
- ½ teaspoon salt
- 4 large eggs, beaten
- 1 15-ounce can 100% pure pumpkin
- ½ cup canola oil
- ¼ cup 1% low-fat milk
- ½ cup mini semi-sweet chocolate chips

1 Preheat the oven to 350°F. Lightly oil or coat a 15 x 10 x 1-inch rimmed baking or jelly roll pan with nonstick cooking spray and set aside.

2 Whisk together the all-purpose flour, whole wheat flour, pecans, sugar, baking powder, cinnamon, baking soda, and salt in a large bowl until well combined.

3 In a separate bowl, whisk the eggs, pumpkin, oil, and milk until well blended. Pour the liquid ingredients over the dry ingredients and stir until just combined. Stir in the chocolate chips.

4 Spread the batter evenly in the prepared pan and bake for 25 minutes, or until a toothpick inserted in the center comes out clean. Transfer the pan to a wire rack and cool for 10 minutes before slicing into thirty 2 x 2½-inch bars.

PER SERVING (1 bar): 140 calories, 8g fat (1g saturated, 0.4g omega-3), 95mg sodium, 16g carbohydrate, 2g fiber, 2g protein, 45% vitamin A

tip For maximum freshness, store leftovers in a plastic container or zip-top bag in the refrigerator.

mom's feedback

My oldest son doesn't like nuts, so I chopped the pecans really fine in my small food processor. If he can't find the pieces he doesn't complain. I got two "Yummies" and "Can I have another piece?" from my boys, which is their version of high praise.

— Wanda, mother of Ian, age 8 and Eric, age 11 ▪ Windham, NH

Lime 'n Honey Black Bean Dip

MAKES 6 TO 8 SERVINGS

If you ask us to name the least beautiful-looking recipe in the book, this one would be it. But looks can be deceiving. Once you try this easy-to-make dip, we're sure you'll like the combo of the sweet honey, tangy lime, and slightly spicy seasonings. If your family's palate is on the adventurous side, kick up the heat with a medium (or even hot) salsa or an extra shake of chili and cumin. Beans are rich in fiber and they're technically a "vegetable" — two of the many reasons we love this recipe so much!

1   15-ounce can black beans, drained and rinsed

⅓   cup salsa

¼   cup light sour cream

2   tablespoons lime juice

1   tablespoon honey

1   teaspoon ground cumin

½   teaspoon chili powder

¼   teaspoon garlic powder

1 Place the beans, salsa, sour cream, lime juice, honey, cumin, chili powder, and garlic powder in the bowl of a food processor and process until smooth and creamy.

2 Serve with baked tortilla or pita chips, baby carrots, or sliced bell peppers.

PER SERVING (about ¼ cup): 60 calories, 0.5g fat (0g saturated fat), 180mg sodium, 13g carbohydrate, 3g fiber, 3g protein

mom's **feed**back

I made this dip at a family gathering and my husband's younger brother, Andrew, was a huge fan. We like our food spicy, so I'll probably use a medium or hot salsa the next time I make it. The lime added great flavor.

— Miriam, mother of Hezekiah, age 1 and sister-in-law to Andrew, age 15 ▪ Upland, IN

Re-Deviled Eggs

MAKES 6 SERVINGS

Deviled eggs are so basic and old fashioned that we decided to give them a modern twist. We use omega-3 eggs and light mayonnaise, and we mix in some finely diced vitamin C-rich bell pepper to add sweetness and crunch to the creamy yolk filling. Serve them for snacks, appetizers, or as a picnic finger food.

6 hard-cooked large eggs, shelled

3 tablespoons minced orange or red bell pepper

3 tablespoons light mayonnaise

1 teaspoon honey mustard

⅛ teaspoon kosher salt

1 generous pinch black pepper

Paprika

1 Cut the eggs in half, lengthwise. Remove the yolks and place in a bowl. Mash the egg yolks with the back of a fork. Add the bell pepper, mayonnaise, mustard, salt, and pepper and stir to combine.

2 Place the egg yolk mixture in a zip-top sandwich bag. Seal the bag and snip half an inch off one bottom corner. Squeeze an equal amount of the mixture into each egg white half. Sprinkle with paprika to garnish.

PER SERVING (2 halves): 100 calories, 6g fat (1g saturated, 0.4g omega-3), 180mg sodium, 1g carbohydrate, 0g fiber, 6g protein, 10% vitamin C

---

tip How to Hard Cook an Egg:

Have you ever hard boiled an egg only to end up with an unsightly greenish ring between the yolk and the white? This occurs when the egg is overcooked and/or not chilled quickly enough. For a perfect egg every time, follow these four steps eggs-actly:

- Place eggs in a saucepan in a single layer and add enough cold water to cover by an inch.

- Bring the water to a boil. Remove from heat, cover, and let stand for 17 minutes.

- Remove eggs from saucepan and place in a bowl filled with cold water and ice. Cool for 5 minutes.

- To peel, gently tap eggs on a kitchen counter to crack. Then roll gently, pressing down just enough to crush the shells all over. Peel under cool running water starting at the large end.

mom's **feed**back

We all thought the flavor was great. I liked red bell peppers the best — they seemed to be the sweetest — and they're so colorful. We'll use them instead of the orange peppers the next time we make these.

Elizabeth, mother of Caleb, age 2, Lydia, age 5, Cameron, age 7, Cargill, age 9 and Ellie, age 11 ▪ Southfield, MI

Juicy Strawberry Wigglers

Jell-O® Jigglers: What can we say? They contain artificial colors and about a tablespoon of sugar per square. We decided to give them one of our healthy makeovers after hearing from a blog reader whose son was hooked on the wiggly little squares. By using 100% fruit juice, frozen fruit, and plain gelatin, we create an all-natural treat that is just as fun to eat and a lot lower in sugar. We use just one tablespoon for the entire recipe.

1½ cups 100% strawberry kiwi juice, divided

1 cup frozen strawberries

2 envelopes unflavored gelatin

1 tablespoon granulated sugar

1 In a blender, blend together 1 cup of the juice and the frozen strawberries until smooth. Pour into a small saucepan and bring to a boil. If you think your kids will object to the tiny strawberry seeds, strain the mixture into the saucepan. Stir occasionally to break up any frothy bubbles.

2 Meanwhile, place the remaining ½ cup juice in a large bowl. Sprinkle the gelatin over the juice and let stand 1 minute. Add the hot juice mixture and stir, or gently whisk, until the gelatin completely dissolves, about 5 minutes. Stir in the sugar.

3 Pour the mixture into an 8 x 8-inch pan or dish. Refrigerate until firm, about 3 hours. Cut into twenty-four 2 x 1⅓-inch rectangles. (Use an off-set spatula to remove them from the pan.)

PER SERVING (2 pieces): 20 calories, 0g fat, 0mg sodium, 4g carbohydrate, 1g protein, 25% vitamin C

tip For a mango version of our wigglers, use 1½ cups 100% tropical mango juice blend, 1 cup frozen mango, 2 envelopes unflavored gelatin, and 1 to 2 tablespoons granulated sugar.

mom's feedback Everyone liked this recipe. My son said, "Mmmmm, momma this is good," and my husband added, "This is better than anything you could make from a box!"

Nikki, mother of Jonathan, age 2 ▪ Louisville, KY

Turkey and Cheese Pretzel Sticks

MAKES 1 SERVING

Sometimes the simplest recipes are the ones kids like the best. This three-ingredient snack has the crunch kids love and the protein and calcium that keep moms happy. If your supermarket deli counter does not carry part-skim mozzarella cheese, switch to reduced-fat American.

2 slices lower-sodium deli turkey (about 1½ ounces)

1 slice part-skim mozzarella cheese (about ½ ounce), cut into four strips

4 whole wheat pretzel sticks

1 Cut each slice of turkey in half. Lay the four slices on a cutting board. Place one cheese strip and one pretzel stick at the bottom edge of each turkey slice. Roll up around the pretzel.

2 Serve as an after-school snack, or place in a container in your child's lunch box.

PER SERVING 120 calories, 3.5g fat (2g saturated), 430mg sodium, 10g carbohydrate, 1g fiber, 13g protein, 10% calcium

---

tip **Small Bites**

Stumped for a healthy mid-morning snack for your child's lunch box or something to serve when your kids get home from school? These easy snack stuffers are just what you need.

Fresh Fruit
It comes in its own wrapper, requires little or no preparation, and is naturally packed with vitamins, minerals, phytonutrients (plant nutrients), and fiber.

Mini Applesauce
Look for an all-natural brand and avoid the ones with added sugar and the fake blue, green, red, or pink coloring.

Veggies with Dip
Baby carrots, red bell pepper strips, sugar snap peas, or cucumber rounds with a ranch dressing dip are fun for kids and help to weave a vegetable into the lunch box.

Squeeze Yogurt
Go for the all-natural brands made without artificial colors and flavors.

Popcorn
Kids love popcorn and moms love the fact that it's a whole grain. Look for popcorn made without partially hydrogenated oils. (Popcorn isn't recommended until the age of four because it is a choking hazard.)

Make-Your-Own Trail Mix
Combine mixed nuts, raisins or dried apricots, mini pretzels, sunflower seeds, whole grain breakfast cereal, and a few semi-sweet chocolate chips in a zip-top bag.

mom's **feed**back

The best part about this recipe is that it's so easy the boys can make it themselves.

Jennifer, mother of Walker, age 4, Cooper, age 6 and Dawson, age 7 ▪ Wichita, KS

Sugar & Spice Pecans

MAKES 16 SERVINGS

This snack has everything your taste buds could possibly want: sweet, spicy, salty, and oh-so crunchy. We're big fans of nuts, because they're packed with good nutrition. Pecans are rich in heart-healthy monounsaturated fats, and a handful (¼ cup) has a respectable 3 grams of fiber. Walnuts would also work well with this recipe.

1 egg white

1 teaspoon water

1 pound pecan halves (about 4½ cups)

½ cup granulated sugar

1 teaspoon ground cinnamon

½ teaspoon kosher salt

¼ teaspoon allspice

⅛ teaspoon cayenne pepper

1 Preheat the oven to 325°F. Lightly oil or coat a rimmed baking sheet with nonstick cooking spray and set aside.

2 Whisk together the egg white and water in a large bowl until well blended. Add the pecans and toss to coat evenly with the egg white.

3 In a separate bowl, whisk together the sugar, cinnamon, salt, allspice, and cayenne pepper, and sprinkle over the nuts. Toss until well coated.

4 Spread the pecans in a single layer on the prepared baking sheet, and bake until the glaze is crisp and golden brown, 15 to 18 minutes. Cool completely and store in an airtight container.

PER SERVING (about ¼ cup): 220 calories, 20g fat (2g saturated, 0.3 omega-3), 40mg sodium, 10g carbohydrate, 3g fiber, 3g protein

---

tip **How to Toast Nuts:**

Toasting nuts brings out the flavor and aroma. Whether you are snacking on nuts or adding them as an ingredient to a recipe, use either one of these two toasting methods.

1 Place the nuts in a single layer on a baking sheet and bake at 325°F in the oven or toaster oven until golden brown, about 6 minutes. Stir the nuts or shake the sheet occasionally to ensure even toasting.

2 Place the nuts in a dry skillet over medium heat. Cook, stirring frequently, until golden brown, about 5 minutes.

If you're toasting sliced or slivered almonds or pine nuts, the toasting time will probably be less. We've burned a lot of nuts in our day, so be sure to keep a watchful eye.

mom's feedback

This recipe was easy, it tasted great, and I wouldn't change a thing about it. My whole family gave it two-thumbs up, and my teenage daughter, Jocelyn, said, "These are amazing."

Melissa, mother of Kaitlin, age 8, Hannah, age 10 and Jocelyn, age 16 ▪ Euless, TX

Banana Zucchini Squiggle Loaf

MAKES 16 SERVINGS

Everyone should have a go-to banana bread recipe. This is ours. What makes it different is that we add zucchini, a nutritious vegetable that works really well in baked goods. Just a head's up: Don't be freaked by the little green bits of zucchini in this loaf. You'll get extra fiber if you keep the skin on, but if it's a deal breaker with your kids, by all means, peel before shredding. As for the sugar, we only use ¾ cup because the natural sweetness of the bananas really comes through.

1 cup all-purpose flour

1 cup whole wheat flour

½ cup walnuts, finely chopped

¼ cup wheat germ

2 teaspoons baking powder

1 teaspoon ground cinnamon

½ teaspoon salt

2 large eggs, beaten

¾ cup granulated sugar

⅓ cup canola oil

1 teaspoon vanilla extract

2 ripe large bananas, mashed (about 1 cup)

1 small 6-ounce zucchini, unpeeled and shredded (about 1 cup)

1 Preheat the oven to 350°F. Lightly oil or coat a 9 x 5-inch loaf pan with nonstick cooking spray and set aside.

2 Whisk together the all-purpose flour, whole wheat flour, walnuts, wheat germ, baking powder, cinnamon, and salt in a large bowl.

3 In a separate bowl, whisk the eggs, sugar, oil, and vanilla until well blended. Stir in the bananas and zucchini. Pour the liquid ingredients over the dry ingredients and stir until just combined.

4 Spread the batter evenly into the prepared pan. Bake 50 to 55 minutes, or until a toothpick inserted in the center comes out clean. Cool about 15 minutes in the pan, then turn the loaf onto a wire rack and cool before slicing.

PER SERVING (1 slice): 170 calories, 8g fat (0.5g saturated, 0.6g omega-3), 130mg sodium, 24g carbohydrate, 2g fiber, 4g protein

mom's feedback

The bread was moist, and I like how the banana flavor takes over and the zucchini is kind of hidden. My son, Aidan said, "Can I take some in my lunch box tomorrow?"

— Tina, mother of Tristan, age 4 and Aidan, age 6 ▪ West Hills, CA

Magical Mango Snack Cake

MAKES 24 SERVINGS

Even though they only rank 24th among the top 25 fruits consumed in the U.S., juicy, sweet mangoes are one of the most popular fruits in the rest of the world. Rich in vitamins A and C and a good source of fiber, we use one as the star ingredient in this delicious snack cake. We also use walnuts, because they're one of the nuts highest in omega-3 fat (the good, heart-healthy kind). If your kids turn their noses up at nuts, we have two suggestions: Chop them up until they're very fine — almost like rough grains of sand — or cut the amount from one cup to a half cup.

1 cup all-purpose flour

1 cup walnuts, finely chopped

¾ cup whole wheat flour

1 teaspoon baking soda

½ teaspoon ground cinnamon

¼ teaspoon ground nutmeg

¼ teaspoon ground cloves

¼ teaspoon salt

2 large eggs, beaten

1 cup brown sugar

½ cup canola oil

1 very ripe large mango, peeled, pit removed, and pureed in a food processor (to yield about 1 cup)

⅓ cup mini semi-sweet chocolate chips

Powdered sugar, optional

1 Preheat the oven to 350°F. Lightly oil or coat a 9 x 13-inch baking pan or dish with nonstick cooking spray and set aside.

2 Whisk together the all-purpose flour, walnuts, whole wheat flour, baking soda, cinnamon, nutmeg, cloves, and salt in a large bowl.

3 In a separate bowl, whisk the eggs, brown sugar, and oil until well blended. Add the mango and whisk to combine.

4 Pour the liquid ingredients over the dry ingredients and stir until just combined. Stir in the chocolate chips.

5 Spread the batter evenly in the prepared pan and bake about 22 minutes, or until golden brown and a toothpick inserted in the center comes out clean. Cool on a wire rack and cut into twenty-four 2¼ x 2¼-inch squares. Sprinkle with powdered sugar as desired.

PER SERVING (1 square): 160 calories, 9g fat (1.5g saturated, 0.9g omega-3), 85mg sodium, 17g carbohydrate, 1g fiber, 3g protein

dad's feedback This recipe was fun and easy to make with my daughter. My son had two words to describe our results: fantastic and perfect!

David, father of Dahlia, age 8 and Asher, age 10 ▪ Pacific Palisades, CA

Apple Butterscotch Squares

MAKES 20 SERVINGS

After our first cookbook was published, we got an email from the editors of *Nick Jr. Family Magazine* asking if we were interested in writing a monthly column. Of course we said, "Yes," and for the next few years we contributed recipes to the magazine. Our delicious *Apple Butterscotch Squares* was one of those recipes, written for the magazine's October, 2006 issue. This snack is incredibly easy to make (okay, shredding the apples will definitely take some time), and it's truly fabulous. Liz remembers Simon (who was eight at the time) saying, "Mom, this is the best recipe you ever made!" The reason we don't peel the apples is because half the fiber is in the skin, plus it blends right in to the batter.

2 large Golden Delicious apples

1 cup all-purpose flour

¾ cup whole wheat flour

¾ cup granulated sugar

¼ cup ground flaxseed or wheat germ

1 teaspoon baking powder

1 teaspoon pumpkin pie spice or ground cinnamon

½ teaspoon baking soda

½ teaspoon salt

3 large eggs, beaten

½ cup unsweetened applesauce

½ cup canola oil

⅓ cup butterscotch chips

1 Preheat the oven to 350°F. Lightly oil or coat a 9 x 13-inch baking pan or dish with nonstick cooking spray and set aside.

2 Cut the unpeeled apples into quarters, core them, and shred, using the large holes of a box grater (the yield will be about 2 cups). Set aside.

3 Whisk together the all-purpose flour, whole wheat flour, sugar, flaxseed, baking powder, pumpkin pie spice, baking soda, and salt in a large bowl.

4 In a separate bowl, whisk the eggs, applesauce, and oil until well blended. Stir in the apples.

5 Pour the liquid ingredients over the dry ingredients and stir until just combined. Stir in the butterscotch chips.

6 Spread the batter evenly in the prepared pan, and bake about 35 minutes, or until the top is golden and a toothpick inserted in the center comes out clean. Cool on a wire rack and cut into twenty 2¼ x 2½-inch pieces.

PER SERVING (1 piece): 170 calories, 8g fat (1.5g saturated, 0.8g omega-3), 120mg sodium, 23g carbohydrate, 2g fiber, 3g protein

mom's feedback

I love how it's sweet without having too much sugar, and it has lots of fiber from the flaxseed, apple skins, and whole wheat flour. I also like that it got some extra fruit in my kids' diets.

— Brianna, mother of Wesley, age 1, Clarine, age 3 and James, age 6 ▪ Sun Prairie, WI

Moms' Ultimate Guacamole

MAKES 6 SERVINGS

Avocados are technically a fruit, not a vegetable, but what's in a name? They are rich in heart-healthy monounsaturated fat, and so tasty that we can honestly say that avocado is one of our favorite foods in the world. While we love avocados on sandwiches and in salads, our children prefer them mashed into guacamole. Serve this satisfying version with baked tortilla chips or pita chips for a nutrient-filled after-school snack. For an extra kick of protein and creaminess, you can also stir in a quarter cup of plain 0%-fat Greek yogurt.

- 2 medium ripe avocados (about 8 ounces each), halved and pitted
- 2 tablespoons lemon or lime juice
- 2 tablespoons minced red onion
- 1 tablespoon finely chopped cilantro
- ½ teaspoon kosher salt
- ½ teaspoon chili powder
- 1 pinch black pepper
- 1 pinch onion powder
- 1 pinch garlic powder

1 Slice the avocado halves in half again, peel away the skin, and place the avocado in a large bowl. Mash with the back of a fork until smooth.

2 Stir in the lemon juice, onion, cilantro, salt, chili powder, pepper, onion powder, and garlic powder. Season with additional salt and pepper to taste.

PER SERVING (about ¼ cup): 110 calories, 10g fat (1.5g saturated), 100mg sodium, 6g carbohydrate, 5g fiber, 1g protein, 15% vitamin C

> **tip** When left uncovered, avocados or guacamole quickly turn brown. Adding an acidic ingredient such as a spritz of lemon or lime juice can reduce browning. Storing guacamole in an airtight container and covering the surface directly with clear plastic wrap also helps.

mom's feedback Jake made this by himself. Although he has never really liked guacamole, he said this one was exceptionally good!

— Robin, aunt of Jake, age 14 ▪ Dallas, TX

Ginger Drizzle Cookies

CHAPTER 13

Dreamy Desserts

When it comes to mealtime complaints, we haven't met too many kids (or adults, for that matter), who say, "UGH! I hate dessert!" So our goal with this chapter is to create a line-up of treats that were lip-smacking good as well as healthy. Even though we still use sweets like sugar and chocolate — but not too much — we make a lot of ingredient swaps to boost the good nutrition. We add whole wheat flour when possible, toss in finely chopped nuts, replace shortening, margarine or butter with heart-healthy canola oil, and even use a bit of ground flaxseed or wheat germ. The result: treats you really can feel good about serving to your family.

Four-year old Kaila bakes a batch of our *Ginger Drizzle Cookies* with a smidgen of guidance from her mom, Heather.

See more photos of our young cooks and moms cooking their favorite desserts on Flickr http://www.flickr.com/photos/mealmakeovermoms

I-Love-Chocolate Party Torte

MAKES 16 SERVINGS

Imagine a chocolate torte that's good for you! If you listen to our podcasts, you know that chocolate ranks pretty high on our list of favorite foods, and our kids clearly take after their moms. For this decadent-sounding (and tasting) cake, we lighten things up by using canola oil instead of butter, and whole wheat flour versus the usual white. The pièce de résistance is the berry topping. It's amazing how many vitamin C–rich strawberries kids will eat when there's some chocolate to go with them. The key with this cake is to stick with the suggested portion size. Our torte is so good that you'll only need a small piece to satisfy your chocolate craving.

8 ounces semi-sweet chocolate chips (about 1¼ cups)

½ cup canola oil

1 cup granulated sugar

½ cup whole wheat flour

½ cup unsweetened cocoa powder, sifted

5 large eggs, beaten

Powdered sugar

1 16-ounce container fresh strawberries, washed and sliced

Light whipped cream, optional

1 Preheat the oven to 350°F. Butter the bottom and sides of a 9-inch springform pan and dust the bottom with granulated sugar. Set aside.

2 Place the chocolate chips and oil in a medium saucepan over low heat and stir until the chips melt, about 2 minutes. Remove from the heat.

3 Whisk together the sugar, flour, and cocoa powder in a large bowl until well combined. Whisk in the eggs until well blended. Add the melted chocolate and stir to combine.

4 Pour the batter into the prepared pan. Smooth the top with a rubber spatula. Bake 35 minutes, or until a toothpick inserted in the center comes out clean.

5 Transfer the pan to a wire rack and cool completely. When cool, remove from the pan, sprinkle with powdered sugar, and serve with the strawberries and the whipped cream as desired.

PER SERVING (1 slice): 230 calories, 13g fat (3.5g saturated, 0.7g omega-3), 25mg sodium, 28g carbohydrate, 2g fiber, 4g protein, 25% vitamin C

tip If you use a 10-inch springform pan, the cook time should be about 5 minutes less. You can also use this recipe to make little torte "muffins." Just divide the mixture between mini muffin cups and bake for 12 to 15 minutes. The yield will vary from 24 to 30 depending on the size of your mini muffin tin.

mom's feedback

We turned the torte into small muffins, and my daughter, Victoria, said they were the best "muffins" she had ever eaten. All those eggs gave them a light and airy texture.

Jennifer, mother of Alyssa, age 4 months, Christina, age 4 and Anthony and Victoria, age 7 ▪ Norcross, GA

Pumpkin Spice Bundt Cake

MAKES 16 SERVINGS

The next time you're invited to a Halloween party (or any party for that matter), consider bringing along this sweet, hint-of-spice bundt cake. Made with an entire can of pureed pumpkin, each slice is brimming with good nutrition. There's nothing tricky about this treat. It's easy to prepare and the flavor can't be beat, especially when it's dusted with powdered sugar or topped with a small scoop of frozen low-fat vanilla yogurt.

1¼ cups all-purpose flour

1¼ cups whole wheat flour

1¼ cups granulated sugar

¼ cup wheat germ
or ground flaxseed

1 tablespoon baking powder

2 teaspoons ground
cinnamon

¾ teaspoon ground ginger

¾ teaspoon salt

¼ teaspoon ground cloves

¼ teaspoon ground nutmeg

3 large eggs, beaten

1 15-ounce can 100% pure
pumpkin

⅓ cup low-fat milk

⅓ cup canola oil

2 teaspoons vanilla extract

⅓ cup dried currants

2 tablespoons powdered
sugar, optional

1 Preheat the oven to 350°F. Generously oil or coat a 10-cup bundt pan with nonstick cooking spray and set aside.

2 Whisk together the all-purpose flour, whole wheat flour, sugar, wheat germ, baking powder, cinnamon, ginger, salt, cloves, and nutmeg in a large bowl until well combined.

3 In a separate bowl, whisk the eggs, pumpkin, milk, oil, and vanilla until well blended. Pour the liquid ingredients and the currants over the dry ingredients and stir until just moistened.

4 Pour the batter into the prepared pan, and smooth the top with a rubber spatula. Bake about 50 minutes, or until a toothpick inserted in the center comes out clean. Transfer to a wire rack and cool for 15 minutes before removing from the pan.

5 Cool the cake completely, and dust the top with powdered sugar as desired.

PER SERVING (1 slice): 210 calories, 6g fat (0.5g saturated, 0.5g omega-3), 230mg sodium, 36g carbohydrate, 3g fiber, 5g protein, 80% vitamin A

mom's feedback Anna said the cake reminded her of the pumpkin bread I sometimes make. I used mini chocolate chips because I ran out of currants and it worked just fine!

Kristin, mother of Sam, age 5 and Anna, age 7 ▪ San Jose, CA

Fudgy Black Bean Brownies

Admittedly, black bean brownies sound a bit strange, so you may want to wait to mention the black bean thing until after the kids try them. Just trust us: when black beans are pureed and then combined with eggs, oil, sugar, and cocoa powder, they turn into luscious, hard-to-resist brownies. This recipe is perfect for people following gluten-free diets or for anyone interested in lowering the saturated fat and calories in dessert. When a friend of Josh's tried them, he declared, "These brownies are so good, I could eat black beans for the rest of my life."

1 15-ounce can black beans, drained and rinsed

3 large eggs

3 tablespoons canola oil

¾ cup granulated sugar

½ cup unsweetened cocoa powder

1 teaspoon vanilla extract

½ teaspoon peppermint extract, optional

½ teaspoon baking powder

1 pinch salt

½ cup mini semi-sweet chocolate chips, divided

1 Preheat the oven to 350°F. Lightly oil or coat an 8 x 8-inch baking pan or dish with nonstick cooking spray and set aside.

2 Place the black beans in the bowl of a food processor and process until smooth and creamy. Add the eggs, oil, sugar, cocoa powder, vanilla, peppermint extract as desired, baking powder, and salt and process until smooth. Add ¼ cup of the chips and pulse a few times until the chips are incorporated.

3 Pour the batter into the prepared pan, smooth the top with a rubber spatula, and sprinkle with the remaining ¼ cup chocolate chips.

4 Bake 30 to 35 minutes, or until the edges start to pull away from the sides of the pan and a toothpick inserted in the center comes out clean. Cool in the pan before slicing into 2-inch squares.

PER SERVING (1 brownie): 120 calories, 5g fat (1.5g saturated, 0.3g omega-3), 95mg sodium, 18g carbohydrate, 2g fiber, 3g protein

mom's feedback I like the brownies because they're a good source of fiber. Alexa said they were, "Delish." And no one even tasted the beans!

Lori, mother of Nathan, age 5 and Alexa, age 7 ▪ Boxborough, MA

Carrot Patch Cupcakes

MAKES 12 SERVINGS

Carrot cake always sounds so "healthy," but that's not necessarily the case — especially when the cake is made with a stick of butter and there's a thick layer of cream cheese frosting on top. For our carrot cake makeover, we control the portion size by making kid-friendly cupcakes, but we still keep a hefty helping of carotene-rich carrots. We also switch from butter to canola oil, use some whole wheat flour, and whip up a frosting with light cream cheese. The carrots blend into the batter if you grate them into miniscule bits using the smallest side of a box grater. Decorate each cupcake with a jelly bean, a raisin, or sprinkles, or just keep things plain and simple.

1 cup granulated sugar

½ cup canola oil

2 large eggs

¼ cup 1% low-fat milk

1 teaspoon vanilla extract

1¼ cups finely grated carrots (about 8 ounces)

¾ cup all-purpose flour

¾ cup whole wheat flour

1½ teaspoons baking powder

¼ teaspoon salt

4 ounces light cream cheese

¾ cup powdered sugar

1 Preheat the oven to 350°F. Line 12 muffin cups with paper liners and set aside.

2 Combine the sugar, oil, eggs, milk, and vanilla in a large bowl and beat on medium speed until well blended, 2 minutes. Add the carrots and stir to combine. Scrape down the sides of the bowl if necessary.

3 In a separate bowl, whisk together the all-purpose flour, whole wheat flour, baking powder, and salt. At low speed, gradually beat the flour mixture into the liquid mixture until just combined.

4 Spoon the batter evenly into the prepared muffin cups. Bake for 20 minutes, or until a toothpick inserted in the center comes out clean. Transfer the pan to a wire rack and cool for 5 minutes. Remove the cupcakes and cool completely before frosting.

5 To make the frosting, beat the cream cheese and sugar at low speed until blended. Raise the speed to medium once the sugar is incorporated and continue to beat until creamy. Spread the frosting over the cupcakes, and garnish as desired.

PER SERVING (1 cupcake): 270 calories, 12g fat (2g saturated, 0.9g omega-3), 170mg sodium, 38g carbohydrate, 1.5g fiber, 4g protein, 40% vitamin A

mom's feedback

These actually got my 7-year old son to eat some vegetables. None of the kids noticed the carrots at all, and I might even add some shredded zucchini next time!

Martha Anne, mother of Cara, age 3, Jordan, age 6 and Jake, age 7 ▪ Atlanta, GA

Nutty Fruit Crumble

MAKES 6 SERVINGS

Fruit crisps may start out healthy, but the rich, buttery topping can be a nutritional deal breaker. We choose two fruits for our crisp — apples and blueberries — both antioxidant powerhouses and fruits kids typically like. From there, we stir up a nutty, oat topping with 2 tablespoons of canola oil and no butter at all. Don't get us wrong: We like butter, but quite frankly, this topping doesn't need it. You can make this dessert nut-free by replacing the walnuts with an extra half cup of oats. Top it with low-fat vanilla frozen yogurt or a dollop of light whipped cream, and watch how quickly it disappears.

3 large Red or Golden Delicious apples (about 2 pounds), unpeeled and cut into ½-inch pieces (4 cups)

2 tablespoons brown sugar

2 tablespoons whole wheat flour

1 teaspoon vanilla extract

½ teaspoon ground cinnamon

1 cup fresh or frozen blueberries

½ cup walnuts, very finely chopped

½ cup old-fashioned or quick-cooking oats

2 tablespoons brown sugar

2 tablespoons whole wheat flour

2 tablespoons ground flaxseed or wheat germ

½ teaspoon ground cinnamon

⅛ teaspoon salt

2 tablespoons canola oil

1 Preheat the oven to 400°F. Place the apples, brown sugar, flour, vanilla, and cinnamon in a large bowl and stir until the apples are well coated. Gently stir in the blueberries.

2 Place the apple mixture in an 8 x 8-inch baking pan or dish and set aside.

3 To make the topping, place the walnuts, oats, brown sugar, flour, flaxseed, cinnamon, and salt in a medium bowl and stir to combine. Add the oil and stir until the oat mixture is well coated. Spread the topping evenly over the fruit mixture.

4 Bake 40 to 45 minutes, or until the fruit is tender and the topping is golden brown (cover with foil about halfway through if the topping browns too quickly).

PER SERVING 260 calories, 13g fat, (1g saturated, 1.8g omega-3), 55mg sodium, 34g carbohydrate, 5g fiber, 4g protein, 10% vitamin C

tip If you use tart apples such as a Granny Smith, you may want to add an extra tablespoon or two of brown sugar to the apple mixture.

mom's feedback
I loved serving a dessert with very little sugar and lots of whole grains and fruit. The texture was also great for my young daughter.

Elizabeth, mother of Abigail, age 9 months ▪ Brighton, CO

Ginger Drizzle Cookies

MAKES 3 DOZEN COOKIES

For the past (uh-hum) 20 years, Janice has been part of a neighborhood holiday cookie swap. Her best pal, Mary, always bakes gingersnap cookies, and they're the first cookies Janice's girls look for when she brings home her holiday bounty. To health-ify Mary's "famous" recipe, we swap half the white flour with whole wheat, use canola oil in place of (gasp!) shortening, add some ground flaxseed, and create a simple sugar glaze. These cookies are great for the holidays — or for any time of the year. Just don't tell Mary our secret.

1 cup all-purpose flour

1 cup whole wheat flour

2 tablespoons ground flaxseed or wheat germ

2 teaspoons baking soda

1½ teaspoons ground ginger

1 teaspoon ground cinnamon

½ teaspoon salt

1 cup granulated sugar

½ cup canola oil

1 large egg

¼ cup molasses

1 cup powdered sugar

2½ tablespoons 1% low-fat milk

1 Preheat the oven to 350°F. Lightly oil or coat two large baking sheets with nonstick cooking spray and set aside. Whisk together the all-purpose flour, whole wheat flour, flaxseed, baking soda, ginger, cinnamon, and salt in a medium bowl.

2 Combine the sugar and oil in a large bowl and beat on medium speed until well blended, 1 minute. Add the egg and molasses and continue to beat until smooth. Scrape down the sides of the bowl if necessary. At low speed, gradually beat in the flour mixture until just combined.

3 With your hands, roll the dough into 1¼-inch balls and place on the prepared baking sheets, about 2 inches apart.

4 Bake, 1 sheet at a time, 10 to 12 minutes, or until the cookies are golden brown. Cool for 5 minutes on the baking sheet before transferring the cookies to a wire rack. Repeat with the remaining dough.

5 To make the glaze, place the powdered sugar and milk in a bowl and stir until well combined. If the glaze is too thick, add a few drops of milk as needed. Drizzle over each cookie in a lattice or squiggle design.

PER SERVING (1 cookie): 90 calories, 3.5g fat (0g saturated, 0.3g omega-3), 105mg sodium, 14g carbohydrate, 1g fiber, 1g protein

mom's feedback I loved the added nutrition of the flaxseed and molasses. Kaila told our guests that these yummy cookies were very healthy "because they have flaxseed."

Heather, mother of Kaila, age 4 ▪ Honolulu, HI

Peppermint Meringue Snowballs

MAKES 3 DOZEN MERINGUES

As many as one in 133 Americans may be affected by celiac disease, a genetic intolerance to gluten, the protein found in wheat, rye, and barley. These cookies should hit the spot for people on gluten-free or wheat-free diets … but they're certainly A-OK for anyone with a sweet tooth. We first created this recipe with the holidays in mind, but as far as we're concerned, they're amazing 365.

4   egg whites

¼   teaspoon cream of tartar

1   cup granulated sugar

¼   teaspoon peppermint extract, optional

¼   cup finely crushed candy canes or peppermint candy

1 Line two large baking sheets with aluminum foil and set aside.

2 Combine the egg whites and cream of tartar in a large bowl and beat on medium speed until frothy. Gradually add the sugar, one tablespoon at a time, beating until the whites stand in stiff, glossy peaks, about 10 minutes. Beat in the peppermint extract as desired.

3 Preheat the oven to 200°F. Drop meringues by rounded tablespoons onto the baking sheets, about 1 inch apart. Sprinkle the tops with the crushed candy. Bake for 1½ hours. Turn off the oven and leave meringues in the oven for an additional 30 minutes.

4 Let meringues cool completely before removing from foil. Store in an airtight container.

PER SERVING (1 meringue): 30 calories, 0g fat (0g saturated), 5mg sodium, 7g carbohydrate, 0g fiber, 0.5g protein

tip For best results, use imitation peppermint extract. Do not use peppermint extract containing peppermint oil because the meringues will deflate.

mom's feedback

These cookies are a sweet treat without a lot of calories. They were easy to make and only called for a few ingredients. My daughter smiled and said, "Mmmmm!" when she tried one.

— Carrie, mother of Katie, age 17 months ▪ McKinney, TX

Peanut Butter Power Cookies

MAKES 3 DOZEN COOKIES

These soft and chewy cookies get high marks from all of our kids. Dotted with mini chocolate chips and brimming with peanut butter flavor, they're hard to resist. As moms, we appreciate the nutritional value of peanut butter ... it's a good source of high-quality protein and rich in heart-healthy monounsaturated fat. The addition of ground flaxseed or wheat germ ups the nutritional quotient even more.

1 cup all-purpose flour

1 cup whole wheat flour

½ cup mini semi-sweet chocolate chips

¼ cup ground flaxseed or wheat germ

1 teaspoon baking powder

½ teaspoon baking soda

½ teaspoon salt

1¼ cups granulated sugar

¾ cup creamy peanut butter

2 large eggs

¼ cup 1% low-fat milk

¼ cup canola oil

2 teaspoons vanilla extract

1 Preheat the oven to 350°F. Lightly oil or coat two large baking sheets with nonstick cooking spray and set aside.

2 Whisk together the all-purpose flour, whole wheat flour, chocolate chips, flaxseed, baking powder, baking soda, and salt in a medium bowl and set aside.

3 Combine the sugar, peanut butter, eggs, milk, oil, and vanilla in a large bowl and beat on medium speed until well blended, about 2 minutes. At low speed, gradually beat in the flour mixture until just combined. Scrape down the sides of the bowl if necessary.

4 Scoop the dough by slightly rounded tablespoons into 1¾-inch "blobs," and place on the prepared baking sheets, about 2 inches apart.

5 Bake, 1 sheet at a time, about 15 minutes, or until the cookies are golden brown (when done, the cookies will be about 2½ inches in diameter). Cool for 5 minutes on the baking sheet before transferring the cookies to a wire rack. Repeat with the remaining dough.

PER SERVING (1 cookie): 120 calories, 6g fat (1g saturated, 0.3g omega-3), 90mg sodium, 15g carbohydrate, 1g fiber, 3g protein

mom's feedback I can't believe these don't have any butter in them. All of my kids repeatedly asked, "Can I have another cookie?"

Sheri, mother of Richard, age 3, April, age 6 and Myranda, age 8 ▪ Dexter, MI

Crunchy Currant Oatmeal Cookies

MAKES 3 DOZEN COOKIES

This is a treat any health-conscious mom can happily add to her cookie jar. We start with oats — a whole grain — as the star ingredient, then we build our cookie with pecans, whole wheat flour, ground flaxseed or wheat germ (a heart-healthy, vitamin E powerhouse) and little dried currants. You can use dried blueberries instead if they're available (and affordable) in your area. These cookies get a resounding "wow" from our kids, even though there's no chocolate in them!

1½ cups quick-cooking oats
1 cup pecans, finely chopped
¾ cup all-purpose flour
¾ cup whole wheat flour
½ cup dried currants
¼ cup ground flaxseed or wheat germ
1 teaspoon baking powder
½ teaspoon salt
2 large eggs
1 cup brown sugar
½ cup canola oil
1 teaspoon vanilla extract

1 Preheat the oven to 375°F. Lightly oil or coat two large baking sheets with nonstick cooking spray and set aside.

2 Whisk together the oats, pecans, all-purpose flour, whole wheat flour, dried currants, flaxseed, baking powder, and salt in a large bowl until well combined.

3 In a separate bowl, whisk the eggs, brown sugar, oil, and vanilla until well blended. Pour the liquid ingredients over the dry ingredients, and stir until just combined.

4 Working in batches, scoop the batter by slightly rounded tablespoons into 1½-inch "blobs," and place on the prepared baking sheets, flattening slightly with the heel of your hand to create circles about 2 inches in diameter. Leave about 1 inch between each cookie.

5 Bake, 1 sheet at a time, 10 to 12 minutes, or until the cookies are golden brown (when done, the cookies will be about 2½-inches in diameter). Cool for 5 minutes on the baking sheet before transferring the cookies to a wire rack. Repeat with the remaining dough.

PER SERVING (1 cookie): 120 calories, 6g fat, (0.5g saturated, 0.5g omega-3), 75mg sodium, 14g carbohydrate, 1g fiber, 2g protein

mom's feedback We all agreed: these had a crunchy, nutty, chewy and satisfying flavor and texture! Next time we make them, we'd like to try adding dried cranberries or raisins.

Karen, mother of Niki, age 14, Sean, age 17, Erin, age 20, and Marc, age 22 ▪ Steilacoom, WA

Double Strawberry Smoothie Pie

MAKES 8 SERVINGS

Every month on our blog, we take a recipe from a reader and give it a *Recipe Rescue*. So when Jennifer, a mom of two from Pennsylvania, asked us to take the classic recipe for graham cracker pie crust and give it a healthy makeover, we accepted the challenge. We cut the butter from over half a stick down to one tablespoon each of butter and canola oil, and we reduced the sugar from four tablespoons to one. We also added some ground flaxseed for a boost of heart-healthy omega-3 fat. After perfecting our crust recipe, we took our makeover one step further by crafting a delicious strawberry filling.

1¼ cups graham cracker crumbs (about 12 squares)

2 tablespoons ground flaxseed or wheat germ

1 tablespoon granulated sugar

1 egg white, slightly beaten

1 tablespoon unsalted butter, melted

1 tablespoon canola oil

1½ cups frozen strawberries, thawed

1 cup 100% cranberry strawberry or cranberry raspberry juice, divided

2 envelopes unflavored gelatin

¾ cup low-fat strawberry yogurt

3 tablespoons granulated sugar

Light whipped cream, optional

1 Preheat the oven to 350°F. For the pie crust, stir together the graham cracker crumbs, flaxseed, sugar, egg white, butter, and oil in a large bowl until well combined.

2 Using the back of a large spoon, press the crumb mixture firmly on the bottom and up the sides of a 9-inch pie plate. Bake about 8 minutes (the color of the crust won't change). Cool before filling.

3 Meanwhile, in a blender, blend together the strawberries and ½ cup of the juice until smooth. Pour into a small saucepan and bring to a boil. Stir occasionally to break up any frothy bubbles.

4 Place the remaining ½ cup juice in a large bowl. Sprinkle the gelatin over the juice and let stand 1 minute. Add the hot juice mixture and stir, or gently whisk, until the gelatin completely dissolves, about 5 minutes. Stir in the yogurt and sugar.

5 Pour the mixture into the prepared pie crust. Carefully transfer to the refrigerator, and chill, uncovered, until firm, about 3 hours. Serve with light whipped cream as desired.

PER SERVING (1 slice): 180 calories, 6g fat (1.5g saturated, 0.5g omega-3), 130mg sodium, 29g carbohydrate, 1g fiber, 4g protein, 20% vitamin C

mom's feedback

I have two picky eaters at home, so I make sure every little bite counts. I liked this crust recipe better than my original one, and I know that it's healthier. Ainsley and I thought the pie was amazing.

Jennifer, mother of Ainsley, age 7, and Max, age 9 ▪ Kansas City, MO

Trio of Pops

MAKES 4 SERVINGS

For our weekly radio podcast, *Cooking with the Moms*, we created three naturally nutritious pops, and invited Liz's niece, Andrea, to be our taste tester. Watermelon Pomegranate was her favorite, but she liked the others too (phew!). Each features fruit or 100% fruit juice and no artificial anything! If you don't own ice pop molds, use small paper cups and craft sticks to make these refreshing treats.

Watermelon Pomegranate Pops

1½ cups cubed seedless watermelon

½ cup 100% pomegranate blueberry juice

1 Combine the watermelon and juice in a blender and blend until smooth. Pour into four 3-ounce ice pop molds and freeze until firm, about 3 hours. To remove the pops from the molds, run under warm water to loosen.

PER SERVING (1 pop): 30 calories, 0g fat (0g saturated), 0mg sodium, 9g carbohydrate, 0g fiber, 0g protein, 15% vitamin C

Chocolate Banana Pops

1 cup 1% low-fat chocolate milk

1 ripe medium banana

1 Combine the chocolate milk and banana in a blender and blend until smooth. Pour into four 3-ounce ice pop molds and freeze until firm, about 3 hours. To remove the pops from the molds, run under warm water to loosen.

PER SERVING (1 pop): 60 calories, 0g fat (0g saturated), 30mg sodium, 13g carbohydrate, 1g fiber, 2g protein

Creamy Orange Pops

1 cup orange juice

⅓ cup low-fat vanilla yogurt

2 teaspoons pure maple syrup

¼ teaspoon vanilla extract

1 Combine the juice, yogurt, maple syrup, and vanilla in a blender and blend until smooth. Pour into four 3-ounce ice pop molds and freeze until firm, about 3 hours. To remove the pops from the molds, run under warm water to loosen.

PER SERVING (1 pop): 50 calories, 0g fat (0g saturated), 15mg sodium, 10g carbohydrate, 0g fiber, 1g protein, 45% vitamin C

mom's feedback

Ruby ate almost all the watermelon pop which was a total "win" for her, and Ava really liked the banana flavor in the chocolate pop. If you don't own a pop mold, I'd recommend you buy one.

Jennifer, mother of Ava, age 5 and Ruby, age 7 ▪ Columbia, PA

Super Sundae with Strawberries

MAKES 1 SERVING

We have an issue with ice cream. While we would both consider ourselves ice cream lovers, the portion sizes have increased so much over the years that now, even some "kiddie" cones and cups are bigger than most adults should eat. Our sundae puts the kibosh on portion distortion, but by adding two kinds of syrup, whipped cream, nuts, and fruit it looks a lot more decadent than it is. The thinly sliced strawberries on top are a favorite with our families, but any fruit — blueberries, sliced bananas, bits of pineapple — would be scrumptious too.

1 small scoop low-fat vanilla frozen yogurt or light ice cream (about ⅓ cup)

2 strawberries, thinly sliced or diced, divided

1 drizzle chocolate syrup

1 drizzle caramel syrup

2 teaspoons toasted chopped walnuts or pecans

1 small dollop light whipped cream

1 Spoon the ice cream into a bowl or parfait glass. Place all but one of the strawberry slices around the ice cream, drizzle with the chocolate syrup and caramel syrup, and sprinkle with the nuts.

2 Garnish with a dollop of light whipped cream, and top with the remaining strawberry slice.

PER SERVING 160 calories, 6g fat (2g saturated), 50mg sodium, 23g carbohydrate, 1g fiber, 4g protein, 35% vitamin C, 10% calcium

mom's feedback

My daughter, Meagan, has decided to call this her "favorite, fabulous ice cream sundae!" I diced the berries for 2-year old Kyle to make them easier to eat.

— Mollie, mother of Kyle, age 2 and Meagan, age 4 ▪ Cincinnati, OH

One-Pot Sausage, Potatoes and Green Beans

Bloggers' Best

There are over 200 million blogs on the web featuring everything from politics and religion to travel and the environment. But of course, the ones we're drawn to are written by fellow moms and dietitians whose primary focus is food and family. On any given day, we visit about a dozen blogs between us, and what we like best is reading about bloggers' adventures in the kitchen, their recipes, and their clever ways of getting wholesome meals on the family table. For this chapter, we asked some of our favorite mom bloggers to share a recipe and a personal tip for getting their kids to try new foods. Their unique ideas and perspectives made us smile ... and made us hungry! If you want more ideas from a particular blogger, we've listed the URLs at the end of each recipe.

Big Boo and Little Boo make their favorite one-pot dinner with mom, Jenna, from *Food with Kid Appeal*.

See more photos of our young cooks and moms cooking their favorite recipes on Flickr
http://www.flickr.com/photos/mealmakeovermoms

Honey Mustard Chicken Bites

MAKES 4 SERVINGS

Written by Aggie, a stay-at-home mother of two who loves to cook and eat good food, *Aggie's Kitchen* features healthy, family-friendly recipes … but the occasional treat is certainly permitted! Aggie's mission is to inspire everyone to use their kitchens more often. We think she's made her point with these homemade chicken nuggets.

2½ tablespoons honey

2 tablespoons yellow mustard

1½ cups panko or regular bread crumbs, seasoned to taste with salt and pepper

1 pound boneless, skinless chicken breast halves, cut into large "nuggets"

Nonstick cooking spray or olive oil

1 Preheat the oven to 400°F. In a bowl, stir together the honey and mustard until completely combined.

2 Place the bread crumbs in a large rimmed dish or bowl. Season chicken pieces with salt and pepper and gently dredge chicken in the honey mixture. After dredging, coat the chicken well with the bread crumbs.

3 Place the breaded chicken onto a cooling rack that is placed inside a rimmed cookie sheet. Coat each chicken piece with nonstick spray or drizzle lightly with olive oil.

4 Place the cookie sheet in the oven and bake the nuggets until golden brown, 15 to 20 minutes. Serve with your favorite dipping sauce.

PER SERVING 280 calories, 3g fat (1g saturated), 170mg sodium, 36g carbohydrate, 0g fiber, 26g protein, 10% iron

click Visit Aggie on the web at AggiesKitchen.com

aggie's tip Get your family involved in the kitchen. Start with small steps like "decorating" pizza by sprinkling chopped onions or bell peppers on top, or stirring up a dipping sauce. It gets everyone interested and opens their eyes to new things.

Aggie, mother of Gina, age 3 and Sammy, age 5

Cranberry Pear Applesauce

MAKES 8 SERVINGS

At *Family Fresh Cooking,* blog host Marla features healthy, fresh, and clean foods, using as many organic and sustainable ingredients as she can find to feed her family. On her vibrant blog, you'll find traditional recipes with unique twists. This applesauce, for example, is made with so much more than apples. It gets "a little zing" from juicy ripe pears, tart cranberries, orange zest, and cinnamon and ginger.

3 large apples, cleaned, unpeeled, cored, and cut into chunks

2 pears, cleaned, unpeeled, cored, and cut into chunks

1 cup cranberries

1 cup water

1 cinnamon stick or 1 teaspoon ground cinnamon

½ teaspoon ground ginger

½ tablespoon orange extract or 1 tablespoon orange zest

1 In a medium saucepan, combine the apples (I used 2 Honey Crisp and 1 Granny Smith), pears (I used D'Anjou), cranberries, water, cinnamon stick (or ground cinnamon), and ginger.

2 Bring to a boil and then lower the heat to a simmer. Simmer about 30 minutes, gently stirring occasionally.

3 Remove the saucepan from the stove, and carefully discard the cinnamon stick if you used one. With a ladle, place the mixture in a blender or food processor. Add the orange extract or orange zest and the sweetener of your choice (see note below). Puree until smooth and enjoy!

Note: Sweeten to your taste. This applesauce can use some extra sweetness to balance the tartness of the cranberries. The overall sweetness of your apples will be a factor in how much additional sweetener you add. Use one or a combination of the following: Stevia powder; maple syrup; or agave. Keep tasting to determine desired flavor.

PER SERVING (½ cup): 80 calories, 0g fat (0g saturated), 0mg sodium, 22g carbohydrate, 4g fiber, 0g protein, 15% vitamin C

click Visit Marla on the web at FamilyFreshCooking.com/blog

marla's tip

I love using my kids (and husband) as my recipe testers. It is so cool to watch them become little foodies. As they grow their taste buds grow with them. To encourage them to try new foods, I often ask them if they would like to add "sprinkles" to their food. A little salt or some spices can entice the pickiest eaters. Kids love to be a part of the creating as well as the eating.

— Marla, mother of "The Nugget," age 3 and "Sunshine," age 6

One-Pot Sausage, Potatoes and Green Beans

MAKES 6 SERVINGS

As a recovering picky eater, *Food with Kid Appeal* blogger Jenna can relate to the challenges of feeding reluctant eaters. She's a mom of two, so her blog showcases family-friendly recipes and practical tips for motivating kids to eat. Jenna believes that making the connection between food and its benefits to overall health and daily activities entices children to taste new foods, and later, to like them. For example, Jenna's youngest son likes how the sausage in this dish makes his muscles big and strong!

1½ pounds red-skin potatoes, cut into ¾-inch dice

2 tablespoons canola oil, divided

2 cloves garlic, diced, crushed or minced

1 medium yellow or white onion, sliced or diced

1 12-ounce package chicken sausage, sliced lengthwise, then into ½-inch-thick half moons

1 16-ounce bag frozen petite whole green beans, partially thawed

½ teaspoon kosher salt

Freshly ground black pepper

1 Steam the potatoes until nearly fork tender, about 8 minutes. Remove from heat, uncover, and set aside.

2 Meanwhile, place 1 tablespoon of the oil in a large Dutch oven or nonstick skillet over medium heat. Add the garlic and cook, stirring frequently, until golden, 30 seconds to 1 minute. Add the onion and continue to cook, stirring frequently, until softened, about 7 minutes.

3 Add the sausage and cook until both sides are brown (the time may vary depending on whether it was precooked or not). Pour off any fat. Add the remaining 1 tablespoon oil, and gently stir in the potatoes. Add the green beans on top, cover with a lid, and cook for 5 minutes.

4 Remove the lid, stir the mixture, cover, and cook until the potatoes and green beans are fork tender, about 5 more minutes. Season with the salt and pepper to taste.

PER SERVING (about 1½ cups): 230 calories, 9g fat (1.5g saturated, 0.4g omega-3), 500mg sodium, 24g carbohydrate, 4g fiber, 13g protein, 45% vitamin C, 10% iron

click Visit Jenna on the web at FoodWithKidAppeal.blogspot.com

jenna's tip

I listen to my kids. If they're put off by something new, I don't insist they eat it. I've taught them that it's okay to like some foods a little and some foods a lot. I expect them to eat a lot of the food they like a lot, and a little of the food they like a little. Empowering kids to eat only a few bites generally leads to them liking the food.

— Jenna, mother of "Little Boo," age 4 and "Big Boo," age 6

Sweet Chili Glazed and Walnut Crusted Tilapia

MAKES 4 SERVINGS

Picky Palate is a blog hosted by Jenny, a mom of two little boys with picky little palates. Her goal is to "dress up" new dishes to add fun and excitement to the family's table. This dinner recipe uses a slightly sweet, spicy, and salty bread crumb coating for tilapia, a fish that's so mild it doesn't even taste like fish.

- 3 tablespoons honey
- ¼ teaspoon chili powder
- 1 teaspoon warm water
- ¾ cup panko (Japanese bread crumbs)
- ½ cup walnuts, finely chopped
- ½ teaspoon kosher salt
- ½ teaspoon chili powder
- ¼ teaspoon fresh cracked black pepper
- 4 tilapia fillets (about 1 pound)
- 2 tablespoons extra virgin olive oil

1 Place the honey, chili powder and water in a small bowl; mix to combine. Place bread crumbs, walnuts, salt, chili powder, and pepper in a shallow dish; mix to combine.

2 Season both sides of the tilapia fillets with pinches of salt and pepper. With a pastry brush, brush the honey glaze on both sides of the tilapia, then press into the bread crumb mixture. Continue until all fillets are coated.

3 Heat the oil in a large skillet over medium heat. When hot, place the coated tilapia fillets in the skillet; cook until golden brown and the fish flakes easily with a fork, about 4 minutes per side. Remove and serve warm.

PER SERVING (1 fillet): 420 calories, 19g fat (2.5g saturated, 0.4g omega-3), 250mg sodium, 28g carbohydrate, 1g fiber, 35g protein, 10% iron

click Visit Jenny on the web at Picky-Palate.com

jenny's tip

Enticing my boys to eat their vegetables takes some creativity, so I offer a lot of different "dippers." They like to dip carrot sticks and broccoli florets in a light ranch dressing dip, apple slices and celery sticks in a mixture of warmed peanut butter and honey, and marinara sauce works wonders for sautéed veggies.

— Jenny, mother of Brady, age 4 and Mason, age 7

Apple Caramel Salad

MAKES 6 TO 8 SERVINGS

At *Super Healthy Kids,* Amy is passionate about making nutritious food so delicious and enjoyable that kids would rather eat healthy things like apples and oranges than gooey things like candy and cake. Amy's three children ask for her crispy, sweet apple salad most nights of the week.

- 2 medium Golden Delicious apples, unpeeled and cut into ½-inch dice
- 1 cup finely chopped or shredded green cabbage (about ¼ small cabbage)
- 2 tablespoons chopped pecans
- 1 6-ounce container plain 0%-fat Greek yogurt
- 2 tablespoons brown sugar
- 1 teaspoon vanilla extract

1 Combine the apples, cabbage, and pecans in a large bowl. In a separate bowl, mix together the yogurt, brown sugar, and vanilla.

2 Pour the dressing over the apple–cabbage mixture and stir to combine. Chill in the refrigerator for 30 minutes or longer before serving.

PER SERVING (about ½ cup): 70 calories, 1.5g fat (0g saturated), 15mg sodium, 12g carbohydrate, 2g fiber, 3g protein, 10% vitamin C

click Visit Amy on the web at SuperHealthyKids.com

amy's tip

Kids like to win, so give them the power! Get silly with their options, especially when they are young. You: "Suzy, I need you to eat 100 bites of broccoli." Child: "No! I'm only two years old." You: "Well, how many bites should a 2-year old eat?" Child: "Two bites." You: "OK, fine. You win. Have two bites!"

— Amy, mother of TJ, age 7, Erica, age 9 and Nathan, age 11

Greek Chicken Salad Sandwiches

MAKES 4 SERVINGS

Sarah's Cucina Bella is a food blog about cooking for a young family. Written by Sarah, a mother of two, the featured recipes are tested in Sarah's kitchen and are taste-tested by her own children. Her blog emphasizes making healthy choices, cooking together as a family, and raising knowledgeable, curious eaters. This recipe — which requires a bit of mixing, chopping, and stirring — was made with the help of pint-size sous-chef, 2-year old Paige.

½ cup peeled, seeded, and diced (½ inch) cucumber

¼ teaspoon kosher salt

1 cup diced (½ inch) cooked chicken

½ cup crumbled feta cheese

¼ cup chopped kalamata olives

2 tablespoons olive oil

1 tablespoon white wine vinegar

½ teaspoon dried basil

Kosher salt and ground black pepper

4 small pita breads or 2 regular-size ones

1 Combine the cucumber and salt in a mesh sieve (AKA wire-mesh strainer) over a bowl or the sink and let sit for about 10 minutes. (Cucumbers are watery, so this step allows them to release some of their liquid. You can skip this step if you plan to eat the salad right away.)

2 Meanwhile, combine the chicken, feta cheese, and olives in a medium bowl. Set aside.

3 In a small bowl, whisk together the olive oil, vinegar, and dried basil. Set aside.

4 Press gently on the cucumbers to remove any excess water, and shake the sieve. Then, pour the cucumbers into the bowl with the chicken mixture. Stir to combine. Pour the olive oil dressing over the mixture and stir well. Season with salt and pepper to taste. Let stand for a minute or 2 before serving.

5 Cut the pita bread into two half-moons. Divide the chicken salad evenly among the halves. If using small pita breads, 2 halves is a serving. For regular-size pitas, one-half is a serving.

PER SERVING (1 sandwich): 280 calories, 16g fat (4.5g saturated), 670mg sodium, 18g carbohydrate, 1g fiber, 16g protein, 15% calcium

click Visit Sarah on the web at SarahsCucinaBella.com

sarah's tip

Get your kids involved in the food. From selecting veggies at a farm stand or in the produce aisle to washing, prepping, and cooking, letting your kids see, feel and smell unfamiliar or new foods can help inspire them to try them. Who knows? It may turn out to be a favorite food.

Sarah, mother of Paige, age 2, Will, age 5 and stepmother of Chris, age 10

Carrot Sesame Salad

MAKES 4 SERVINSG

Rachael, who writes the beautiful blog, *La Fuji Mama*, features recipes that are a fusion of different tastes, influenced by the places she has lived and visited and the people she's met. Rachael doesn't believe food should be "dumbed down" for children, and she shares ideas for making time spent in the kitchen and at the dinner table playful, delicious, and educational for children. Rachael's *Carrot Sesame Salad* is fun to eat, and it provides a great opportunity for kids to practice their chopstick skills (see Rachael's *tip* below).

3-4 medium-size carrots (about 8 ounces), washed and peeled

1 tablespoon reduced-sodium soy sauce

1 tablespoon seasoned rice vinegar

1 tablespoon toasted sesame oil

2 teaspoons toasted white sesame seeds

½ teaspoon granulated sugar

1 With a vegetable peeler, slice the carrots into long ribbons (using a "Y"-shaped peeler works well). Set the ribbons aside in a serving bowl.

2 In a separate bowl, or liquid measuring cup, mix together the soy sauce, vinegar, oil, sesame seeds, and granulated sugar. Pour over the carrot ribbons, and toss the ribbons to coat in the dressing. The salad can be served immediately, or it can be refrigerated up to a day before serving.

PER SERVING 70 calories, 4.5g fat (0.5g saturated), 260mg sodium, 7g carbohydrate, 2g fiber, 1g protein, 170% vitamin A

click Visit Rachael on the web at LaFujiMama.com

rachael's tip

My best tip for getting my kids to try healthy meals and new foods without complaints is chopsticks! My girls love eating with their chopsticks, and I keep multiple sets of made-just-for-kids on hand. My favorite chopsticks are called Rookie Stix Chopsticks. They are inexpensive, easy to wash, easy for even small children to use, and provide a good grip on food.

Rachael, mother of "Bug," age 1½ and "Squirrel," age 3½

Smooth-as-Silk Hummus

MAKES 8 SERVINGS

At *Nutrition Unplugged*, Janet, a registered dietitian, is on a mission to help people cut through the clutter on nutrition and focus on the fad-free facts instead. On her blog, you'll find the latest scoop on diet books, nutrition myths, new food products, and trends. She believes food should be enjoyed, not feared. Janet's husband is Lebanese, so she often includes recipes and articles about Middle Eastern cuisine — such as this one.

2 small cloves garlic, peeled and halved

1 15-ounce can chickpeas, drained and rinsed

⅓ cup tahini, well stirred

1 lemon, juiced

2 tablespoons extra virgin olive oil

½ teaspoon kosher salt

Water (as needed)

Optional garnish: Whole chickpeas, toasted pine nuts, chopped parsley, paprika, cumin, or sumac

1 Combine the garlic, chickpeas, tahini, lemon juice, olive oil, and salt in the bowl of a food processor and process until smooth. Add water to thin the mixture to the desired consistency (about ¼ cup).

2 Transfer to a bowl and drizzle with additional olive oil to keep the hummus from crusting. Add garnish as desired. Refrigerate until ready to use, and serve with pita chips or raw veggies.

Note: Even though we like the plain garlic/lemon-y version best, we often experiment by adding different ingredients, including canned chipotle in sauce, roasted red peppers, chopped jalapeno, olives, cilantro, or pomegranate molasses. My husband also likes a version without tahini called balila hummus (he refers to it as hummus "unplugged").

PER SERVING (¼ cup): 150 calories, 10g fat (1.5g saturated), 85mg sodium, 11g carbohydrate, 2g fiber, 6g protein

click Visit Janet on the web at NutritionUnplugged.com
Janet is also founder of NutritionBlogNetwork.com, a collection of blogs written by registered dietitians.

janet's tip

My husband is Lebanese, so for our kids, we try to instill a sense of pride in their heritage. One way is to introduce them to Lebanese food. When we get excited about it, our kids are more likely to try it. As for getting the twins to eat more vegetables, I will frequently serve them as a first course — and often raw. When the kids come to the table hungry, their plates will be piled with crunchy carrots so they get started on those first.

— Janet, mother of Layla and Sami, age 7

Garlicky Black Beans

MAKES 4 SERVINGS

Maryann, a dietitian from *Raise Healthy Eaters*, provides parents with research-based, simple ways to raise healthy and happy eaters. On her blog, she talks a lot about exposing children to a wide variety of healthy foods and role modeling good eating habits. She reminds parents that forcing kids to eat nutritious foods or using sweets as a reward ("eat your veggies before dessert") can backfire because it makes healthy foods less desirable. As for this simple black bean side dish — which Maryann serves every time Mexican food is on her menu — she and her husband gobble it up, so their kids do too.

1 15-ounce can black beans, drained (liquid reserved)

2 cloves garlic, minced

1 tablespoon olive oil

2-3 teaspoons ground cumin

Kosher salt and freshly ground black pepper

1 Heat the olive oil in a small nonstick skillet over medium heat. Add the garlic and cook, stirring frequently, until golden, 30 seconds to 1 minute.

2 Stir in the black beans, 2 to 3 tablespoons of the reserved liquid, and the cumin until well combined. Cook until heated through, and season with salt and pepper to taste.

PER SERVING (about ⅓ cup): 90 calories, 3.5g fat (0.5g saturated), 220mg sodium, 15g carbohydrate, 5g fiber, 4g protein

click Visit Maryann on the web at RaiseHealthyEaters.com

maryann's tip

Serve foods your children like with foods they don't. Research shows that kids are more likely to try a new food if it's prepared in a familiar way (i.e. a favorite sauce or dressing). This technique works especially well with salads. Making a new dinner recipe you're not sure your little ones will like? Serve it with a well-liked side dish and you'll have better luck getting them to try it.

Maryann, mother of David, age 1 and Anna, age 3

Peter Rabbit's Mixed-Up Garden

MAKES 2 TO 4 SERVINGS

Mandy, a mother of three from *Gourmet Mom on the Go*, is passionate about "taking back dinnertime" and bringing the family together around the table. In her house, Mandy cooks up an array of whimsically colored and shaped foods … perfect for kids (and adults) of all ages. Playing with food is a major focus of Mandy's blog, and her "recipe" for *Peter Rabbit's Mixed-Up Garden* is guaranteed to get kids excited about eating their veggies.

1 cupcake pan or mini muffin tin

Various fruits and vegetables, cut into bite-size pieces

Tissue paper

Tape

Peter Rabbit's Mixed-Up Garden cards (see note below)

1 Fill the cupcake or mini-muffin tins with various fruits and veggies. Cover with a sheet of tissue paper and tape down to secure. Two layers of tissue paper work best (just fold a piece in half) so no one can peek.

2 Print the Peter Rabbit's Mixed-Up Garden cards, fold in half, and place next to the muffin tin. Let the kids "dig" and discover what yummy treats are in the "garden."

click Visit Mandy on the web at GourmetMomOnTheGo.com

While you're there, print off some of Mandy's Peter Rabbit's Mixed-Up Garden cards. The following message is written on each: Peter Rabbit's seeds got all mixed up this year and now he doesn't know what has grown in his lovely garden! Will you help him eat his yummy treats and figure out what they are? Help Peter by digging in each hole, nibbling the food and deciding what it is. Use your taste, smell, and sight to figure out this mystery. Good luck!

mandy's tip

Sit down at the table all together as a family, and talk while you eat. Ask questions like, "If you were an animal, what would you be?" Have everyone take a bite before they answer. Even if you have already eaten or are not eating that dinner, find something to eat or drink and sit down with your family.

Mandy, mother of "Little H," age 3, "Little C," age 5 and "Big C," age 7

Crispy Kale Chips

MAKES 4 SERVINGS

Wicked Tasty Harvest is a blog written by April and two fellow food writers. April, a mother of an adventurous little eater, features stories about food, where it comes from, and how it's been grown. As a member of a local CSA (Community Supported Agriculture), April blogs about the locally-grown food she receives each week. For this recipe, she takes deep green, super-nutritious kale (which was in her CSA basket for many weeks in a row) and turns it into chips. They're light and crispy, and eating just one is impossible!

1   big bunch kale

1-2 tablespoons olive oil

½   teaspoon smoked paprika (or more)

½   teaspoon ginger powder (or more)

1   pinch chili powder, optional

Sea salt

1 Preheat the oven to 250°F. Remove the stems and woody ribbing from the tender leaves of the kale. Tear the leaves into bite-size pieces. Wash and dry.

2 Add the olive oil to a large bowl. Whisk in the paprika and ginger. Add the chili powder as desired. Add the kale leaves to the oil and toss with your hands, coating each leaf, front and back.

3 Lay the kale out on a parchment paper–covered cookie sheet. Sprinkle with the salt. Wash your hands so you don't rub chili powder into your eyes!

4 Working in batches, bake in the oven, until the chips are flat and crisp. (It took about 17 minutes for mine, although the recipe that inspired it online said 33 minutes.)

5 Remove with a spatula and let cool. Serve them to someone who will try one and say, "Kale chips?" as they bite into one. In about a minute, they'll come back for 10 more.

PER SERVING 100 calories, 6g fat (1g saturated, 0.2g omega-3), 50mg sodium, 11g carbohydrate, 2g fiber, 4g protein, 350% vitamin A, 230% vitamin C, 15% calcium, 10% iron

click Visit April on the web at WickedTastyHarvest.com

april's tip

To encourage my daughter to eat new things and find new favorites, I talk about the farmers she has met through our CSA share. She talks to "her farmers" — the ones who grow the food — and she knows what they do. Since she was really young, she has called them "farmer-chefs" because for her (as well as our whole family), the source of our food is tied into the meals we eat.

April, mother of Esmé, age 4

Blueberry Banana Smoothie

MAKES 3 SERVINGS

Bringing food and families together around the dinner table is Tina's mission at *Mommy's Kitchen*. Today's on-the-go families are short on time, so Tina's recipes are fast, easy, and family-focused. She enjoys cooking up old classics with her kids as well as creating new recipes that entice them to the table.

1½ cups ice cubes

½-1 cup fresh or frozen blueberries

1 cup 1% low-fat milk, plain or vanilla soy milk, or almond milk

1 cup low-fat blueberry or vanilla yogurt

1-2 ripe bananas

1 Add the ice cubes, blueberries, and milk to a blender. Blend on ice breaker or icy drink to break up the ice a bit. Add the yogurt and bananas and blend until smooth. Pour into glasses and enjoy.

PER SERVING (about 1 cup): 140 calories, 1.5g fat (0.5g saturated), 55mg sodium, 29g carbohydrate, 3g fiber, 5g protein, 10% vitamin C, 15% calcium

click Visit Tina on the web at MommysKitchen.net

tina's **tip**

My youngest is particular about vegetables and beans so I get a little sneaky. I puree them into muffins, breads, and smoothies. Sometimes we make up fun names for our smoothies to encourage everyone to try them: Spinach smoothies become Green Monsters or Green Slime Smoothies. I also involve my children in food preparation, so they're more likely to eat what we make.

Tina, mother of Carson, age 7, Mackenzie, age 10 and Travis, age 16

Fresh Fruit and Veggie Snack

CHAPTER 15

50 Moms' Secrets
For Getting Picky Eaters to Try New Foods

In a perfect world, every child would eat a well-balanced diet overflowing with fruits, vegetables, and whole grains. But in reality, most children fall short of the daily recommendations. Our goal in this book (and in life) is to close the gap between what kids do eat and what kids should eat. As moms — Liz has two boys, and Janice, two girls — and more important, as dietitians who constantly experiment with new foods, we have faced the gamut of mealtime challenges.

We've weathered eye rolls, "yucks," and even the devastating "that's gross." We've tried what we thought was every trick in the book to put the kibosh on complaints. But what we learned from our network of moms is that there's always a new way to encourage kids to be adventurous eaters (or at least, tasters).

Eight-year old Anthony adds maple syrup to our *Sweet and Hearty Beef Stew*. When kids help with food prep, they're more likely to eat what's for dinner with a smile.

The advice that's most often given to entice kids to eat well can be highly effective: Eat together as a family; model good eating habits; offer new foods over and over again; and maintain a positive attitude at the table. However, if this advice worked one hundred percent of the time, supermarkets would be hard pressed to keep spinach and broccoli on their shelves, and moms across America would be a lot less stressed during mealtime.

In the summer of 2009, we sent a survey to our online community of moms to gauge their greatest mealtime challenges and find out how they encouraged healthy eating. From the nearly 600 people who took the survey, we learned the following:

- The number one obstacle to getting children to eat healthy, well-balanced meals is "picky eaters who whine and complain."
- The foods children refuse to eat most often are vegetables, beans, and seafood.
- When children complain about what's for dinner, 30% of moms insist they try at least one bite before offering an alternative, 30% ignore the complaints and say, "This is dinner," and 11% make a separate meal for their kids.
- The biggest downfalls for families when it comes to eating a healthy diet are snacking on empty-calorie foods, relying on frozen and boxed processed foods, and turning to take-out or pizza.

Despite these struggles, when we asked our moms to share their best strategy for encouraging their children to try new foods and eat a healthy diet without complaint, we received over 300 creative "secrets," and the majority of them were playful and positive. Instead of using tactics like sneaking, coercing, and begging, we heard advice about involvement, encouragement, and fun.

As you read these tips, you'll see that most aim to change the mealtime paradigm from one in which mom stands apart, preps the food, and expects everyone to eat it, to one where the kids become actively involved in the choices presented to them. This ultimately creates a kitchen culture where kids buy into the concept of healthy food and actually want to eat the good stuff.

After much deliberation, we narrowed the tips down to 50 of our favorites. Why so many? Because kids — and families — come in all shapes and sizes, so no single method will serve everyone. With this many choices, whether you have an adventurous eater who may need a little nudge every now and again, or the pickiest, most fickle, exasperating eater on the planet, we guarantee you'll find at least one strategy that will work at your table.

1 The Three Pennies Game

When my children were younger, we played the "Three Pennies Game" at the dinner table. Each person, including mom and dad, got three pennies. The object was to get rid of your pennies before the meal was over. I would often try new recipes. The family had to give three compliments, paid with a penny each, about the main meal. The compliments had to come after eating a bite. So, not only did the family have to try the meal and eat at least three bites, they had to say something nice too. That meant talking at the dinner table … YEAH! Each night the kids would get so excited to get their three pennies to play. At the end of the meal, the family could do a thumbs-up or thumbs-down which meant, "make it again," or "no thank you."

Kelly, mother of Julia, age 12 and Claudette, age 15 ▪ Marietta, GA

2 Put Parsley on Everything

I keep a bottle of dried parsley in the fridge and dust every dish with a little dried, or even better, fresh parsley. This helps the kids realize there is no such thing as "white food" and it gets them used to the idea that herbs are supposed to be in food. Nothing goes out of my kitchen that is one color — ever. My reward for this is that they don't pick the rosemary out of the chicken when we are at a dinner party.

Kim, mother of Edie, age 3 and Lucy, age 4 ▪ New York, NY

3 Adjust Your Recipes

When my children complain about something I'm serving, I still request they eat a small amount, but I listen to why they don't like it and make adjustments. I used to serve broccoli with a cheese sauce on top because I know my children love cheese. But they apparently prefer broccoli plain — whether it is raw or cooked. If raw, they like it with ranch dressing for dipping. When it's cooked, they prefer it barely cooked — not soggy, and separate from the cheese sauce.

Teena, mother of Aaron, age 5 and Angelica, age 11 ▪ Flossmoor, IL

4 Dinner in a Box

We have a special box full of dinner ideas that my two kids have chosen from cookbooks and cooking magazines. Once a week, I sit down with both of them and we make a game of looking through the books and magazines for new ideas. My daughter likes to page through her collection of kids' cookbooks and write lists of different main and side dishes that complement each other, while my son loves cutting out magazine pictures of foods and making them into a collage. After we've gathered some new ideas, they choose a few from the box, and we add those to the next week's meal plan. I try to involve them in the preparation of the recipes they've chosen as much as possible and have found that both of them are much more willing to try new foods when they've had a chance to pick out the recipes and help in the preparation. While they aren't always thrilled with some of the dishes we've tested this way, they are always more interested in giving them a chance if they've been involved in the process. After a little tweaking, the majority of the recipes we test make their way into our regular mealtime repertoire.

Melissa, mother of Elias, age 4 and Clio, age 9 ▪ Oxnard, CA

5 The Sharing Plate

I put a plate of vegetables and ranch dressing on the table before every meal and let the kids dip and snack on it while I'm cooking. It keeps them out of my way and has greatly increased their vegetable consumption! I always serve carrots and broccoli and will vary what else I put out. My 3-year old will ask, "What's this?" I'll tell her, "It's green," (or whatever color it is) and then she'll try it!

Laura, mother of Sarah, age 3 and Christopher and Rachel, age 5 ▪ West Henrietta, NY

6 Connect Food with Feelings

I talk with my kids about how the food they eat affects them. I ask them how they feel after eating fast foods (usually grumpy) versus a balanced, home-cooked meal. We've even talked about how fiber helps us poop (after listening to one of your podcasts), and we discuss good choices and better choices. For example, it's okay to have a chocolate chip waffle or pancake with some fruit because it's a healthier choice than a toaster pastry.

Alex, mother of Sammie, age 5 and Sean, age 7 ▪ Jackson, MI

7 Create Your Own Kebabs

Kebabs seem to do the trick with my son. He has fun cutting his own fruit with a table knife — melon, bananas, apples and grapes — and piercing the pieces with wooden skewers. He then creates his own kebab patterns. I was shocked when he downed four of the kabobs. He told me to watch out because there is a new "chef" in the house!

Vicky, mother of Aidan, age 7 ▪ Ft. Thomas, KY

8 Choose Colorful Words to Describe Your Recipes

Whenever I make a new dish, I use colorful words to describe the flavors instead of just talking about the main ingredient or cooking technique. For example, my boys would typically frown at me if I told them we were having salad for dinner. Yet when I say we're having Crunchy Fajita Salad (in which I incorporate every vegetable in my crisper) they can't wait. When I say we're having chicken for dinner, I usually get the "Not chicken again!" response. But if I call it Italian Chicken or Curry Chicken or Spicy Chicken Finger Wraps, they go wild. I haven't fried anything in my home for years, but I serve up baked fries every other week, and as long as I don't call them "baked," the boys think they're getting a real treat (and they are)!

Meredith, mother of Matthew, age 8 and Zachary age 12 ▪ Aurora, CO

9 Take a "Family Bite"

My son is only two so we haven't gone too far with this, but when he's hesitant to try something new, we do a "family bite" where we each take the same food and eat a bite of it at the same time. Often he will at least try it after seeing Mom and Dad eat it like that.

Lois, mother of Alexander, age 2 ▪ Chicago, IL

10 Bring Your Restaurant Meals Home

Sometimes we order something at a restaurant that we'd like our daughter to eat at home. Then when we re-create it at home, we say, "Just like they make at Prairie Joe's," which is quite exciting when you're three!

Marla, mother of Sarah, age 3 ▪ Evanston, IL

11 Follow the Food Groups

I have posted the food groups on our refrigerator and the kids put magnetic stars next to the ones that they have eaten after each meal. This way they're able to see which food groups they still need. They often ask if they can have something from the food groups they haven't eaten so they can put a star next to it.

Rachel, mother of Alyssa, age 3 months, Gavin, age 2 and Kayla, age 4 ▪ Blue Ridge, VA

12 Pretend Not to Share the Good Stuff

When my daughter does not want to try a specific food, her daddy tells her that the food she refuses to eat is his and that she better not eat it all up from him. She laughs and starts eating the food so that her daddy can't get it. My daughter is now four and this has worked since she was about two. My husband makes it a big game, and my daughter gets very excited about trying new foods or eating the foods that are good for her. She responds so much better when we make it fun.

Cassondra, mother of Victoria, age 4, John, age 20 and Jerrod, age 23 ▪ Norcross, GA

13 Offer Tiny Tastes to Spark Curiosity

Not only do I cook for my family, but I am an in-home childcare provider as well. For new foods, we do many "little tastes" before an item is actually offered as a component of a meal (especially unfamiliar fruits and veggies). Occasionally I will prepare something new and different for myself at lunchtime. When the children express curiosity about what I'm eating, I may offer "just a taste" to be kind and share, then tell them that maybe sometime I will make it for them too. This helps them look forward to a new food, rather than wrinkling their noses at something I simply put on their plates.

Molly, mother of Gavin, age 6 and Gwen, age 9 ▪ Coon Rapids, MN

14 Saucy Siblings

When my teenage son, who is an athlete, tells his two younger sisters they need to eat better to perform better, they listen. A healthy dose of sibling rivalry and competition play into this positive form of role modeling.

Peggy, mother of Talia, age 11, Ali, age 13 and Scoop, age 16 ▪ Lexington, MA

15 Eat the Rainbow

I encourage my girls to eat the "rainbow." We take turns calling out a color and everyone at the table takes a bite of the food that's that color.

Julie, mother of Dagny, age 7 and Valerie, age 9 ▪ Alpharetta, GA

16 Choose a "Try It" Food Every Time You Shop

We always pick out a "try it" item when we go to the grocery store. One rule: NO junk food! We have tried star fruit, kefir, and plantains. Each week we pick one new thing and look up what to do with it. My kids are always excited to try it, and as a result, we have added quite a few new foods to our diet.

Kim, mother of Emily, age 3, Libby, age 5 and Andrew, age 7 ▪ Dexter, MI

17 Food Pyramid Power

I go to the *MyPyramid.gov* website with my 7-year old and help him enter his food choices into the food log. He likes to see the bar graph with the different food groups and it's another way for him to see he's low in veggies. He'll say, "Uh-oh, I guess I'm low in veggies." Then I ask him what he thinks he should do about it. This way, he's in charge. He likes raw carrots and corn on the cob, and so I try to include those with as many dinners as possible, while also asking him to "take a taste" of the other veggies. It's a very slow process, but by staying upbeat with the whole thing we avoid having food fights.

Karen, mother of Adam, age 7 ▪ Lincoln, RI

18 Join a CSA

We belong to a CSA (Community Supported Agriculture), so I talk with the kids about the farmer, and I make a big deal out of discovering what's in our bag this week. I also try to incorporate my kids' favorite veggies in sauces. My son is a fan of mushrooms, so I'll put them in pasta sauce or eggs.

Jill, mother of Grant, age 6 and Anna, age 8 ▪ Austin, TX

19 Gross Out the Kids

I have four boys. To get them to try new vegetables I let them know the "gas factor." When they found out that broccoli would make them gassier or asparagus would make their urine smelly, they were ready to try. Such is life in my animal house!

Pam, mother of Elizabeth and Emily, age 6 months, Ethan, age 6, Owen, age 8, William, age 11 and Andrew, age 14 ▪ Bismarck, ND

20 Recipe Reviewer Chart

We "hire" our own children to become recipe reviewers. It's an instant mood changer at the dinner table. After each "review," the kids get a check mark. Five or ten tries earn a reward. For younger kids, the "payment" ideas include stickers, school supplies, or sports equipment. For older kids, the incentive may be an iTunes gift card. To "hire" your own kids to taste and critique your recipes, use our Recipe Reviewer Chart. You can download the chart at *MealMakeoverMoms.com.*

Liz (Meal Makeover Mom), mother of Simon, age 11 and Josh, age 15 ▪ Lexington, MA

Janice (Meal Makeover Mom), mother of Leah, age 10 and Carolyn, age 18 ▪ Melrose, MA

21 Invest in a Kid's Cookbook

My 4-year old received a couple of kid cookbooks for her birthday. When she picks a recipe from her cookbook, she gets to make it "herself" (with help from us, of course) and is usually so excited to try "her" special dish. We've mostly used recipes from *Pretend Soup*, which are all fairly healthy, so I feel good about her trying them.

Amy, mother of Alyce, age 18 months and Kelli, age 4 ▪ La Mirada, CA

22 Establish "Mommy and Me Time"

I let my daughters pick one meal every week that they shop for and help prepare. It's special "mommy and me" time with each girl at least once a week. We also play games in the grocery store. I ask them to find one food they have never eaten but are willing to try. They usually pick a fruit or vegetable. I think it is because they are easy to touch and pretty to look at in their raw state. Fruits and veggies are no longer a battle!

Bonnie, mother of Reagan, age 6 and Peyton, age 7 ▪ Henderson, NV

23 Build a Meal

"Build-your-own" anything seems to work best with my crew: build your own tacos, taco salad, green salad, pasta salad, smoothies, subs, and even build-your-own stir fry.

Cindy, mother of Emilie, age 9, Anna, age 13 and Alex, age 15 ▪ Green Bay, WI

24 Be the Boss but Don't be Bossy

Here's the deal: I decide what's for dinner, and the kids decide how much of it they want to eat. Once the meal is over, that's it until the next one.

Laura, mother of Carson, age 4, Dylan, age 10 and Keira, age 13 ▪ Whitecourt, Alberta, Canada

25 Toothpicks to the Rescue

Anything cut up small and served on frilly toothpicks seems to be a hit in my house. Also, as long as my 5-year old can "dip" her food in something, she'll often get past the initial "ick" reaction and be okay eating the new food without the dip by the third or fourth try. Instead of using ranch dressing, I mix plain fat-free yogurt with a small dollop of ranch to make a healthier white dip alternative.

Jennifer, mother of Emily, age 5 ▪ Delaware, OH

26 Serve Soup

Soup and chili are great ways to get the kids to eat vegetables. Having rolls on hand makes them much more amenable to trying them. They can dip the bread into the soup and become familiar with it, without having to jump in all at once.

Melanie, mother of Olivia and Julianne, age 11 and Athena, age 13 ▪ Acton, MA

27 The Power of Superheroes

My 4-year old, Aidan, loves superheroes. In order to get him to eat his veggies or whatever else he doesn't want to eat on a particular night, I will tell him that his favorite superhero eats that food … and that is how he got his superhero powers! Aidan is sure to at least try some after that.

Sara, mother of Kellan, age 1 and Aidan, age 4 ▪ Nashua, NH

28 Take the "P" Out of "Picky" and Let the Kids Get Icky

To encourage my boys to try new foods, I let them eat like "pigs" and even let them squeal à la "Christmas Story." You'd be surprised what becomes more palatable when you can really be a pig. The weekly "pig out" at our house leads to a mess, but I don't feel too bad about it because I always stick a vegetable in the piggy's "slop." They only get the piggy opportunity on new foods, and it amazes me how after a "pig session," we always get a few "squeals" when the same dish comes back around!

Amy, mother of Ben, age 5 and Daniel, age 6 ▪ Houston, TX

29 Positive Peer Pressure

I have found that my daughters will try a new food when at a friend's house. My 10-year old came home one day and told me she tried this great new food and that I should buy it. It was edamame! This is now a favorite snack/food at our house. She never would have tried it at home.

Lisa, mother of Sarah, age 10 and Elizabeth, age 13 ▪ Lexington, MA

30 Grow Your Own Food

A surprising way to get my kids to try new things has been growing our own food. Ever since my daughter helped grow and harvest, she has become a true fan of broccoli, radishes, arugula, grape tomatoes, and more. These are all vegetables she would NEVER have tasted before.

Denise, mother of Emma, age 10 ▪ Lacombe, LA

31 Foster Mealtime Independence

My kids pack their own school lunch every day. The lunch always includes at least one fruit and one vegetable as well as one serving of whole grain (usually whole wheat bread, Triscuits®, or a dry cereal like raisin bran), and a serving of protein (usually lunch meat or peanut butter). A small water bottle goes in each lunch too. They can also pick one small "snack" such as pudding, Jell-O®, etc. By packing their own lunch, they have learned how to look for and create a well-balanced meal. Sometimes I sneak a special note in the lunch telling them what a great job they did packing that day. At the grocery store, they read labels to see if the first ingredient is whole wheat, or they check the amount of fiber and protein in a breakfast cereal. I no longer have to stand over their shoulders to make them eat vegetables and whole grains — they look for them. And to think, it all started from packing their own school lunches!

Deb, mother of Zachary, age 6, Claudia, age 10 and Morgan, age 12 ▪ Springfield, OH

32 Assign Silly Names to Vegetables

I started giving foods fun names like X-ray Carrots or Ogre Toes (baby tomatoes), and it often intrigues my kids enough to give them a try! The sillier the name the better.

Andrea, mother of four ▪ Lake Village, IN

33 Theme Nights

Recently, I started serving Theme Dinners. They're a huge success (and fun, too)! One theme that worked well was dessert first. We tried fruit kebabs with a flaxseed and yogurt dip, and ended with healthy chicken fingers! Other theme night ideas are:

- Italian Night: Serve lasagna roll ups or baked ziti, Caesar salad, and mini garlic buns.
- Hockey Night: While watching a game, serve healthy finger-friendly foods such as chicken fingers with a coating of cereal/whole grains, cheese sticks, and cups of hot chocolate to drink.
- Breakfast for Dinner Night: Serve pancakes, waffles, or French toast.

Jennifer, mother of Kennedy, age 3 and Jaxon, age 7 ▪ Little Britain, Ontario, Canada

34 Use a Bento Box

I create cute bento boxes for my son to take to school for his lunch, and I often use these same techniques when I'm serving him food at home. Here are a few ideas:

- Use cookie cutters to cut sandwiches, cheese, or tofu into various shapes. I use animal, star, heart, gingerbread man, and circle cutters. Use a regular knife to cut sandwiches into strips or triangles or cheese and tofu into matchsticks or cubes.
- Use mini-versions of regular foods: Mini muffins, bagels, and crackers seem to go over better with preschoolers than regular size.
- Use lots of color. I try to have at least three different colors in each lunch. It looks good, and is a good way to ensure that your child is getting lots of fruits and veggies.

Wendy, mother of Augie, age 1 and Wyatt, age 4 ▪ El Cerrito, CA

35 Plan a Family Tasting Party

We've had "tasting parties" where we line up several new foods in a row and ask the kids to rate them like restaurant critics.

Dina, mother of Josh, age 10 and Hannah, age 13 ▪ Lexington, MA

36 Serve Yourself Meals

Instead of me loading my kids' plates with a small serving of everything, we now serve the food family style so the kids can help themselves. They can take whatever they want or pass the plate along. I use fun serving utensils such as different tongs and scoops that the kids always want to use. It has been super successful with my daughter who has tried several foods she used to refuse to eat.

Stacy, mother of Henry, age 3 and Molly, age 5 ▪ Maryland Heights, MO

37 Create Healthy Options

We have small plastic bins in both the fridge and pantry. Each bin contains a certain food group. I make up single serving size amounts of vegetables, fruit, whole grain crackers, string cheese, etc. and place them in the corresponding bin. My children know to grab one of each for a healthy snack. They feel a little bit of control when they get to choose their own snack and seem open to trying new things when I slip them into the bins. The older kids know how to choose and it's easy for them to help their little brother.

Kimberly, mother of Spencer, age 2, Kendall, age 5 and Jaden, age 8 ▪ San Diego, CA

38 Offer Lots of Hugs & Tickles

My kids love getting lots of hugs and tickles so I started the, "I tried something new hug." Every time they eat or try something new they get a big hug followed by a giggly tickle. They love it!

Joanne, mother of Madeline and Elliot, age 5 ▪ Stoneham, MA

39 Challenge Your Children's Palates

We have begun challenging our kids to test their palates and expand their tastes. Even if they are unsure of what's in a particular dish, they are always eager to pick out flavors, guess the ingredients, and use their words to describe why they do or don't like something new that they've tried.

Nathalie, mother of Emerson, age 5 and Julia, age 8 ▪ Van Nuys, CA

40 Yummy in My Tummy

I have always talked about fruits and vegetables as, "yummy," as in, "Do you want yummy green beans?" and "You love yummy green beans." By the time they were old enough to argue, they already thought of green beans (and other vegetables and fruits) as "yummy."

Jill, mother of Tommy, age 2, Alix, age 8, Geoffrey, age 10 and Gregory, age 16 ▪ Moraga, CA

41 Plan the Weekly Menu Together

In our household, we plan our weekly meals as a family. My kids and husband will pick a new or favorite entree and I will introduce new or favorite sides. The result: Meals each night are filled with something everyone is looking forward to eating! The whole strategy behind my family's meal planning is to prevent the whining before it even happens or becomes a problem. Once the schedule is done, it's printed and hung up on the refrigerator for everyone to see. This eliminates the infamous question, "What we are having for dinner tonight?" My children actually look forward to family mealtime.

Lisa, mother of Zack, age 12 and Sara, age 17 ▪ Melrose, MA

42 Don't Join the Clean Plate Club

I never pressure my son to eat anything that he doesn't like. I don't label foods as "good" or "bad." Some foods are "special occasion" foods that we don't eat very often, but I don't offer dessert as a reward for eating vegetables or fruits. I let him decide when he's had enough, so that has minimized the battles at the dinner table. However, when he chooses not to eat what I've prepared or offered for dinner, he has to live with that decision. He doesn't get to have a separate dinner or snack before bed if he gets hungry. This is slowly starting to work.

Jill, mother of Joseph, age 4 ▪ Big Bear Lake, CA

43 Say Bye-Bye to Baby Taste Buds

I do a lot of kids' cooking classes for third and fourth grade school children. When I begin, I comment on how tall they are and how they must be getting close to becoming teenagers. Then I tell them that when they turn 13, they will develop new taste buds on their tongues; their "baby food" habits of disliking foods will be a thing of the past. Since most of these kids are 10- and 11-year olds and want to be teenagers yesterday, they tell me that they already have the new taste buds. From there, I prepare several recipes with ingredients such as yogurt, fruits, and vegetables, and herbs such as basil and cilantro. The kids who still claim to have the "baby" taste buds often try the new foods so they can join the kids in the "new" taste buds group. It really works.

Rosalind, grandmother of Nicholas, age 2 and Katie, age 5 ▪ San Antonio, TX

44 Read "Healthy" Books

We read books about health and fitness (such as the *Magic School Bus* books) and my kids want to eat healthy. They know a cookie here and there is all right — as long as we are getting healthy meals otherwise.

Danielle, mother of Tara, age 3, and Kade, age 5 ▪ New Cumberland, WV

45 New Dish Night

Saturday night is always new dish night at our house. Everyone agrees to try something new on that night with no argument. My son and my husband even tried (and liked!) stuffed eggplant. I also have my son cook together with me one night a week, and I let him be adventurous and try adding new ingredients to whatever we're making. He calls these "science experiments" and loves making them (admittedly, some turn out gross)!

Laura, mother of Jacob, age 8 ▪ Culver City, CA

46 Set a Pretty Table

When my kids were younger I would set the table with colorful napkins and placemats, and even light a candle or two. They would feel so grown up, and I found that they not only behaved better at the table, but were more willing to try new and different foods.

Lori, mother of David, age 19, Nicole, age 22 and Jen, age 23 ▪ Olympia, WA

47 Smile ... Even if You Don't Like Something

Never turn your own nose up at food, especially when you're in front of your children! Recently, I was making a salad and added some chopped red bell pepper. In front of all of the kids, my sister said, "Ewww, why did you ruin that salad?" To turn her reaction into a positive, I told her kids how much my family really enjoys having red peppers in their salad. As it turned out, her 8-year old son tried them and loved them!

Wendy, mother of Caeli, age 7 and Corinna, age 10 ▪ Bel Air, MD

48 Go Crazy with Condiments

Make up a condiment tray for vegetables to serve with meals. For instance, put out vegetables prepared in a way your child will eat them. Then, in small ramekins, lay out some condiments from which they can dip. The idea here is to get the kids to try something besides ranch dresssing. Set the ramekins on a Lazy Susan so they can have fun spinning the tray around. Try these condiments for a start: hoisin sauce, chutney, BBQ sauce, peanut sauce, salsa, and ketchup. Go ahead and include the usual ranch dressing as well!

Robyn, stepmother of Michael, age 25, Laurie, age 35 and Darrin, age 38 ▪ Alexandria, VA

49 Give them the Tools to Help

We gave our son his own apron, chef's hat, and bought some age-appropriate kitchen tools. Having him help in the kitchen gets him excited to try his own creations!

Valerie, mother of George, age 4 ▪ Waipahu, HI

50 Eat Your Age

Each of my children has to "eat their age" in bites, which means that Anthony has to have at least eight bites, Jackson, five bites, and Taylor, three bites.

Lisa, mother of Taylor, age 3, Jackson, age 5 and Anthony, age 8 ▪ Marana, AZ

Acknowledgments

Over the years, we have connected with thousands of fellow moms through our blog, *Meal Makeover Moms' Kitchen,* our Facebook fan page, our weekly radio podcast, *Cooking with the Moms,* and our monthly e-newsletter. It was these virtual connections that inspired us to write *No Whine with Dinner.* Thanks to the 231 moms (and one dad) who tested and had their kids taste our recipes, and shared their insights and photos. We've named each of these invaluable testers on the following page. Thanks also to the 300-plus moms who shared a mealtime "secret" for feeding their children nutritious meals. Their humor and help tickled both our taste buds and our funny bones.

Wendy Smolen, our cookbook editor, and Carol Shufro, our designer, worked tirelessly to bring our recipes and vision to life on these pages. We thank them for their creative input and attention to details, and for spending the summer of 2010 immersed in *No Whine with Dinner.*

Coordinating our testers — assigning recipes, gathering feedback, answering questions, uploading photos to Flickr — would not have been possible without the hard work and extraordinary organizational skills of Callie Gordon and Chelsea Hobgood.

Building our online community and maintaining our presence on the Internet laid the foundation for this book. We thank Susan Getgood of *Marketing Roadmaps* for helping us map out our blog, and our favorite web guys, Brian Johnson and Eric Strathmeyer of BKJ Productions, for keeping our website afloat. With a push from fellow dietitian, Rebecca Schritchfield, inspiration from Erin Kane and Kristin Brandt, the *Manic Mommies,* technical assistance from Evans Travis and Janice's husband, Don, and sponsorship support from Eggland's Best Eggs, our podcast, *Cooking with the Moms,* has been going strong since 2008.

When we set out to write *No Whine with Dinner,* we decided to go the self-publishing route with encouragement from fellow self-published registered dietitians, Nancy Clark, Zonya Foco, and Jill Nussinow. Bob Johnson, Julee Hicks, and Powell Ropp from FRP (Favorite Recipes Press) provided us with expert guidance ... and patience. Our sponsors of the book, the U.S. Potato Board and the California Raisin Marketing Board, believed in our mission and supported our efforts.

Twelve bloggers generously contributed recipes to our *Bloggers' Best* chapter: Aggie from *Aggie's Kitchen,* Marla from *Family Fresh Cooking,* Jenna from *Food with Kid Appeal,* Jenny from *Picky Palate,* Amy from *Super Healthy Kids,* Sarah from *Sarah's Cucina Bella,* Rachael from *La Fuji Mama,* Janet from *Nutrition Unplugged,* Maryann from *Raise Healthy Eaters,* Mandy from *Gourmet Mom on the Go,* April from *Wicked Tasty Harvest,* and Tina from *Mommy's Kitchen.*

Many thanks also go to photographer Lynne McGraw, who shot the photo on the front cover, and Jess Lindley for offering her kitchen as a beautiful backdrop. To ease our work load, we were lucky to have dedicated dietetic interns from Boston University, Brigham & Women's Hospital, and Tufts University: Nina DiBona, Jennie Galpern, Callie Gordon, Laura Hodgdon, Mary Kate Keyes, Sara McGowan, Beth Morse, Maggie Shapiro, Amy Taylor, Leah Traverse, and Susanne Wakerly.

We thank the following individuals for reviewing our book and providing a quote for the back cover: Kristin Brandt, Erin Kane, Dr. David Katz, Ellie Krieger, RD, Jen Rehberger, and Vicky Thornton.

Writing this book required endless time in the kitchen, sinks full of dirty dishes, and friends and family willing to taste and test our ideas. Those who had no choice included our husbands, Tim Carruthers and Don Bissex, and our children, Josh and Simon Carruthers and Carolyn and Leah Bissex, and our extended families. Those who also contributed a cup of coffee, a cup of flour, or a cup of advice include Janice's friends Catherine Cezeaux,

Maryellen Fitzgibbon, Mary Hayward, Paul Locke, Anne Noonan, and Molly Phillips; and Liz's friends Marcia Gordon, Michele Hagan, Wendy Horn, Meg Kimball, and Carolyn O'Neil.

Finally, we'd like to thank each other for staying focused, sticking to deadlines, and keeping each other sane when recipes and life intruded. Being able to work together made writing this book worth every ounce of effort.

A personal thank you to these amazing recipe testers:

Aj, Dundee, OR ▪ Alicia, Washington, DC ▪ Alicia, Alexandria, MN ▪ Alyssa, Arlington, MA ▪ Amanda, Louisville, KY ▪ Amanda, Arnold, MO ▪ Amy, Acton, MA ▪ Amy, Westford, MA ▪ Amy, La Mirada, CA ▪ Amy, Kewaunee, WI ▪ Amy, Weston, CT ▪ Andrea, Brookfield, CT ▪ Andrea, Shrewsbury, MA ▪ Angela, Boxborough, MA ▪ Angela, Athens, GA ▪ Ann, Marietta, GA ▪ Ann, Boulder, CO ▪ Ann, Frisco, TX ▪ Anne, Melrose, MA ▪ April, Centralia, MO ▪ Ashley, Tallahassee, FL ▪ Ashley, La Mesa, CA ▪ Becky, Minneapolis, MN ▪ Beth, Garner, NC ▪ Beth, Wilmington, NC ▪ Beth, San Diego,CA ▪ Betsy, Sioux Falls, SD ▪ Bonnie, West Valley City, UT ▪ Brandy, Eagle River, AK ▪ Brenda, Tewksbury, MA ▪ Brenda, Sugar Land, TX ▪ Brianna, Sun Prairie, WI ▪ Brooke, Marietta, GA ▪ Cara, Beaverton, OR ▪ Carey, New Brighton, MN ▪ Caroline, Melbourne Beach, FL ▪ Carrie, McKinney, TX ▪ Catarina, San Ramon, CA ▪ Celestin, Hatfield, PA ▪ Charlotte, New Orleans, LA ▪ Christa, Plymouth, WI ▪ Christina, American Fork, UT ▪ Christina, Sultan, WA ▪ Christy, Acton, MA ▪ Cindy, De Pere, WI ▪ Colleen, Sandy Hook, VA ▪ Cory, Wakefield, MA ▪ Courtney, Calgary, AB, Canada ▪ Danielle, Chelmsford, MA ▪ Danielle, Gardnerville, NV ▪ Darcey, Port Jervis, NY ▪ David, Pacific Palisades, CA ▪ Dawn, Urbandale, IA ▪ Deanna, Havertown, PA ▪ Deborah, Lexington, MA ▪ Desiree, Calgary, AB,Canada ▪ Diane, Ashland, MA ▪ Donna, Kingston, NY ▪ Elaine, Vienna, VA ▪ Elisia, Sharpsburg, GA ▪ Elizabeth, Southfield, MI ▪ Elizabeth, Apex, NC ▪ Elizabeth, Brighton, CO ▪ Elizabeth, Reading, MA ▪ Heather, Laytonsville, MD ▪ Heather, London, England ▪ Heather, Honolulu, HI ▪ Heidi, Rothschild, WI ▪ Helen, Elmesthorpe, England ▪ Helen, Douglasville, GA ▪ Jackie, Roseville, MN ▪ Jamie, Cantonment, FL ▪ Jamie, Wenatchee, WA ▪ Jamie, Unionville, MI ▪ Jamie, Marinette, WI ▪ Jane, Aalen, Germany ▪ Janet, Rib Lake,WI ▪ Jen, Ft. Thomas, KY ▪ Jenette, Surprise, AZ ▪ Jennifer, Wailuku, HI ▪ Jennifer, Norcross, GA ▪ Jennifer, Jackson, MI ▪ Jennifer, Van Buren Twp, MI ▪ Jennifer, Fairfax, VA ▪ Jennifer, Columbia, PA ▪ Jennifer, Louisville, KY ▪ Jennifer, Framingham, MA ▪ Jennifer, Kansas City, MO ▪ Jennifer, Laurinburg, NC ▪ Jennifer, Wichita, KS ▪ Jessica, Surprise, AZ ▪ Jill, Austin, TX ▪ Jill, Valparaiso, IN ▪ Jill, Moraga, CA ▪ Jill, Bedford, MA ▪ Jill, Big Bear Lake, CA ▪ Joyann, Menasha, WI ▪ Judy, Huntington Beach, CA ▪ Judy, Groton, MA ▪ Julia, Holyoke, MA ▪ Julie, Mercer Island, WA ▪ Julie, Camarillo, CA ▪ Karen, Steilacoom, WA ▪ Karen, King of Prussia, PA ▪ Karen, Dublin, CA ▪ Karen, Melbourne, FL ▪ Karen, Omaha, NE ▪ Karen, Mobile, AL ▪ Kari, St. Paul, MN ▪ Kate, Cheshire, CT ▪ Katherine, Miami Lakes, FL ▪ Kathi, Grand Blanc, MI ▪ Kathy, Bloomington, IN ▪ Katie, Littleton, MA ▪ Katie, Olympia, WA ▪ Kelli, Windermere, FL ▪ Kelly, Downers Grove, IL ▪ Kim, North Augusta, SC ▪ Kim, Quitman, AR ▪ Kim, Tulsa, OK ▪ Kimber, Gilbert, AZ ▪ Kirsten, Danville, CA ▪ Kris, Denham Springs, LA ▪ Kelly, Marietta, GA ▪ Kristen, Cartersville, GA ▪ Kristen, Bothell, WA ▪ Kristin, O Fallon, IL ▪ Kristin, Ashland, MA ▪ Kristin, San Jose, CA ▪ Lara, Arlington, VA ▪ Lara, Los Gatos, CA ▪ Laura, La Crosse, WI ▪ Laura, West Henrietta, NY ▪ Laura, Newmarket, ON, Canada ▪ Laura, Melrose, MA ▪ Laura, Whitecourt, Alberta, Canada ▪ Leah, Leander, TX ▪ Lee, Aurora, IL ▪ LeighAnn, Chelmsford, MA ▪ Leslie, Edmond, OK ▪ Linda, Lexington, MA ▪ Linnea, Grand Blanc, MI ▪ Lisa, Tallahassee, FL ▪ Lisa, Marana, AZ ▪ Lisa, Ashton, IL ▪ Lisa, Melrose, MA ▪ Lisa, San Carlos, CA ▪ Lisa, Lexington, MA ▪ Lisa, North Reading, MA ▪ Lisa, Frisco, TX ▪ Lori, Carmel, NY ▪ Lori, Boxborough, MA ▪ Lorraine, Metuchen, NJ ▪ Lucy, Midland, TX ▪ Margaret, Seattle, WA ▪ Margot, Glen Burnie, MD ▪ Marissa, League City, TX ▪ Marla, Evanston, IL ▪ Martha, Atlanta, GA ▪ Melissa, San Jose, CA ▪ Melissa, Euless, TX ▪ Michele, Lexington, MA ▪ Michelle, Bedford, MA ▪ Michelle, Trussville, AL ▪ Michelle, Shawnee, KS ▪ Michelle, Aurora, CO ▪ Mindy, Vernon Hills, IL ▪ Miriam, Upland, IN ▪ Mollie, Cincinnati, OH ▪ Molly, Coon Rapids, MN ▪ Molly, Melrose, MA ▪ Nancy, Winkler, MB, Canada ▪ Nicole, Havertown, PA ▪ Nikki, Louisville, KY ▪ Pamela, Bismarck, ND ▪ Patricia, Wakefield, MA ▪ Peggy, Lexington, MA ▪ Rachel, Lexington, MA ▪ Rachel, Columbus, OH ▪ Rebecca, Plover, WI ▪ Rebecca, Wichita, KS ▪ Robin, Arlington, MA ▪ Robin, Dallas, TX ▪ Rose, Santa Barbara, CA ▪ Rosey, Camano Island, WA ▪ Sandi, Port Orange, FL ▪ Sara, Hanover, MN ▪ Sarah, Middletown, OH ▪ Sarah, Indianapolis, IN ▪ Sarah, Littleton, MA ▪ Sari, Garnet Valley, PA ▪ Shanon, Newington, CT ▪ Sharon, Sonoma, CA ▪ Sheri, Dexter, MI ▪ Simera, Beavercreek, OH ▪ Stacy, Maryland Heights, MO ▪ Stephanie, Boise, ID ▪ Susan, Du Quoin, IL ▪ Susan, Vienna, VA ▪ Suzanne, Winchester, CA ▪ Tamar, Southfield, MI ▪ Tamara, Cumberland, RI ▪ Tanya, Stillwater, MN ▪ Tatja, Stow, MA ▪ Teresa, Vancouver, WA ▪ Terri, Twinsburg, OH ▪ Tina, West Hills, CA ▪ Valerie, Waipahu, HI ▪ Vicky, Ft. Thomas, KY ▪ Wanda, Windham, NH ▪ Wendy, San Jose, CA ▪ Wendy, Jacksonville, FL ▪ Yvette, Mason, OH

Index